'Abdullah ("El") Faisal Al-Jamayki

A CRITICAL STUDY OF HIS STATEMENTS, ERRORS AND EXTREMISM IN TAKFEER

'ABDULLĀH ("EL") FAISAL AL-JAMAYKĪ - A CRITICAL STUDY OF HIS STATEMENTS, ERRORS AND EXTREMISM IN TAKFEER

1st Edition © Jamiah Media 2011 C.E. / 1432 A.H.

ISBN: 978-0-9551099-9-7

Published by:
Jamiah Media
www.jamiahmedia.com
Email: admin@salafimanhaj.com

In conjunction with:
Call to Islam
116 Bury Park Road
Luton LU1 1HE

Note:
There have been contributions to this book from those who actually used to listen to Faisal's lectures from eight years ago, so this should not merely be viewed as a mere 'slanderous attack' on Faisal, rather as an in-depth analysis and assessment of his very dangerous ideas, beliefs, views and assertions. As for the line of argument that states "They should not be spoken about as they are being oppressed by the kuffār" then this is bogus as their horrific lectures and audios are still being widely circulated, disseminated, listened to and blindly followed, therefore a study and refutation of them is necessary.

Cover design & Typesetting:
Ihsaan Design - www.ihsaandesign.co.uk
Edited by Abū Fātimah Azhar Majothī

عبد الله فيصل الجميكي

دِراسَةٌ نَقْدِيّة لِتَصْرِيْحاتِهِ وِأَخْطائِهِ الْمُتَطَرِّفةِ

فِيْ مَسْأَلَةِ التَّكْفِيْرِ

'Abdullah ("El") Faisal Al-Jamayki

A CRITICAL STUDY OF HIS STATEMENTS, ERRORS AND EXTREMISM IN TAKFEER

By Abū Ameenah 'AbdurRahmān as-Salafi
and 'AbdulHaq al-Ashantī

Forewords by 'Umar al-Jamaykī,
Abū Saifillāh 'AbdulQādir and Tālib Alexander

Contents

Foreword by 'Umar al-Jamaykī

(Graduate of Faculty of Hadeeth Studies, Islamic University of Madeenah and Imām of Brixton Mosque, London, UK)

It gives me great pleasure to write these words to applaud our two brothers 'AbdulHaq Al-Ashanti and Abū Ameenah 'AbdurRahmān for their efforts in putting together this thesis in clarifying some of the erroneous views, fatawaa and slandering of the 'Ulama of the Sunnah that has emanated from Abdullāh Faisal, a self proclaimed "Shaykh". It is recorded in many books of Ahlus-Sunnah the importance of refuting and warning against those who have showed clear errors in opposition to some of the fundamentals principles of this Deen.

This book will highlight some of these misguided ideas and statements which are to rectify the deception of this particular individual who has poisoned many innocent Muslims. This is only intended to uphold and protect the prestige and beauty of Islām and also in keeping within Islām's emphasis on encouraging good and forbidding evil, as in the Statement of Allāh Ta'ala:

﴿ وَلْتَكُن مِّنكُمْ أُمَّةٌ يَدْعُونَ إِلَى ٱلْخَيْرِ وَيَأْمُرُونَ بِٱلْمَعْرُوفِ وَيَنْهَوْنَ عَنِ ٱلْمُنكَرِ وَأُوْلَـٰٓئِكَ هُمُ ٱلْمُفْلِحُونَ ﴾

"Let their arise out of you a group of people inviting to all that is good, enjoining Al-Ma'ruf (good) and forbidding Al-Munkar (evil) and these are the successful." *{Aal-Imran (3): 104}*

9

We ask Allāh to guide us all and keep us on the Straight Path and aid those that are courageous to defend against those that wish to distort the purity of our Deen that Allāh has chosen for our Islam.

Omar Jamaykee

Imām of Masjid Ibn Taymeeyah

Brixton, London

Thursday 27 Dhu'l-Qa'dah 1431 AH/4 November 2010 CE

Foreword by Abū Saifillah 'AbdulQadir
(Call to Islam Centre, Luton, UK)

This book is of great importance in dealing with the infamous misguidance and misinterpretations of Islam spread by 'Abdullāh Faisal over the past two decades or more here in the UK. These misinterpretations have subsequently been propagated by his followers. From the early 1990s I have personally witnessed the effects of his misguidance in my community here in Luton and in different parts of London. His ignorant legacy persists even to this day in the minds of some disaffected youth in UK generally, as well as other parts of the world such as Africa, Jamaica and the USA.

It is clear the fundamental basis upon which this book has been compiled is sincere advice (*naseehah*) to all. People whom Allāh granted knowledge to should warn from false words and clarify corruption which has been attributed to Islām. One of the most important duties of a Muslim is sincerity for Allāh, His Book, His Messenger and for the leaders and the Muslim public.

'Abdullāh Faisal is responsible for issuing Islamic *fatāwā* targeted at the vulnerable youth, who do not have enough knowledge nor realize that they are based on weak evidence, to trick them into false aims. All such actions are atrocious in Islam; no one who knows the limits of the Islamic Sharee'ah and its objectives would accept them. The words of those who speak without enough knowledge are among the reasons that spilt the Ummah and spread enmities. Exposing such individual's teachings is incumbent upon those who have the ability. Allāh said in the Qur'ān:

﴿ وَإِذْ أَخَذَ ٱللَّهُ مِيثَٰقَ ٱلَّذِينَ أُوتُواْ ٱلْكِتَٰبَ لَتُبَيِّنُنَّهُۥ لِلنَّاسِ وَلَا تَكْتُمُونَهُۥ ﴾

"(And remember) when Allāh took a covenant from those who were given the Scripture to make it known and clear to mankind, and not to hide it." *{Aal-Imran (3): 104}*

'Abdullāh Faisal was a caller to the corrupt *Takfīrī* methodology which has been present in the UK for over two decades. The book in your hands explains what is meant by '*Takfīrī* methodology' namely the incorrect methodology to excommunicate Muslims from the religion of Islām through distorted interpretations of the Quran and *Sunnah*. He studied at Imām Muhammad bin Saud Islamic University and with his limited knowledge, coupled with an uncontrollable rage over the present dire state of the Muslim world, he came up with a 'cure' for the *ummah's* crisis. Many traverse the path of acquiring knowledge but only few attain its correct understanding. That is what is meant by the hadith of Mu'awiyah ﷺ where the Messenger ﷺ said: *"He who Allāh wants good for, He gives him the understanding of the deen (religion)."*[1] One of the characteristics of a caller to Islām is that he/she must be able to control his/her

---

[1] Bukhārī and Muslim

12

emotional state. The *shariah* must be superior to our feelings, the *shariah* must dictate to the *da'ee* his/her position or opinion even in the face of tyranny, hardships or loss of life. Unfortunately Faisal was unable to subject his emotions to the dictates of the *shariah*, rather he subjected the *shariah* to the dictates of his emotions and hence Allāh misguided him.

Shaykh 'Abdullāh al-Qarnī[1] explained that desires are made up of emotions.[2] If one does not control his emotions, then his emotions will control him, he will no longer be in control, and then eventually a strong desire will develop based on that emotion. If that desire is in opposition to the *shariah* then we fear that such an individual will end up worshiping his desires. This is what we fear for 'Abdullāh Faisal. As Allāh said:

$$ \text{﴿ أَفَرَءَيْتَ مَنِ ٱتَّخَذَ إِلَٰهَهُۥ هَوَىٰهُ ﴾} $$

"So have you seen the one who took his own desires as a god?"
{Al-Jaathiyah (45):23}

We can confirm from recent historical facts that one's need for food (desire) has been a major cause for some Muslims around the world to rebel against their leaders and adopt *Takfīrī* beliefs due to their poverty. For example in the Algerian revolt of 1988, Muslims took to the streets in protest and later joined violent extremist (*Takfīrī*) groups due to the lack of the basic necessities

---

[1] He is not the infamous Āid al Qarnī.
[2] In a Dawrah 'Ilmiyyah which I attended in Riyadh in April 2010 CE

provided by their Muslim government. It is well documented that the lack of basic necessities, as well as oppression by their leaders gives birth to the *Takfīrī* ideology.

'Abdullāh Faisal's longing and desire for Allāh's law and His system of justice to be implemented throughout the world was partly influenced by his personal experience of the poverty he saw in the Muslim world and how wealth was massed distributed unjustly on a worldwide scale. Such a desire is not blameworthy; unless it trespasses other human rights legislated by Allāh. But this is exactly what 'Abdullāh Faisal did. His infatuation with the implementation of *shariah* led him to oppose other aspects of the *shariah* such as the sanctity of a persons life, wealth and honour as Allāh's Messenger ﷺ said in a *hadeeth* narrated by Abū Bakrah: *"indeed your wealth, your lives, your honour are sacred for you like the sacredness of this month, this day and this place"*[1] 'Abdullāh Faisal rendered Muslim blood, honour, and wealth *halāl* in order to justify violence and bloodshed in pursuit of the implementation of Islamic law. As for the non-Muslim's honour, blood and wealth, 'Abdullāh Faisal allowed them to be abused and taken without hesitation and with no conditions or barriers. For 'Abdullāh Faisal "the end justified the means", which is a principle alien to the true teachings of Islām. Allāh said:

---

[1] Bukhārī and Muslim

$$\left\{ \text{قُلْ يَا أَهْلَ ٱلْكِتَٰبِ لَا تَغْلُوا۟ فِى دِينِكُمْ غَيْرَ ٱلْحَقِّ وَلَا تَتَّبِعُوٓا۟ أَهْوَآءَ قَوْمٍ قَدْ ضَلُّوا۟ مِن قَبْلُ وَأَضَلُّوا۟ كَثِيرًا وَضَلُّوا۟ عَن سَوَآءِ ٱلسَّبِيلِ} \right\}$$

"Say (O Muhammad ﷺ): 'Oh people of the book do not go to extremes in your religion'" *{Al-Maa'idah (5):77}*

A warning which Abdullah Faisal did not take heed of. Furthermore, Allāh Most High said:

$$\left\{ \text{وَلَوِ ٱتَّبَعَ ٱلْحَقُّ أَهْوَآءَهُمْ لَفَسَدَتِ ٱلسَّمَٰوَٰتُ وَٱلْأَرْضُ وَمَن فِيهِنَّ ۚ بَلْ أَتَيْنَٰهُم بِذِكْرِهِمْ فَهُمْ عَن ذِكْرِهِم مُّعْرِضُونَ} \right\}$$

"And if the truth had been in accordance to their desires, verily the heavens and the earth, and whosoever is therein would have been corrupted. Rather we have brought to them their reminder but they turn away from their reminder." *{Al-Mu'minūn (23): 71}*

Abdullah Faisal is not even close to the level of scholarly knowledge which is a pre-requisite to articulating a cure for this *ummah*. His 'cure' is in reality a disease, similar to the disease being propagated by others similar to him: Abū Qatādah, Abū Hamza, Omar Bakrī, Safar al-Hawālī and Salmān al-'Awdah just to name a few. None of them are known to have been from the grounded scholars who give *fatawa* on such tremendous matters as 'the cure for this *ummah* in times of crises.' It brings to mind the time about which the Messenger ﷺ foretold would come to pass: *"Allāh will not lift the knowledge by taking it from the hearts of the scholars but He will lift it by the death of the scholars. Until there will be no scholar left, people will make the ignorant people their chiefs. These ignorant chiefs will be asked religious issues. They will issue decrees without knowledge. In this way, they will themselves go astray and send astray others also.*[1] 'Abdullāh Faisal is indeed one of these ignorant chiefs who have gone astray and sent many others astray. The dangerous cocktail of emotion, ignorance, and distance from the scholars led him to the path of misguidance. The Prophet ﷺ said: *"And he who calls (people) to error, he shall have to carry (the burden) of its sin, like those who committed it, without their sins being diminished in any respect."*[2]

For this reason I see it pertinent that some from those who have correct guidance and access to the scholars expose his distorted beliefs, incorrect teachings and his overall misguidance from the true path of *Ahl us-Sunnah wa'l-Jama'ah*. Our two brothers Abū Ameenah AbdurRahmān as-Salafī and AbdulHaq al-Ashantī have taken this task to hand in this book. I would encourage the readers to not just read the book, but rather to study it and be sure to focus on the references that the compilers of this book have supplied. The references and disseminated knowledge make this book irrefutable. Some may question why such a book is being compiled arguing that it will further disunite this *ummah* and give more ammunition to the disbelievers against the Muslims. They may also claim that such a book is tantamount to hanging the

---

[1] Bukhari
[2] Bukhari and Muslim

16

dirty laundry of the Muslims out in public. These are words that I have heard often. I have observed that the common factor was that these words came from people who did not have knowledge or they had some knowledge but void of scholarly guidance. In reply I say to them what our scholars have told us:

1. That we must enjoin the good and forbid the evil even if it be against our own selves. This of course, is done with applying all the conditions and rules of enjoying good and forbidding evil and is not done with just raw emotion and a lack of evidences.

2. Ibn Taymiyyah said: *fighting the enemy within is a priority over fighting the external enemy.* We know this from when Ali left fighting the disbelievers in Persia and Rome and turned to fighting the *khawārij*.

3. 'Abdullāh Faisal's teachings are innovations in Islam and misguidance, and the way of the early generations in refuting the innovators is the way that we follow today. For example, examine the statements of the following three early scholars: Sa'eed bin Jubair said: *"my son accompanies a sinful and cunning scoundrel who is a Sunni is more beloved to me than that he accompanies a devoted and worshipful Innovator."*[1] Imām ash-Shāfi'ī (d. 204H) said that: *"A servant meets Allāh with every sin except Shirk is better than meeting Him upon any one of the innovated beliefs."*[2] Imām Ahmad said: *"The graves of Ahl us-Sunnah from the people of major sins are a garden. And the graves of Ahl*

---

[1] Reported in Ibn Battah, *al-Ibānah*, no. 89.
[2] As reported by al-Bayhaqī in *al-I'tiqād*, p.158; *Tārīkh Dimashq*, p. 309 and Ibn Katheer, *al-Bidāyah wa'n-Nihāyah*, vol.10, p.254.

ul-Bid'ah from the pious abstemious ones are a pit. The sinful of Ahl us-Sunnah are the Awliyā of Allāh, and the pious, abstemious of Ahl ul-Bid'ah are the enemies of Allāh."[1]

An intelligent person will recognise that Imām Shāfi'ī, Sa'eed Ibn Jubayr and Imām Ahmad warned the Muslims against innovations and innovators. This was the way of all the scholars. They did not hold back out of fear of what the non-Muslims would think, or what divisions it may cause in the *ummah*. This is because they knew very well the evil and corruption that would arise from the innovators if they were to remain silent was far worse than the consequences of them exposing the misguided ones. Furthermore the compilation of this book is a necessity. No sensible person could argue it is a 'cause' of *fitnah*, rather it is 'the cure' of the *fitnah*.

Abū Saifillāh 'AbdulQādir
Luton, October 2010 CE

---

[1] *Tabaqāt al-Hanābilah*, vol.1, p.184.

Foreword by Abū Safiyah Tālib Alexander
(Head Teacher, Olive Tree School, Luton, UK)

Indeed, all praise is due to Allaah. We praise Him, seek His assistance and we ask for His forgiveness. We seek refuge in Allaah from the evil of our souls and our actions. Whosoever Allaah guides then none can misguide him and whomsoever He misguides then none can guide him. I bear witness and testify that none has the right to be worshipped (in truth) but Allaah, alone without partners, and that Muhammad (the son of Abdullah) is his slave and messenger.

To proceed:

I remember, vividly, as if only yesterday when Faisal el-Abdullāh was first introduced to the *dawah* scene in the UK. This was way back in 1992 and at a time Brixton Mosque was engaged in a progressive transition in management. It was after a study circle held after the *Maghrib* prayer that we were first introduced to the man who was to gain international notoriety as 'Shaykh Faisal'. As we were preparing to leave the mosque, putting on our shoes, engaging in idle banter and chitchat, unexpectedly, the main door opened and in popped Dr. Abū Ameenah Bilāl Philips. We were pleasantly surprised to see Dr. Philips, whom we greeted warmly and cordially. We noticed that behind him was a young man of African heritage, small in stature and like most of us neatly dressed in Middle Eastern clothes. Dr. Philips introduced this elusive figure as Faisal Abdullāh who was one of his 'students.'

Our initial reaction was joy and elation. We hoped that Faisal would continue the good work of his mentor in educating both Muslims and non-Muslim on the fundamentals of Islām, building and promoting community cohesion based upon mutual respect and cultural independence. Unfortunately, Faisal proved to be the diametric opposite of his mentor, promoting communalism and obfuscating the fundamentals of Islām. Unfortunately, like most heretics of the *Khārijī* ('*Takfīrī*') brand, Faisal concealed his true aims: the desire to propagate a crude and vulgar form of *Takfīrism*, with a Jamaican twist. Capturing the imagination of disaffected youth, he worked arduously to promote the ideas of the Takfīrī movement that was prevalent at that time.

This book therefore, written by two of the foremost Salafī researchers in the UK, is a timely and scholarly analysis of the deviated and heretical beliefs of a man who undeservedly was described as being a '*Shaykh*', a man of Islamic learning and scholarship. This individual – Faisal al-Abdullāh – while hiding under the mantle of scholarship was, like Shukrī Mustapha and the other Khārijī (i.e. *Takfīrī*) intelligentsia and literati, took their spiritual impetus not from the pure sources of the Qur'ān and Sunnah but rather from the constricted understanding of confused and astray ideologues such as Sayyid Qutb. This book, a tome of over three hundred pages, is a much needed study which not only highlights the theological errors of Faisal Abdullāh; addressing some of his most heinous deviations in some detail, but also attempts to shed light on the fundamentals of Orthodox Sunnī Islam in relation to issues of politics, excommunication, apostasy, and revolt.

We ask Allāh that he makes this book a good deed in the scale of good deeds on the Day of Judgement being a means in which He, The sublime and Exalted, grants the highest level of Paradise, to the authors of this study and all those good people who have aided them and supported them in its publication.

Aboo Safeeyah Taalib Alexander
15 Muharram 1432 AH / 21 December 2010 CE
London

Acknowledgments

We would firstly like to thank Allāh, all praise is due to Him. We then have to extend our thanks to Abu Saifillah AbdulQadir Baksh and the Salafi brothers from the Call to Islam Centre in Luton for helping to raise the funds to make it possible to print this important book. We would also like to send our thanks to Abu Hibbān for his help.

Thanks and appreciation also go out to the Brixton Salafi 'old school' who have been an inspiration to many and helped to establish Salafiyyah in London since 1992, brothers like: Abū Uthmān AbdulMālik, Abū Safiyah Tālib Alexander, Abū Dāwud Samīr, AbdulHaqq Baker, Abu Hajirah AbdurRahmān, Shaykh Kamāl, Abū Ilyās Idrīs and Abu AbdurRahmān Dāwud, Abū Yūsuf AbdulHakīm and Abdullāh, enough respect! Indeed they have been trustworthy narrators in regards to the subject matter of this book, may Allāh reward them.

Prelude: Introductory Principles

Indeed, all praise is due to Allāh, we praise Him, we seek His aid, and we ask for His forgiveness. We seek refuge in Allāh from the evil of our actions and from the evil consequences of our actions. Whoever Allāh guides, there is none to misguide, and whoever Allāh misguides there is none to guide. I bear witness that there is no god worthy of worship except Allāh, and I bear witness that Muhammad is the servant and Messenger of Allāh. To proceed:

Before we start with this critique it is important that we begin with some introductory principles:

First Principle

From the greatest features of those who preach for Allāh is calling to *Tawheed* in the way traversed by the Prophet ﷺ and all of the Prophets, as Allāh said:

﴿ وَلَقَدْ بَعَثْنَا فِى كُلِّ أُمَّةٍ رَّسُولاً أَنِ ٱعْبُدُواْ ٱللَّهَ وَٱجْتَنِبُواْ ٱلطَّـٰغُوتَ ﴾

"And We certainly sent to every nation a Messenger, [saying],
'Worship Allāh and avoid Tāghūt.'" *{an-Nahl (16): 36}*

Allāh said to His Prophet Muhammad ﷺ:

$$\langle\!\langle \, \text{قُلْ هَـٰذِهِۦ سَبِيلِىٓ أَدْعُوٓاْ إِلَى ٱللَّهِ} \, \rangle\!\rangle$$

"Say, 'This is my way; I invite to Allāh...' *{Yūsuf (12): 108}*

Meaning "*to Tawheed*" to singling out Allāh in worship,

$$\langle\!\langle \, \text{قُلْ هَـٰذِهِۦ سَبِيلِىٓ أَدْعُوٓاْ إِلَى ٱللَّهِ عَلَىٰ بَصِيرَةٍ أَنَا۠ وَمَنِ ٱتَّبَعَنِى وَسُبْحَـٰنَ ٱللَّهِ} \, $$

$$\text{وَمَآ أَنَا۠ مِنَ ٱلْمُشْرِكِينَ} \, \rangle\!\rangle$$

"Say, 'This is my way; I invite to Allāh with insight, I and those who follow me. And exalted is Allāh; and I am not of those who associate others with Him.'" *{Yūsuf (12): 108}*

Thus, if you want to know a true caller from others, then look at his condition, and if he is concerned with Tawheed, calls to Tawheed and strives hard in that, then you will know that he is a true caller.

Second Principle

Mistakes are not all on the same level, there are errors in *ijtihād* wherein if a man makes *ijtihād* he is between one reward or two rewards. There are also errors wherein *ijtihād* within those matters are unacceptable as in the case of most of the errors in matters of belief. There are errors wherein if a man falls into them he is deemed sinful, errors wherein a man is deemed an innovator and errors wherein a man is to be deemed a disbeliever. For this reason, when you mention to some people that so and so has erred, they say *"there is no one except that he makes mistakes, and the Prophet judged that we are prone to error"* –

this is correct; however errors are not all on the same level and all are taken to account based on the level of error committed.

Third Principle

The criteria for truth are that you look at a man's condition and assess: is his *da'wah* based on the Book of Allāh and the Sunnah of His Messenger 饜, and what the *Salaf us-Sālih* from the Sahābah, Tābi'een and those who followed them, traversed or not? If so, then he is a caller to truth. An error with many ignorant people is that they think that the criteria of *da'wah* is that a man has a lot of followers or that those who attend his lessons and lectures are many, yet this is a huge misunderstanding. For the Prophet 饜 stated, as reported in the Saheeh from the hadeeth of Ibn 'Abbās 饜: *"A Prophet will come on the Day of Judgement and he will have a man or two with him. Then another Prophet will come with a group of men with him, while another Prophet will come with a small group of followers. Then another Prophet will come with no followers with him whatsoever."* This is in regards to a Prophet, Allāh chose him to have this great status and yet with that he will come with no one with him; his *da'wah* is still successful without doubt because he is Prophet.

So the criteria of truth is not having many followers, rather from what the Prophet 饜 informed of, is that, in the hadeeth of Abū Hurayrah and Ibn 'Umar, and in the wording of Abū Hurayrah (as reported in Saheeh Muslim): The Messenger of Allāh 饜 said: *"Islām began as something strange, and will return (to being) strange as it began, Tūbah is for the Ghurabā (strangers)."* Thus,

25

the people of truth are a few yet this is not a proof of their *da'wah* being erroneous. Rather, when you read the Book of Allāh you will find that Allāh in many verses clarifies that the people of bāṭil are many and the people of truth are few. Allāh says,

﴿ وَلَقَدْ أَرْسَلْنَا نُوحًا وَإِبْرَٰهِيمَ وَجَعَلْنَا فِى ذُرِّيَّتِهِمَا ٱلنُّبُوَّةَ وَٱلْكِتَٰبَ ۖ فَمِنْهُم مُّهْتَدٍ ۖ وَكَثِيرٌ مِّنْهُمْ فَٰسِقُونَ ﴾

"...and among them is he who is guided, but many of them are defiantly disobedient." *{Hadeed (57): 26}*

And Allāh says,

﴿ وَإِن تُطِعْ أَكْثَرَ مَن فِى ٱلْأَرْضِ يُضِلُّوكَ عَن سَبِيلِ ٱللَّهِ ۚ إِن يَتَّبِعُونَ إِلَّا ٱلظَّنَّ وَإِنْ هُمْ إِلَّا يَخْرُصُونَ ﴾

"And if you obey most of those upon the earth, they will mislead you from the way of Allāh." *{al-'An'ām (6): 116}*

Therefore, having many followers is neither the criteria for the truth nor is eloquence, articulacy or heroic speech. Many people see an eloquent man who is articulate, poetic and a strong speaker who *"says it as it is"* and think that he is on the truth due to that, and this is a mistake. Yes, eloquence, being articulate and bravery if used in order to support Allāh's *deen* is sought-after; yet it is not the criteria for truth or *bāṭil*. This eloquence and articulacy has to be looked at to see: if it is being used to support the *deen* or not. If it is being used to support Allāh's Book, the Sunnah of His Messenger ﷺ and the way of the first and foremost ones then bring this (eloquence)! But if it (such eloquence and articulacy) is being used in a way which opposes Allāh's *Shar'* then it is unacceptable.

Fourth Principle

There is a big difference between giving advice and *gheebah* (backbiting); many people do not differentiate between the two and many common people are confused about this. On the contrary, how many of those who want good have been blocked from good due to this? They say *"they are backbiting so-and-so"* and *"how can you read that when they are backbiting so-and-so?"* etc. It is therefore important for us to know that *naseehah* and *gheebah* can be interlinked and also distinguished from each other in important matters. As for the matter wherein they are connected, then this is in regards to mentioning something about a person that he dislikes, but advice is mentioning those things that a person dislikes out of giving advice and warning people from his error, as an advice to him initially and then an advice to the general public secondly.

As for *gheebah*, then it is not applied to matters related to the *deen*, so if a man is mentioned for things that he dislikes without a religious benefit then this is *gheebah*. This is *harām* as Allāh forbade it in His Book and so did the Messenger ﷺ as mentioned in his Sunnah. But if a clarification of a person's condition is in order to advise people and to warn them from his errors so that Allāh's creation is not misguided due to his statements then this is sought-after. Imām Ibn 'AbdulBarr stated:

The Sharee'ah has permitted speaking about a man in matters wherein there is a specific benefit such as in marriage.

As is found in the hadeeth in Saheeh Muslim of Fātimah bint Qays wherein the Prophet ﷺ was asked by Fātimah about Abū Jahm and Mu'awiyah and the Prophet said: *"As for Mu'awiyah then he is poor and has no money, and as for Abū Jahm then his stick does not leave his side, marry Usāmah."* So pay attention: this is mentioning things about a man which he dislikes, but it is permissible as there is a benefit in mentioning that to the woman; so then what about a greater issue, such as the Ummah of Muhammad ﷺ? The error of the one who erred is to be clarified so that the error will neither be followed nor will people be misguided and oppose the *Sharee'ah* of Muhammad ibn 'Abdillāh ﷺ.

Imām Ahmad ﷺ recorded in his *Musnad* (hadeeth no. 21453) from the hadeeth of Abū Dharr al-Ghifārī ﷺ that the Prophet ﷺ advised him saying:

«وأمرني أن أقول بالحق وان كان مرا»

"And he ordered me to say the truth even if it is bitter."

Look at the statement of the Tābi'ī Imām, Muhammad ibn Sīrīn ﷺ, which is recorded in the *Muqaddimah* of Saheeh Muslim, vol.1, p.15:

«إن هذا علم الدين، فانظر عمن تأخذون دينكم»

"This is the knowledge of your religion, so look to whom you take your religion from."

28

Imām Muslim ﷺ also recorded in the *Muqaddimah* of his *Saheeh* (vol.1, p.15) that Muhammad ibn Sīrīn said:

لم يكونوا يسألون عن الإسناد فلما وقعت الفتنة قالوا سموا لنا رجالكم فينظر إلى أهل السنة فيؤخذ حديثهم وينظر إلى أهل البدع فلا يؤخذ حديثه

They had not used to ask about the Isnād (chains of narration) but when the Fitnah arose they said, "Name us your men!" so they looked to Ahlus Sunnah and they took their narrations and they looked to the people of innovation and they did not take their narrations.

The Imām Abū 'Abdillāh Muhammad bin 'Abdillāh ﷺ, also well known as Ibn Abī Zamanayn, and is one of the top four most well-known scholars of the Madhhab of Imām Mālik, said:

ولم يـــزل أهل السنة يعيبون أهل الأهواء المضلة، وينهون عـــن مجالستهم، ويخوفون فتنتهم، ويخبرون بخلاقهم، ولا يرون ذلك غيبـــة لـــهم، ولا طعناً عليهم

And Ahlus Sunnah never ceases to expose the people of desires, the deviants. And they prohibit sitting with them, and fear their trials and narrate in opposition to them, and this is neither seen as backbiting them nor insulting them.[1]

---

[1] Reported in *Usūl as-Sunnah*, p. 293.

29

Regardless of who is the speaker or caller, Ahlus Sunnah wal-Jamā'ah were firm upon this affair of exposing and criticizing the callers to falsehood and making clear this religion. Imām adh-Dhahabī ﷺ recorded in Volume 2 of his *Tadhkirat ul-Huffādh* that Imām Abū Dāwūd as-Sijistānī ﷺ said:

«ابنى عبد الله كذاب»

"My son 'Abdullāh is a habitual liar."

Al-Hāfidh Ibn Hajar al-'Asqalānī ﷺ mentioned in volume 11 of his *Tahdheeb at-Tahdheeb* under the biography of Yahya bin Abī Unaysah that Zayd ibn Abī Unaysah said about his brother:

«أخي يحى يكذب وحجاج وأشعث وابن إسحاق كل هؤلاء أحب إلي من يحيى»

"My brother Yahya lies, and Hajjāj and Ash'ath and Ibn Ishāq, they are all more beloved to me than Yahya."

Fifth Principle

All are to be held accountable for their statements, Allāh says,

﴿ مَّا يَلۡفِظُ مِن قَوۡلٍ إِلَّا لَدَيۡهِ رَقِيبٌ عَتِيدٌ ۝ ﴾

"Man does not utter any word except that with him is an observer prepared [to record]." *{Qāf (50): 18}*

This is regarding the one who speaks as no one else will be held accountable for his word; so what about if he was to speak to the masses? He speaks and addresses his words to all of them so he is accountable for his words. All of us are sought to refer to this, whether the words are in a lecture, class, "lesson", book, interview or whatever. When statements are highlighted which oppose the *Sharee'ah*, some people may say *"akhī this is a literary writer and they are vast in their speech,"* etc.[1] Yet the *Sharee'ah* does not differentiate between a literary writer, a poet, a speaker, a preacher or others! Rather, poets are censured because they say that which they do not do, Allāh says,

﴿ وَٱلشُّعَرَآءُ يَتَّبِعُهُمُ ٱلۡغَاوُۥنَ . أَلَمۡ تَرَ أَنَّهُمۡ فِى كُلِّ وَادٖ يَهِيمُونَ . وَأَنَّهُمۡ يَقُولُونَ مَا لَا يَفۡعَلُونَ ﴾

"And the poets – [only] the deviators follow them; do you not see that in every valley they roam and that they say what they do not do?" *{ash-Shu'arā' (26): 224-226}*

Thus, everyone is accountable for their statements whether the person is a preacher, a speaker, a literary writer, a poet, a prose writer or whatever. Articulacy, literary skill, poetry or "saying it as it is" does not grant a person freedom to say whatever he likes, rather every statement that he makes he will be held accountable for. This is especially the case if many people are influenced by his words, for his sin will affect more than just him alone as is verified in Saheeh Muslim in the hadeeth of Jareer ibn 'Abdillāh al-Bajalī ☙ that the Prophet ﷺ said: *"Whoever starts a bad thing in Islam, and others do likewise after him, there will be written for him a burden of sin like that of those who followed*

---

[1] **Translator's note:** this is a common excuse which is made to defend Sayyid Qutb and some of his erroneous views within his *'tafseer'*.

him up until the Day of Judgement, without it detracting in the least from their burden."[1]

Sixth Principle

In order to reject criticisms of people, some people say *"this speech (that you are refuting) is cut and out of context"* – this is sometimes suggested when a critique is forwarded. There are two aspects to this:

❖ Cutting and pasting which changes the meaning (of what was intended) and this is *dhulm* (oppression) and *kadhib* (lying) about which a person will be held accountable. And it is not permitted for anyone to follow the statement of a person about another person if it is solely based on statements which have been cut, taken out of context and have changed the meaning of what was intended by the speaker being critiqued.

❖ Cut statements which have further attestation and do not change the meaning.

This is what the Imāms of Islām adhered to and you will see that if the Imāms refuted anyone they would make reference to further supporting evidences from the person's statements and then refute. If they also wanted to use as evidence Allāh's Book and the Sunnah of His Messenger ﷺ then they would use that which is relevant to what they were discussing. Furthermore, if cut speech does

---

[1] **Translator's note:** The hadeeth is also reported by at-Tirmidhī, an-Nasā'ī and Ibn Mājah.

not change the meaning of the reality (of what was intended) then it has to be accepted. So if one wants to claim that certain speech is cut, taken out of context and has changed the meaning then he has to clarify and bring proof. Mere cutting of statements is not sufficient to refute.

Some people also say: *"your words about so-and-so are delving into his intentions"*. It can be said to this: that this is general, so if a man is refuted on account of what he said or wrote, is this deemed to be "speaking about the person's intentions" or a refutation of what the person himself manifested? How often it is heard, when a deviant person is refuted with clear speech and proofs, that this is *"speaking about his intentions"*? This is a mistake because his speech has to be looked into. If the speech criticising him is based on a statement that he said or an action that he did then it is not *"looking into a person's intentions"*.

Furthermore, the apparent and the internal are interconnected as mentioned in the *hadeeth* of Nu'man ibn Basheer ﷺ in the *Saheehayn*: that the Messenger of Allāh ﷺ said: *"There is a piece of flesh in the body, if it is sound then the whole body will be sound, but if it is corrupted then the whole body will be corrupted – indeed that piece of flesh is the heart."* Therefore, if a man said a statement and by his actions it is known that he wants something then the critique of him is based on his action – this is not considered to be speaking about a person's intentions. What is also used to divert speaking about a person who erred is to say: *"the person has served the deen"*. It can be said to this: *"Yes, the person may have served the deen; however at the same time he is also opposing the deen! And we are sought to stop him opposing the deen so that we will not be held accountable with Allāh, the Lord of the Worlds."* This is especially the case as this is forbidding evil, and of the greatest characteristics of this Ummah of Muhammad is that it is an Ummah established on commanding the good and forbidding the evil. Allāh says,

﴿ كُنتُمْ خَيْرَ أُمَّةٍ أُخْرِجَتْ لِلنَّاسِ تَأْمُرُونَ بِٱلْمَعْرُوفِ وَتَنْهَوْنَ عَنِ ٱلْمُنكَرِ ﴾

"You are the best nation produced [as an example] for mankind. You enjoin what is right and forbid what is wrong..." *{Āli Imrān (3): 110}*

Forbidding the error of the one who makes a mistake and the one who destroys the *deen* with his misguidance is a great reason for curses to be lifted from the Ummah of Muhammad ﷺ. Allāh says,

﴿ لُعِنَ ٱلَّذِينَ كَفَرُوا۟ مِنۢ بَنِىٓ إِسْرَٰٓءِيلَ عَلَىٰ لِسَانِ دَاوُۥدَ وَعِيسَى ٱبْنِ مَرْيَمَ ذَٰلِكَ بِمَا عَصَوا۟ وَّكَانُوا۟ يَعْتَدُونَ . كَانُوا۟ لَا يَتَنَاهَوْنَ عَن مُّنكَرٍ فَعَلُوهُ لَبِئْسَ مَا كَانُوا۟ يَفْعَلُونَ ﴾

"Cursed were those who disbelieved among the Children of Israel by the tongue of David and of Jesus, the son of Mary. That was because they disobeyed and [habitually] transgressed. They used to not prevent one another from wrongdoing that they did. How wretched was that which they were doing." *{al-Mā'idah (5): 78-79}*

Such forbiddance results in evil curses being lifted from the Ummah of Muhammad ﷺ. So it is wājib on the whole Ummah of Muhammad to support

34

those who forbid the evil of doubts, innovations and misguidance. We ask Allāh, who there is no god except He, to make us from those who command the good and forbid the evil of desires and doubts.

How often is it stated when deflecting criticisms that *"the person has some good"*? Yes, the person may have some good, but we have to know that Allāh did not create evil solely, and there is not a creation except that it has some good in it. Imām Ibn ul-Qayyim ﷺ stated in his book *Shifā' al-'Aleel* that Allāh's creation are between good and that there are instances where evil is overpowered, and he mentioned this even in regards to Iblees as is found in his book *Madārij us-Sālikeen*. How many of the creation fall into disobedience due to Iblees and then make *tawbah*? How many of the creation disobey Allāh due to Iblees and then make *tawbah* and their condition after the *tawbah* becomes better than their condition before? So there is nothing from the creation of Allāh except that its good can overpower its evil.

Their statement and principle *"he has some good"* necessitates that even Iblees should not be refuted and this is *bātil* which Allāh has invalidated when He explained the misguidance of Iblees, and the Messenger of Allāh ﷺ also invalidated this by refuting the one who erred openly. A group of men came to the Prophet ﷺ as relayed in Saheeh Muslim in the *hadeeth* of 'Adiyy ibn Hātim where a speaker of this group stood and spoke saying: *"Whoever obeys Allāh and the Messenger, then he is guided, and whoever disobeys the two of them, then he is misguided."* Do you find that the Messenger of Allāh ﷺ was over-courteous with him because he was with a visiting group and their representative speaker? No not at all! Rather, when the man's error was overt, the Messenger of Allāh ﷺ censured the error openly. The Messenger of Allāh said ﷺ: *"What a bad speaker you are! Instead say: 'And whoever disobeys Allāh and His Messenger'."*

As a result, Imām Abu'l-'Abbās Shaykh ul-Islām Ibn Taymiyyah mentioned in *Majmū' al-Fatāwā,* and as did Imām 'Abdul'Azeez bin Bāz ﷻ, that: **Whoever errs openly is to be corrected openly.** It is not to be said *"Leave him and do not criticise him because he has good in him"* and the likes of such unacceptable objections. Also from such unacceptable objections are that some people say: *"His intention is good"*, in response to this it should be said: *"His intention could be good and he could desire good yet you have to know that acts of worship have to have two conditions: ikhlās, a sincere intention and (in) following of the Messenger of Allāh ﷺ."* Allāh says,

$$﴿ قُلْ هَلْ نُنَبِّئُكُم بِٱلْأَخْسَرِينَ أَعْمَـٰلًا . ٱلَّذِينَ ضَلَّ سَعْيُهُمْ فِى ٱلْحَيَوٰةِ ٱلدُّنْيَا وَهُمْ يَحْسَبُونَ أَنَّهُمْ يُحْسِنُونَ صُنْعًا ﴾$$

"Say, [O Muhammad], 'Shall we [believers] inform you of the greatest losers as to [their] deeds? [They are] those whose effort is lost in worldly life, while they think that they are doing well in work.'" *{al-Kahf (18): 103-104}*

Their intention is good, yet when they were in opposition to the way of the Messenger ﷺ their action was evil. Ad-Dārimī reported a *hadeeth* which mentions that some people were gathered praising Allāh ten times while using

36

stones to count the *tasbeeh* and *tahleel*. When Abdullāh ibn Mas'ūd saw them, he forbade what they were doing. One of them said: *"Yā 'AbdarRahmān, by Allāh, we did not intend except good!"* Look my brothers! His intention is good, Ibn Mas'ūd ﷺ however said: *"How many desire the good yet never gain it?"* So a good intention is not sufficient, rather it has to be accompanied by good action in line with the Prophet ﷺ. This is known in reality, because if a man wants to go to Makkah, may Allāh bless him with *Tawheed* and the Sunnah, yet takes a route which does not lead him to Makkah, although he has good intention, will he reach Makkah? No! So along with good intention there has to be good action which is traversing the way that will lead him to Makkah.

Also there are those who say, when objecting to criticisms, that: *"you are just relying on quotes from newspapers and the media when these are not trustworthy"* – this can be refuted from a number of angles. Firstly, those people (who are being criticised) depend on newspapers in order to transmit their own statements, so you will see that they themselves will write an article and then send it to the newspapers or write out a *"fatwa"* and then send it to the newspapers. So this indicates that the person is himself happy with using newspapers and the media as a source of transmitting his statements. Secondly, most of these people (who are being criticised) are media friendly and are often on TV channels and have their articles within the papers (and now there is the web wherein everyone is able to write). So if there was a lie made against him they would not keep quiet if it was speech ascribed to him, and if he did keep quiet, he would be blamed. So if they (those being criticised) were lied against, they would clarify just as they have done when many other matters were falsely ascribed to them, thus absolving themselves from those claims. Therefore, if the newspapers, or any other medium, transmitted anything from those media friendly speakers specifically, or from others generally, and they did not negate the accusations from themselves, this indicates that such statements are affirmed from them and whoever attributes such statements to them is correct.

What is also stated in deflecting criticisms is that it is said: *"We asked so-and-so about the statements and he negate that he made such statements"* and this is what many of the Harakīs (activists) and Hizbīs (biased partisans) do. So you will see that if any of them say something which was widely distributed in the newspapers or gatherings witnessed by *thiqāt* and then their followers go and ask them, they (i.e. the Hizbīs and Harakīs) will say: *"No, this is not true I didn't say that"*. This is unacceptable. So if the person is truthful, he should stand in front of the people and denounce the speech as being false but if trustworthy witnesses were there then show that they were relating falsely. As for the person mentioning something which was then distributed in the newspapers and via other means but then in private sessions he denies that he even said such statements to his followers, this is unacceptable. The person also has to negate the accusations in front of the masses as his speech was disseminated in front of the masses. So it is not correct for a person to just negate the speech ascribed to him within private sessions with his followers. This is playing around, we ask Allāh to grant us all good health.

It will also thus be said that: *"so-and-so has other speech other than this speech"*, so you will see a person say something and then his followers will come and find other speech and say: *"he has other speech which opposes this speech so how can you ascribe what you have to him?"* It can be said to this: Allāh has taught us in His Book that whoever errs, this error is affirmed so that his error be accepted by doing what Allāh mentioned when He said:

$$﴿ إِلَّا ٱلَّذِينَ تَابُواْ وَأَصْلَحُواْ وَبَيَّنُواْ ﴾$$

"Except those who repent, rectify and manifest (the truth)..."

{al-Baqarah (2): 160}

They have to have repented from the sin, rectified themselves from what they corrupted initially and manifest the truth by saying that they erred beforehand and have now retracted. Imām Ibn ul-Qayyim mentioned this in his book *Iddat us-Sābireen.* What also has to be known is that some of them play around in the name of repentance, so you'll find someone making many errors and then say *"all what I stated before I have retracted from is....."* but there has to be a general and clear *tawbah* with an explanation, saying: *"I erred in such-and-such a matter and I repent for it".* One cannot just come with general statements which confuse the common people. This is a matter of the deen and Allāh knows what is in the hearts, glory unto Him.

Some of them also say: *"Did you advise so-and-so before you refuted him?"* Firstly, it can be said that the condition of giving advice has no evidence. Rather, whoever errs openly is to be censured openly, as it was mentioned beforehand that the Prophet ﷺ censured a spokesman from a group of people openly and he did not take him by the hand to advise him initially and then after that refute him. Rather, the Prophet ﷺ censured him openly without giving advice. This is the first matter, the condition of giving advice has no proof for it, whoever wants to obligate people to advice a person before he can be refuted has to bring evidence for this. This advice has to be in the context of the *masālih* (benefits) and *mafāsid* (harms) because sometimes the benefit of giving advice can take precedence over refuting him initially, and sometimes the benefits in refuting the person can take precedence over the benefit of giving advice. As a result, the matter has to be looked into and the greater benefit has to take precedence. Secondly, according to what we know, there is not a man from those famous Harakīs and Takfīrīs except that he has been advised! Not once, but many times! Advised by the 'Ulama and students of (Islamic) knowledge; but with all this they still continue (in their ways).

Seventh Principle

If you loved a person and this person made an error which obligated his *tabdī'* (declaring him an innovator) and *tadleel* (declaring him to be misguided) there will arrive a tribulation. So at this point one has to inquire: is the love of this person for Allāh's sake? If so then you would free yourself from this person because he made an error which obligated his misguidance. If the love was not for the sake of Allāh, or was for the sake of Allāh and then changed, and you remained with your love of him and you did not treat him in the way the

Sharee'ah demands, then your love here is not for the sake of Allāh. So look at yourself because love for the sake of Allāh is a serious matter, as it is verified in the Two Saheehs in the hadeeth of Abū Hurayrah ﷺ that the Prophet ﷺ said: *"There are seven whom Allāh will shade in His (Throne's) Shade on the Day when there is no shade except His Shade..."* We ask Allāh to make us from them, along with our parents, children and wives. He said in the hadeeth: *"...two men who love each other for Allāh's sake, meeting for that and parting upon that..."* So love for the sake of Allāh is a serious matter enough for one to be shaded on the Day when there will be no shade except (the Shade of the Throne of) Allāh. Bishr al-Hāfī and Imām Sufyān ath-Thawrī, as al-Bayhaqī reported in *Shu'b ul-Īmān,* stated:

Love for the sake of Allāh and hate for the sake of Allāh, is when you see a man who loves another for the sake of Allāh but then the man invents a new matter in Islām and yet the other man continues to love him, then know that the man does not love him for the sake of Allāh.

Imām Abū 'Abdir-Rahmān Muqbil bin Hādī al-Wādi'ī ﷺ said a statement which is worthy of being written in gold:

«فأهل السنة ليست لديهم محاباة بخلاف المبتدعة»

"So Ahlus Sunnah do not have with them (blind) love (for individuals) in opposition to the innovators."[1]

We ask Allāh to grant us love for His sake.

---

[1] Muqaddimah of *Tuhafat-ush-Shābir Rabbānī,* p. 4.

Eighth Principle

Of the most important things that the Salaf warned against was *talawwun* (changing colour and assuming various forms) in the *deen* in regards to matters where it is not permitted to differ. As for a person having a different view in a matter where it is permitted to differ, in *fiqh* issues, then this is allowed because the Imāms of the Sunnah had different views which changed over time. Imām ash-Shāfi'ī had certain views when he was in Irāq but his views differed when he went to Egypt. Imām Ahmad also had different views, for which there are differing narrations from him numbering two or three, regarding certain issues. Yet all of this was in matters which it is permitted to differ. As for matters where it is not permitted to differ, pay attention to this, it is incorrect to use the speech of Imām ash-Shāfi'ī for example, and this is what many of the Harakīs and Takfīrīs do. If his (i.e. the Takfīrī's) statement is criticised and he moves onto a next innovation he will say:

"What I am doing is what Imām ash-Shāfi'ī did when he changed his view when he was in Egypt and then changed his view in Irāq".

This is an error, as the *Salaf* censured assuming various views in matters wherein it is not permitted. Ibn 'AbdulBarr reported in *Jāmi' Bayān 'Ilm wa Fadlihi* that Ibrāheem an-Nakhā'ī said: *"Talawwun in the deen is disliked."* It is also reported that Hudhayfah ibn al-Yamān said, and pay attention: *"It is censured to deny what you know and to claim to know that which you deny. Beware of talawwun in the deen because the deen of Allāh is one."* He spoke the truth may Allāh be pleased with him. Assuming various positions (talawwun) in matters wherein it is not permitted to differ is not correct to hold in the Sharee'ah of Muhammad ﷺ. So know that when you see a man nearly everyday assuming various forms in matters where it is not permitted to differ, then you should be aware that he is upon misguidance resulting in him going from one innovation to another.

Ninth Principle

It is a must to differentiate between a scholar, preacher, admonisher, literary writer, student of knowledge, pious worshipper and others. It is incorrect to mix them all together (as being on the same level) otherwise we will fall into a grave calamity. It is verified in the Two Saheehs from the hadeeth of Abū Sa'eed ﷺ that the Prophet ﷺ said: *"Among those who came before you was a man who killed ninety-nine men. So he asked about where he could find the most knowledgeable of the people on earth. He was told to go to a Monk (a pious worshipper), so the man asked him 'I have killed ninety-nine people, is there any tawbah for me?' The monk replied 'No'. So the man killed him too to make the number of those who had killed one hundred. He then asked again about where he could find the most knowledgeable person on the earth and was told to go to a scholar. The man said to the scholar 'I have killed a hundred people, is there any tawbah for me?' The scholar replied 'Yes, what is there between you and tawbah? Go to such and such a land where there are some people worshipping Allāh, go and worship with them.'"* To the end of the hadeeth. Pay attention brothers, when the matter became confused and mixed up and he did not differentiate between the pious worshipper and the scholar this calamity occurred. When did the pious worshipper make a mistake? When he transgressed his bounds, if he remained on what he was doing in terms of worship then his action would not be censured, but when he transgressed this and placed himself into the position of the people of knowledge he erred and his recompense was to be killed. Likewise, those admonishers that you see who give sermons, or those reciters and *du'āt* or others, when they transgress their bounds - then know for certain that they are incorrect in doing so. Thus, the people have to differentiate between the *du'āt*, admonishers and reciters and between the 'Ulama and students of knowledge.[1] Al-Khateeb al-Baghdādī ﷺ reports the hadeeth:

«من أشراط الساعة أن يلتمس العلم عند الأصاغر»

"From the signs of the Hour is that knowledge will be taken from the Smaller ones."

Ibn al-Mubārak ﷺ said:

«الأصاغر من أهل البدع»

"The smaller ones are the people of innovation."

---

[1] These introductory principles have been adapted from the nine introductions provided by our Shaykh, 'Abdul'Azeez bin Rayyis ar-Rayyis' critique of Dr 'Ā'id al-Qarnī which is available to download in audio format from www.islamancient.com and translated into English here:
http://www.salafimanhaj.com/pdf/SalafiManhaj_AlQarni.pdf

Narrated 'Abdullāh Ibn 'Amr Ibn al-'Ās ﷺ: "I heard Allāh's Messenger ﷺ saying: *"Allāh does not take away knowledge by taking it away from (the hearts of) the people, but He takes it away by the death of the scholars till when none of the (scholars) remains, people will take as their leaders ignorant people who when consulted will give their verdict without knowledge. So, they will go astray and will lead the people astray."*[1]

Abū Hurayrah ﷺ narrated that the Messenger of Allāh ﷺ said: *"There will come upon the people years of deceit wherein the liar will be regarded as truthful and the truthful will be considered a liar and the dishonest will be trusted and the trustworthy one will be considered dishonest and the Ruwaybidah will begin to speak!"* Then it was asked: *"What are the Ruwaybidah?"* He ﷺ replied: *"The foolish insignificant man who speaks about general affairs."*[2] The following narration is also important in regards to El-Faisal:

عن ابن مسعود قال : كيف بكم إذا لبستكم فتنة يهرم فيها الكبير ويربو فيها الصغير يتخذها الناس سنة إذا ترك منها شيء قيل : تركت السنة ؟ قيل : يا أبا عبد الرحمن ؟ ومتى ذلك ؟ قال : إذا كثرت جهالكم وقلت علماؤكم وكثرت خطباؤكم وقلت فقهاؤكم وكثرت أمراؤكم وقلت أمناؤكم وتفقه لغير الدين والتمست الدنيا بعمل الآخرة.

---

[1] Saheeh al-Bukhārī vol. 1, no. 100
[2] Reported by Ahmad in his Musnad, Ibn Mājah and others with a weak chain of narration, but Ahmad has another chain of narration for the hadeeth, which makes the hadeeth *hasan*.

From Ibn Mas'ūd who said: *"How will you be if tribulation afflicts you which the old have grown old upon and the young have been cultivated upon, and which the people have taken as Sunnah. To the extent that if these actions are not done it will be said 'the Sunnah has been left'."* It was said: *'O Abā 'AbdarRahmān, when will that be?'* Ibn Mas'ūd replied: *"If your ignoramuses are many, and your 'Ulama are a few, and if your Khutabā' are many and your Fuqahā are a few; and if your leaders are many and your trustworthy people are a few, and when you gain understanding of other than the deen and you try to attain the dunya with the action of the Hereafter."*[1]

[1] Nu'aym bin Hammād, *Kitāb ul-Fitan*. It is also relayed in 'Ali bin Hisāmuddeen al-Muttaqī al-Hindī (d. 975 AH/1567 CE), *Kanz ul-'U'mmāl fī Sunan il-Aqwāl wa'l-Af āl* (Beirut: Mu'assat ar-Risālah, 1989 CE), p.1795. It can be accessed Online from the website of *Imām Muhammad bin Saud Islamic University* here:
http://www.imamu.edu.sa/DContent/BOOKS/arabic_ibook14/part2/home.html

Introduction To 'Abdullah 'El' Faisal And A Study Of His Methodological Background

Indeed, all praise is due to Allāh, we praise Him, we seek His aid, and we ask for His forgiveness. We seek refuge in Allāh from the evil of our actions and from the evil consequences of our actions. Whomever Allāh guides, there is none to misguide and whomever Allāh misguides there is none to guide. I bear witness that there is no god worthy of worship except Allāh and I bear witness that Muhammad is the servant and Messenger of Allāh. To proceed:

﴿ يَـٰٓأَيُّهَا ٱلَّذِينَ ءَامَنُواْ ٱتَّقُواْ ٱللَّهَ حَقَّ تُقَاتِهِۦ وَلَا تَمُوتُنَّ إِلَّا وَأَنتُم مُّسۡلِمُونَ ﴾

"O you who have believed, fear Allāh as He should be feared and do not die except as Muslims (in submission to Him)."

{Āli-Imrān (3): 102}

﴿ يَـٰٓأَيُّهَا ٱلنَّاسُ ٱتَّقُواْ رَبَّكُمُ ٱلَّذِى خَلَقَكُم مِّن نَّفۡسٍ وَٰحِدَةٍ وَخَلَقَ مِنۡهَا زَوۡجَهَا وَبَثَّ مِنۡهُمَا رِجَالًا كَثِيرًا وَنِسَآءً وَٱتَّقُواْ ٱللَّهَ ٱلَّذِى تَسَآءَلُونَ بِهِۦ وَٱلۡأَرۡحَامَ إِنَّ ٱللَّهَ كَانَ عَلَيۡكُمۡ رَقِيبًا ﴾

"O mankind, fear your Lord, who created you from one soul and created from it its mate and dispersed from both of them many men and women. And fear Allāh through whom you ask things from each other, and (respect) the wombs. Indeed Allāh is ever, over you, an Observer." *{an-Nisā (4): 1}*

﴿ يَـٰٓأَيُّهَا ٱلَّذِينَ ءَامَنُوا۟ ٱتَّقُوا۟ ٱللَّهَ وَقُولُوا۟ قَوْلًا سَدِيدًا . يُصْلِحْ لَكُمْ أَعْمَـٰلَكُمْ وَيَغْفِرْ لَكُمْ ذُنُوبَكُمْ ۗ وَمَن يُطِعِ ٱللَّهَ وَرَسُولَهُۥ فَقَدْ فَازَ فَوْزًا عَظِيمًا ﴾

"O you who have believed, fear Allāh and speak words of appropriate justice. He will amend for you your deeds and forgive your sins. And whoever obeys Allāh and His Messenger has certainly attained a great attainment." *{al-Ahzāb (33): 70-71}*

The best speech is the book of Allāh and the best guidance is the guidance of Muhammad ﷺ. The worst of affairs are the newly invented matters, for every newly invented matter into the religion is an innovation, and every innovation (into the religion) is misguidance and all misguidance is in the fire, we seek refuge in Allāh from it (the fire). Then to proceed:

Fundamentally, this book was authored to provide unsuspecting Muslims with an insight into the deviant dogma of Abdullāh Faisal; however, due to Faisal's diversity in deviancy, this book has had to tackle a multitude of malicious beliefs and practices which contradict and oppose the Straight Path laid down by Allāh and His Messenger ﷺ. Thus, this book not only reveals the true colours of Faisal, but it also serves as a miscellaneous handbook for removing contemporary doubts spread by the likes of Abdullāh Faisal and other new-age Takfiris.

The citations and quotations we have gathered between the covers of this book are so disturbing and worrying that it could easily be argued that it was not necessary to critique them. Many of Faisal's statements are so revealing that they stand alone in testimony to his deviant dogma and extremist behaviour. However, despite this fact, there are still Muslims – albeit a small minority - who are prepared to give 'ear' to Faisal and his malevolent maunderings. For that reason, we undertook the task of trying to place hazard signs in front of Faisal and his 'black ice' ideologies so that our unsuspecting brothers and sisters can safely negotiate themselves around this slippery deviant.

Faisal's deviant da'wah was once limited to the shores of Britain but since his deportation back to his homeland of Jamaica he has now embarked on new frontiers via the internet carrying with him his same old pernicious ideologies. As an example of Abdullāh Faisal's recent activities, in August 2010 we came across the following advertisement for his paltalk lectures, which still refer to him as being "Shaykh". Lo and behold, we find him being advertised with other prominent Takfiris and former Muhajiroun leaders:

While in November 2010 the following was advertised:

The great scholar of Basra, Muhammad Ibn Sīrīn said:

إِنَّ هَذَا الْعِلْمَ دِينٌ فَانْظُرُوا عَمَّنْ تَأْخُذُونَ دِينَكُمْ

This knowledge is the (foundation of) religion, so watch from whom you take your religion.[1]

Born 'Trevor William Forrest', in Point St. James (14 miles from Montego Bay) in Jamaica, he has been responsible for issuing a number of erroneous and extreme rulings to the youth in London, the wider UK and in other English speaking countries such as Nigeria, South Africa and the US. Raised as an active member of the Salvation Army he was allegedly nicknamed 'dictionary' due to his academic progress at a young age. He embraced Islām at the age of sixteen after which he studied at an Islamic educational institute in Guyana. After migrating to the UK in the 1980s, he then applied to study at *Imām Muhammad bin Saud Islamic University* where he was accepted to study. He later allegedly graduated from this university.[2] We state "allegedly" as the evidence for his graduation is unsubstantiated and this is all the more pertinent when his statements are assessed. This is because it is very odd for someone to have even studied at, let alone graduated from, *Imām Muhammad bin Saud Islamic University* and say the things that Abdullāh ("El") Faisal does, which even a first year student would not say. As a result, it is more likely that he

---

[1] Narrated by Muslim in the Introduction to his Sahīh

[2] Refer to an article by Mark Titus entitled *'From Church boy to militant Muslim'* in the *Jamaica Gleaner* (dated June 6 2007), the article can be accessed here: http://www.jamaica-gleaner.com/gleaner/20070606/news/news1.html

51

merely studied there for a few years as opposed to have graduated from the university and proof of his certification is yet to be seen.

Faisal supposedly completed his studies in 1988 and some of the elders from the Brixton Masjid have highlighted to us that he failed twice before eventually passing, if he even did pass. Faisal was introduced to the community at Brixton Mosque in 1990/91 and at this time, Faisal was not extreme in his ideas, and in fact the Brixton community was quite hopeful when he was introduced as he emphasised tawhīd. However, even at this early time, there were serious discrepancies in Faisal's approach as not only was there doubt as to his "graduation" from Imam Muhammad bin Saud Islamic University but also because he would make reference to inauthentic narrations in order to bolster his views, with scant referral to authentic hadeeth as a source. Faisal had gone to study in Saudi in the late 1980s and allegedly completed his studies around 1990/91, yet these details are shrouded in a degree of mystery. His certifications and qualifications have not been seen by the Salafis of Brixton, hence the doubt as to his Islamic study credentials. Indeed, it has even been corroborated by some of the elders from Brixton Mosque that in 1990/91, Faisal was even selling Michael Jackson music tapes in Brixton market!!?

In 1992, Faisal's extremism was noticed when he made takfir of the then administration of Brixton Mosque (led by AbdulMājid aka Uthmān Ibrāhīm Morrison) who were members of al-Murābitūn World Sufi Movement which was headed by the shadowy figure of Ian Dallas (AbdulQādir al-Murābit ad-

Darqawī). Faisal suggested that Uthmān Ibrāhīm Morrison (aka AbdulMājid), and those with him from the al-Murābitūn World Sufi Movement, were kuffār as Faisal had supposedly sat with them "and established the proofs on them" and hence they had to be forcibly removed from Brixton Mosque. Faisal asserted that if the brothers in Brixton were "not up to the job" to remove them then Faisal will call upon "brothers from Willesdon (in North-West London) to come and deal with it"! In this same year, Faisal stated, in a class at the house of Sirāt AbdulMālik 鵝, who pioneered Salafiyyah in Brixton and London in the early 1990s, that the Christians are to be counted among the 73 sects mentioned in the hadeeth of the Prophet 鵝. In 1992 Faisal also admitted to reading many books by Sayyid Qutb. After this series of odd rulings from Faisal, coupled with his usage of inauthentic hadeeth, Faisal's class at the house of Sirāt 'AbdulMālik was brought to an end. At this point Faisal began searching for 'pastures new' as it were, in other parts of London as his presence in Brixton was becoming less accepted.

In 1994, Faisal was sacked from his teaching role at Islamia School in West London and this was also the same year that the Salafi administration of Brixton Mosque (who had initially assumed control of the Mosque in 1993) totally relieved Faisal from any teaching that he was involved in at the Mosque's premises. This was exacerbated by Faisal's growing extremism exemplified in Faisal issuing a religious ruling (fatwā) that it is permitted to steal from Gulf Arabs who visit Central London. Faisal, in Brixton Mosque, expressed a recantation from this "ruling" after being challenged over it at Brixton Mosque. Faisal by this time had gathered around him a clique of followers, some of whom inclined towards him based on nationalism (because he was seen as a "Jamaican Shaykh"), and it was also as if Faisal delivered such aggressive "shock rulings" in order to gain attention which was not afforded to him by the Salafi administration of Brixton Mosque.

In 1995, Faisal also turned up at a JIMAS conference dressed in jeans, jumper and jacket exclaiming "I am not in my Shaykh clothes today I am in my Tālib ul-Ilm clothes"(!?) - as he said to AbdulHaqq Baker. By the end of 1995, Faisal had fully deteriorated and was a full blown Takfīrī and "Jihādī" (meaning one who emphasises military Jihād) and he came to Brixton in 1996, with Abū Qatādah al-Filistīnī (!) in order to attempt to debate the community there. From this point on, Faisal began to popularise Takfīrī-Jihādī thought among the youth in English speaking countries.[1]

When Faisal realised that he was unable to herd a flock of blind-followers from the community in Brixton, and from the youth of *Masjid Ibn Taymiyyah (Brixton Mosque)* in particular, his self-consuming frustrations caused him to launch a vicious propaganda campaign against the Salafis. His hate-fuelled

---

[1] One of the authors, AbdulHaq al-Ashanti, obtained this historical account of Abdullah Faisal from the original Brixton Salafis from 1991/92, such as: Abū Uthmān AbdulMālik, Abū Safiyyah Tālib Alexander, Abū Hajirah AbdurRahmān Anderson, Dr AbdulHaqq Baker, Abū Dāwud Samīr, Abū Yusuf AbdulHakīm and Abū Ilyās Idrīs.

mission was callous and simple: it was to fabricate a warped image of the Salafis in the eyes of the Muslim youth around UK and the West in general - an image fashioned from hyperbole, deception and barefaced lies. This was also exacerbated by the fact that Faisal was being abandoned in droves by those who had been with him for years, after they had come to realise his extremism.

Additionally, it is worth adding here that Faisal was never the "Imām of Brixton Mosque" which insinuates that he was the Imām of *Masjid Ibn Taymeeyah* aka *Brixton Mosque and Islamic Cultural Centre*, as some misinformed journalists have claimed in their shoddy and poorly researched articles. For example, Robert Mendick writing in the London *Evening Standard* on Friday 22 July 2005 CE claimed this and so did Martin Bentham in an article on Thursday 12 April 2007 again in the London *Evening Standard*. One of their main reasons for associating him with the *Brixton Mosque* is purely on racial grounds, due to the high population of the African-Caribbean community found in Brixton. However, this is a false and convenient conclusion. So for those out of touch journalists the equation on the blackboard is simple: **black+Muslim+convert to Islam = an associate of Brixton Mosque**! Yet had they actually bothered to contact *Masjid Ibn Taymeeyah (Brixton Mosque and Islamic Cultural Centre)* they would have found that this was not the case. Bentham states that :

"His convictions followed the discovery of a series of venomous taped lectures in which the Brixton Mosque preacher had urged his followers to 'fly planes, drive tanks, load your guns' and 'use nuclear missiles' to kill 'all unbelievers'."

Faisal is known for his extremist statements and blanket *takfeer*, including his 'take no hostage' type *takfeer* of the Salafi scholars whom he has labelled as being "kuffār" and "Jews" as we shall see in this study. He therefore suffers from a condition which we coin 'Excessive Compulsive Takfeer Disorder' (ECTD). In 2003, Faisal was in prison in the UK for kindling hatred amongst communities and as a result, on release was deported out of the UK. Like Abū Hamza, Faisal's own ill-mannered lectures, which were widely dispersed in the non-Salafi bookstores of London, take the stand as multiple witnesses, testifying to the guilt of this deviant defendant. His frustration and unbridled hatred with the *Salafi da'wah* led him to some very extreme and clear-cut *khāriji* statements which the reader will see straight from Faisal's own words.

After Faisal was deported back to Jamaica, where he had not set foot for fifteen years, the Islamic Council of Jamaica restricted his activities and thus banned him from preaching in Jamaican mosques. Some mosques broke this order and allowed him to give khutab in their Mosques, and he also gave khutab and talks at Spanish Town Mosque. Faisal must have had a sense of restriction during his time back on Jamaican soil, as it wasn't long before Faisal left Jamaica for an "African tour". This trip to Africa involved time mainly in Nigeria, South Africa, Botswana and Kenya, yet he also stopped off in Angola, Swaziland, Malawi, Mozambique and Tanzania.

During his time in these countries he lectured on general Islamic topics but his Takfiri approach was the same as ever. In one discussion with a Nigerian Salafi brother Faisal re-iterates his manhaj by speaking against the Salafis of Brixton Mosque and speaking ill of Imām Bin Bāz. Faisal's takfīr of the rulers was also still evident in his African tour and this found Faisal favourable associates in parts of Africa which had come under the influence of rabble-rousing revolutionary political methods in the garb of Islam.

On the 7th January 2010, the Kenyan authorities deported Faisal (once again!); however, deporting him was not a formality because many countries, due to his unsavoury reputation, declined to have him in transit. The deportation of Faisal led to violent protests in Kenya, which resulted in five people losing their lives after clashes with the Kenyan police. The protests allegedly involved youth who were supporters of the Somālī Takfīrī-Jihādī organisation "ash-Shabāb". Faisal chose Gambia as his next destination to pollute the minds and hearts of those who are oblivious to his toxic teachings. However, Gambia later reneged on its offer to accept Faisal because of the negative publicity surrounding the situation. After a brief stint in a Nairobi prison, Kenyan authorities finally chartered a Gulfstream Jet and deported Faisal to Jamaica. At present, Faisal resides back in his country of origin, Jamaica.

Faisal's tapes and audio lectures during his time in the UK were sold mainly in bookstores owned by those who can be classified into three types of people:

- ignorant Muslims who knew little of the true reality of Faisal;
- those who sold them for the purpose of profit;

- the stores of the people of innovation. Indeed, the Hanafi madhhab parochialists and Deobandis of the UK used to stock, sell and promote the lectures of Faisal, which not only demonstrates his harmful reach, but also the temporary collective unity that many partisan elements are prepared to tolerate when the Salafis are the ones caught in the crosshairs.

As for his so-called "refutations" of the Brailwīs and the like, these were scant in comparison to his vitriolic fighting against the people of *Sunnah*, the Salafis, as we shall clearly see from his own words in this treatise. After reading the previous paragraph one might ask himself, 'why does he place so much effort in fighting the Salafis, who in reality are the vanguards of *tawhīd* when we have large contingencies of Muslims (i.e. the Brailwīs) indulging in polytheistic practices?' Perhaps the answer to this, when psychoanalysed, is due to his personal feud with the Salafis.

The lectures of Faisal are available Online and one website in particular (*'Revolution Muslim'*)[1] has actually placed many of Faisal's ignorant lectures

---

[1] It was formerly known as 'Street Da'wah' - named as such in order to create the impression that Faisal relates to 'the street' as it were, and this is just a ploy in order to gain credibility amongst the youth whom Faisal brainwashes and uses. The website 'Revolution Muslim' is now defunct! Its former partisan leader, Yousef El-Khattab (Joey Cohen), split from the organisation and has since openly recanted in the American

Online. This made it easy for us to gather his calamitous errors and beliefs for this refutation. His lectures are still available Online on a variety of websites, which we will refer to throughout this study.

Another site entitled 'Haqunspun', by one of Faisal's blind followers, 'Amar Iqbal' of Manchester, actually tries to make money from Faisal's lectures of *bātil*.[1] Another website named 'Inshallah Shaheed' also promoted Faisal' ignorant lectures and utilises him as a reference point.[2] Before we analyse the ideas of 'Abdullāh ("El") Faisal ("Sheikh Faisal") it is important to note some recurring ideas that he tries to brainwash his audiences with:

[One]

Slander of the Islamic scholars and accusing them of treachery, selling-out and even *kufr*! Actually, it is a customary tactic of the neo-Takfīrīs to employ underhanded methods when attempting to severe the umbilical cord of knowledge, which fastens the youth to the rope of Allāh through their scholars. Faisal states after an hour and 19 minutes into the lecture entitled *No Peace with the Jews*:

---

media (NPR) for his involvement with the organisation Revolution Muslim. Whether this is a real recantation or a political move to avoid pressure from the authorities is unclear due to the comic machinations of Yousef Cohen. 'Revolution Muslim' does have an Online blog and another site 'IslamPolicy.com' which it also uses for its simplistic propaganda. See:
http://www.npr.org/templates/story/story.php?storyId=130519592
[1] See: http://www.haqunspun.com/
[2] As does the following website: www.darulislam.info

"Where the Jews got their {sic} strength from? Where the Jews got {sic} their strength from? The apostasy of the Muslim leaders! The treachery and hypocrisy of your scholars! Shaykh Bin Bāz did he pass any fatwa for us to liberate it? 'Uthaymeen of Saudi Arabia, did he pass any fatwa for us to liberate Masjid al Aqsa? Now which scholar in the Arabian Peninsula passed fatwa for us to liberate it? Shaykh Bin Bāz pass fatwa {sic} for us to have peace treaty {sic} with the Jews. So the Jews got their strength from the apostasy of your leaders! All the countries surrounding Israel have kāfir leaders: Syria, Jordan, Egypt, Lebanon – they're all kāfirs! The scholars in Saudi Arabia who keep quiet about the massacre they are also kāfirs as they refuse to pass fatwa for us to liberate it."

Faisal also stated in his "tafseer" (!?) of Sūrah al-Kāfirūn, after 1 hour and 22 minutes:

"Shaykh Bin Bāz says democracy is halāl and he's the one who told the people in Algeria to go vote and use democracy...he's jāhil of fiqh ul wāqi', current events."

These scholars have been actively involved in disseminating Islamic knowledge since Faisal was in the *'Salvation Army'* with his mother in Jamaica! In fact, Faisal did not return to visit Jamaica or his mother for over fifteen years.[1] So instead of calling the Muslim youth in English speaking countries to *takfeer*,

---

[1] See: http://www.jamaica-gleaner.com/gleaner/20060827/news/news7.html

erroneous ideas of *jihād* and revolting against Muslim governments, the rule of Allāh concerning the rights of the parents should have been implemented first! So how on earth can a so-called "Shaykh" fail to implement the rule of Allāh with regards to looking after the mother? There are many verses of Allāh wherein Allāh says:

﴿ وَٱتَّقُوا۟ ٱللَّهَ ٱلَّذِى تَسَآءَلُونَ بِهِۦ وَٱلْأَرْحَامَ إِنَّ ٱللَّهَ كَانَ عَلَيْكُمْ رَقِيبًا ﴾

"... And fear Allāh, through whom you ask one another and the wombs.[1] Indeed, Allāh is ever, over you, an Observer."

{an-Nisā (4): 1}

﴿ وَوَصَّيْنَا ٱلْإِنسَـٰنَ بِوَٰلِدَيْهِ حَمَلَتْهُ أُمُّهُۥ وَهْنًا عَلَىٰ وَهْنٍ وَفِصَـٰلُهُۥ فِى عَامَيْنِ أَنِ ٱشْكُرْ لِى وَلِوَٰلِدَيْكَ إِلَىَّ ٱلْمَصِيرُ ﴾

"And We have enjoined upon man (to care) for his parents. His mother carried him, (increasing her) in weakness upon weakness, and his weaning is in two years. Be grateful to Me and to your parents; to Me is the (final) destination." *{Luqmān (31): 14}*

Allāh says in a verse, which is particularly pertinent to this study:

﴿ فَهَلْ عَسَيْتُمْ إِن تَوَلَّيْتُمْ أَن تُفْسِدُوا۟ فِى ٱلْأَرْضِ وَتُقَطِّعُوٓا۟ أَرْحَامَكُمْ ﴾

"So would you perhaps, if you turned away, cause corruption on earth and sever your ties of relationship?" *{Muhammad (47): 22}*

---

[1] i.e. fear Allāh in regards to ties of kinship.

It is reported in *Kitāb ul-Jihād* of the Saheeh of Imām al-Bukhārī; *Kitāb ul-Birr wa's-Silah wa'l-Ādab* in the Saheeh of Imām Muslim; *Kitāb ul-Jihād* in the Sunan of Imām at-Tirmidhī; *Kitāb ul-Jihād* in the Sunan of Imām an-Nasā'ī; *Kitāb ul-Jihād* in the Sunan of Imām Abū Dāwud and in the Musnad of Imām Ahmad that:

'Abdullāh Ibn 'Amr ﷺ said: "A man came to the Prophet ﷺ and asked for his permission to go for jihād. He said,

$$((\text{أَحَيٌّ والداك؟}))$$

'Are your parents alive?'

The man replied, 'Yes.' The Prophet ﷺ said:

$$((\text{ففيهما فجاهد}))$$

'Then your jihād is with them.'"

Imāms Ahmad and Abū Dāwud include the additional narrations, authenticated by Ibn Hibbān, from the Prophet ﷺ:

$$((\text{ارجع فاستأذنهما فإن أذنا لك فجاهد وإلا فبرهما}))$$

"Go back and seek their permission and if they grant you permission (then wage armed jihād) and if they do not (grant you permission) then be dutiful to them (and their wishes)."

The hadeeth of the Prophet Muhammad ﷺ from Abū 'Amru ash-Shaybānī who said, *"The owner of this house narrated to us,"* and he indicated with his hand to the house of 'Abdullāh Ibn Mas'ood ﷺ, that he said:

"I asked the Prophet ﷺ: "Which action is the most beloved to Allāh?" He said:

((الصلاة لوقتها))

"Prayer at its correct time."

I said, *"then which action?"* He said:

((ثم بر الوالدين))

"Birr (good treatment, kindness) to the parents."

I said, "Then which?" He said:

((ثم الجهاد في سبيل الله))

"then Jihād in the way of Allāh."[1]

So before jihād, the Prophet ﷺ mentioned being good and dutiful to parents, yet a so-called 'Sheikh of jihād', did not implement this at all himself! A man asked *"O Messenger of Allāh who is most deserving of my birr?"* He said, *"Your mother."* The man asked, *"Then who?"* He said, *"Your mother."* The man asked,

---

[1] Mentioned in *Saheeh Adab al-Mufrad;* the hadeeth is agreed upon and to be found in Saheeh ul-Bukhārī, *Kitāb ul-Mawāqeet us-Salāh* and Saheeh Muslim, *Kitāb ul-Īmān.*

"Then who?" He said, *"Your mother."* The man asked again, *"Then who?"* He said, *"Then your father."*[1]

From Taysalah bin Mayyās who said Ibn 'Umar ﷺ said to me, *"Do you fear the fire and wish to enter the Paradise?"* I said, *"Of course, by Allāh!"* He said, *"Are your parents alive?"* I said, *"I have a mother."* He said, *"Then by Allāh! If you were to speak gently to her and feed her, you would certainly enter paradise, as long as you stay away from the Major sins."*[2]

From Abdullāh bin 'Umar ﷺ who said, a man came to the Prophet ﷺ to give him the *bay'ah* for *hijrah*, and he left his parents crying. So the Prophet ﷺ said:

((ارجع إليهما فأضحكهما كما أبكيتهما))

"Return to your parents and make them laugh as you have made them cry."[3]

In a *saheeh hadeeth*, the Prophet ﷺ was informed by Asmā bint Abī Bakr as-Siddeeq ﷺ that her disbelieving mother was about to visit her saying:

قدمت عليّ أمي وهي مشركة في عهد رسول الله صلى الله عليه وسلم، فاستفتيت

رسول الله صلى الله عليه وسلم، قلت: إن أميّ قدمت وهي راغبة، أفأصل أمي؟

---

[1] Saheeh ul-Bukhārī and Muslim
[2] Mentioned in *Saheeh Adab al-Mufrad*; See Imām al-Albānī, *as-Saheehah*, no.2898.
[3] Mentioned in *Saheeh Adab al-Mufrad*; Sunan, Imām an-Nasā'ī, *Kitāb ul-Bay'ah*; Sunan, Imām Abū Dāwud, *Kitāb ul-Jihād*; Sunan, Ibn Mājah, *Kitāb ul-Jihād*; Ibn Hibbān. See Imām al-Albānī, *at-Ta'leeq ar-Ragheeb*, vol.3, p.213.

"My mother came to me, and she was a *mushrik* at the time of the Prophet 紫. I asked the Prophet 紫: *"My mother has come to me and needs my help, so should I help her?"* He 紫 said:

((نعم، صلي أمك))

"Yes, keep in touch with your mother and treat her well."[1]

Yet 49 minutes into the lecture entitled 'Jihād' by Faisal he claims that the cockroach has more dignity than a non-Muslim and that the Qur'ān teaches this!!? Allāh, the Most High mentions *al-Birr bil Wālidayn* after *shirk*, but it seems that nothing holds more priority to Faisal than his feud against the Salafi Da'wah.

[Two]

By slandering and discrediting the scholars, he subliminally and indirectly puts his own self forward. Since ("el") Faisal's corrupt rules of engagement, in filling the shoes of his Khawārij predecessors, are to undermine the integrity of true possessors of Islamic knowledge by hurling at them all types of disparaging remarks, whilst hoping that some of his vile diatribe sticks. He launches tirades against the Muslim scholars even saying that some of the senior scholars are "more befitting to be called Rabbis" (!!) as he states in the question and answer session of the lecture *Treachery from Within*. This is also aggravated by referring to himself as being a "Shaykh" who has some Islamic credentials. Indeed, from

---

[1] Bukhārī, *hadeeth* no.2620 and Muslim, *hadeeth* no.1003; See *Sharh us-Sunnah*, vol.13, p.13, *Kitāb al-Birr wa's-Silah, Bāb Silat al-Wālid al-Mushrik.*

the characteristics of the khawārij is that the first of them did not believe that the people of knowledge have any kind of virtue, so they viewed themselves as being more knowledgeable than 'Ali Ibn Abī Tālib, Ibn 'Abbās and the other companions ﷺ. Look closely and you will witness a carbon copy characteristic preserved in the mannerisms and rhetoric of Faisal. Indeed, Faisal has also poured scorn on Ibn 'Abbās, we will look at this within this study.

[Three]

He aligns himself with those who are seen as being against the status quo. So in the nineties he used to praise Safar al-Hawālī, Salmān al-'Awda, Ā'id al-Qarnī et al. then from 2001 CE began quoting and referring to Bin Lādin, from whom he never ever used to mention anything, as he did so in the lecture *'Rules of Jihād.'* Faisal also did this with his futile defence of 'Umar 'AbdurRahmān and referring to him as "his Shaykh" when he never even knew him!? In fact, in Faisal's lecture of *takfeer* and extremism entitled *'21st Century House Niggers'*, Faisal purposefully left out the fact that 'Umar 'AbdurRahmān praised the Rawāfid Shi'a pseudo-revolution in Irān as being "a blessed revolution" yet Faisal did not see any problem in praising the Rāfidī al-Khomaynī. What blessings can one find in the axioms of the Rawāfid, such as their polytheistic concept of Imāmah, or the deification of 'Ali ﷺ? Seriously, what could possibly drive a man to praise such a group?

[Four]

An unhealthy pre-occupation with politics with an aim to get his audiences to cast aspersions against, and have evil suspicions about, Muslim countries.

[Five]

Tadlees (deception in narrating and relaying information)[1] – So it has been noted by some of the elder Salafi brothers in London that Faisal used to

---

[1] The scholars of hādeeth have noted that there are five main types of *tadlees*:

Tadlees ul-Isnad – this is where a narrator claims to have heard a *hadeeth* or a narration from a Shaykh who he usually narrates from and studies with, but in this instance he did not hear anything at all from the Shaykh. There is a degree of meeting and correspondence yet in this case he ascribes something to the Shaykh which he did not actually directly hear from him. Ibn 'AbdulBarr ﷺ states *"As for tadlees it is when a man narrates from a man whom he met and lived at the same time as and took from him and narrates from the man what he did not directly hear from him"*, at-Tamheed, vol.1, pp.15-16. So here the narrator will say *"Anna"* (certainly...), *"an"* (from...) or *"Qāla"* (he said) so it is not necessarily a clear and blatant lie.

Tadlees ut-Taswiyah – this is the most serious type as it is when a narrator purposefully leaves out and drops someone in his chain of transmission because he is weak and it will weaken his narrations. So for example, a Shaykh who is *thiqah* heard from one who was weak who heard from one who is *thiqah*, yet the weak one is left out of the chain in order to make it seem as if the two *thiqāt* heard directly from each other without anyone in the middle.

Tadlees ul-Qat' – this is when the narrator of a *hadeeth* pauses and then just mentions any name as if the person named mentioned actually relayed the *hadeeth*. This is also known as *Tadlees us-Sukūt*.

Tadlees ul-'Atf – this is when a narrator narrates from *two Shuyūkh* but actually only heard from one of them.

Tadlees ush-Shuyūkh – this is when a narrator uses a name of a person in a chain of narration that is well known by the people as being credible, when in reality it is a person who is da'eef but with the same name. So for example, the *mudallis* states: *"I heard Abū 'Abdullāh say..."* trying to deceive the people that it is Ahmad ibn Hanbal who is well known by the name "Abū 'Abdullāh" when it is really someone else. Or using "Abū Sālih" for Ahmad ibn Hanbal in order to make it seem as if the narrator is narrating from someone else so as not to be repetitive in narrating from Ahmad ibn

purposefully refer to fabricated *ahādeeth* in order to further his own agenda and beliefs. Furthermore, he pieces together whatever suits him without a detailed or critical assessment of the sources, indicating that according to Faisal the goal justifies the means, no matter how dubious the means may be. It is thus clearly evident that he is motivated by a personal agenda in many cases. He also concocts new definitions for Arabic words to dupe the unsuspecting youth, who have little knowledge of the Arabic language, into believing that his corrupted beliefs originate from statements from the Salaf. He also makes out as if he was one of the main students of Shaykh Ibn Jibreen, when Ibn Jibreen had no idea who Faisal even was!?

Hanbal. Al-Khateeb al-Baghdādī states in *al-Kifāyah* (p. 365) *"...it is where a muhaddith narrates from a Shaykh from whom he heard yet changes his name, kunyah or nisba or alters his well known condition to one which is unknown."* This is prevalent today especially with the explosion of the worldwide web and internet forums wherein people use false names, hide behind false identities and use fake pseudonyms. In any case, in the modern era, it is still practised in relation to knowledge and Omar Bakrī Muhammad Fustuq from Syria (currently in Lebanon) is the best example of contemporary *tadlees*. Not only did he claim to study in *Umm ul-Qura'* and the *Islamic University of Madeenah* but he also claimed to study with "az-Zuhaylī", insinuating by this the famous Wahbah az-Zuhaylī. But when one of the brothers in London went to Syria in the late 1990s and asked Wahbah az-Zuhaylī directly if Omar Bakrī was his student Shaykh Zuhaylī denied even knowing Bakrī. When Bakrī was confronted over this, Bakri said *"No, no, not that Zuhaylī, another Zuhaylī"*!! Clear *tadlees*!

For more on *tadlees* in the science of *hadeeth* see Dr. Misfar bin Ghirmullāh ad-Damīnī (Professor at the Department of Sunnah at *Imām Muhammad bin Sa'ud University*, Riyadh, KSA), *at-Tadless fi'l-Hadeeth: Haqeeqatuhu, Aqsāmuhu, Marātibuhu wa'l-Mawsūfūn bihi* [Tadless in the Hadeeth Literature: Its Reality, Types, Reasons and Those Described as Doing it], Riyadh: n.p., 1996 CE/1416 AH.

[Six]

A lack of condemning extremism, in fact Faisal hardly ever mentioned the many Qur'ānic verses and *ahādeeth* related to extremism. This in itself indicates a dangerous method, as either he was ignorant of all of this or he purposefully refrained from warning against extremism. For example, in a lecture entitled *'Jihād'* Faisal states 20 mintues into the lecture (which we analyse on 'Sample Lecture no.23'):

> "Now is there any peace treaty between us and the Hindus? No! So you can go India and if you see a Hindu walking down the road you're allowed to kill him and take his money. Is that clear?" (!!?)

Hereby neither distinguishing between the guilty and the innocent nor between the aggressors and the peaceful whatsoever. We assess this in the light of the statements of Islamic scholars past and present.

[Seven]

Making *takfeer* of all of the Muslim countries without exception, and even when he does make an exception it was only the rule of the Tālibān that he respected. Indeed, he made *takfeer* of most of the Muslims in the UK saying in the lecture on *'Knowledge'* (!?), sample lecture no.13 in our study:

> "So the Muslims in this country (i.e. the UK) the majority of them they have no īmān and no taqwā, the average Muslim you meet on the street he has no īmān and no taqwā…"

Faisal stated one hour and twenty-five minutes into the lecture entitled '*The Peak of the Matter*', sample lecture no. 22 in our study:

"So can you imagine the hundreds and thousands and millions of Muslims who have apostated from Islām without even realising it?!"

Faisal also stated in his "tafseer" (!?) of Sūrah Yūsuf, 29 minutes into the lecture:

"Most Muslims who leave their countries and come here (to the UK) have apostated. The nightclub prove too much for them {sic}; the betting shop, the National Lottery is too much for them; the alcohol is too much for them; the blue eye {sic} and blond hair is too much for them and so and so forth. The temptations is {sic} too much for them so they can't practice the deen they can't. They don't have any īmān to remain on the deen."

Herein making takfeer on account of sins, in following his predecessors the Khawārij. His Takfīrī temper tantrums are clearly a product of frustration, vented against the people because they refuse to accept his contorted concepts of Islam. In modern times, this sort of blanket emotional takfeer can be sourced back to the likes of Sayyid Qutb and Ayman bin Muhammad az-Zawāhirī. Both became very frustrated after their coup attempts against the Egyptian leaders backfired and the people of Egypt refused to respond to their revolutionary calls. This resulted in not only declaring the state to be an apostate state but the tide of frustration actually took them out further and caused them to declare the general masses as apostates due to their refusal to revolt against the state.

[Eight]

An avoidance of referring back to detailed explanations of Islamic scholars of the past and instead putting forward his own odd and extreme views instead.

[Nine]

His lack of condemnation when members of his audience shout "Takbeer! Allāhu Akbar" three times, as occurs 59 minutes into the lecture *What's Your Aim; What's Your Objective?*[1] Also in the lecture *Ideological Warfare (1)* and in the lecture *Islam Under Siege.*

[Ten]

His 'hyping up' the audience not based on knowledge, encouraging the audience to agitation, revolt, rebellion and *fitna.*

[Eleven]

What is also noticeable is that he opposes the Salafis the most, due to the spread of the *Salafi da'wah* amongst those whom Faisal himself wishes to reach, namely the Muslim youth and revert Muslims. This explains Faisal's hatred, vitriol and enmity against the Salafis in the West, *Brixton Mosque (Masjid Ibn Taymiyyah)* in London in particular. However, whilst Faisal's Takfīrī trend of *da'wah* is being crushed, squashed and destroyed, the Salafi da'wah is still spreading!

---

[1] This also occurs again a further four minutes into the lecture and then again five minutes later in this same lecture!

A Glossary Of Faisal's Most Commonly Used Words, Terms And Expressions That He Regurgitates Throughout His Lectures

There are some terms and expressions that Faisal frequently regurgitates and drones on about repeatedly. These are:

"Shirk al-Hakimiyyah"

This concept is innovated and only gained ground after the ideas of Sayyid Qutb spread and is not found at all in any of the early works of the scholars. Imām Muhammad bin Sālih al-'Uthaymeen ﷺ said about this 'Hākimiyyah' concept: **"This statement is a newly-invented, innovated, evil saying, making the one who uses it repugnant...and it is indeed a misguided innovation."**[1]

This innovated statement is particularly evil because it was not coined by the scholars of al-Islām, and nor was it coined with an aim to facilitate comprehension of the prophetic texts and the Divine Legal Rulings. Rather, it was coined for political machinations with aspirations to undermine the position of Muslim rulers.

---

[1] *Liqā' ul Maftūh* (no. 150) 20th *Shawwāl* 1417 AH

"Dismantling The Shari'ah"

Faisal constantly refers to this, in doing so attempting to show that those Muslims who have shortcomings in regards to applying Islām are therefore *kuffār* as they have 'dismantled' the Divine Legislation, when the reality is merely that they have shortcomings or are sinful, not that they have purposely 'dismantled' the Divine Legislation of Allāh. Furthermore, the term "dismantle" is not used in the works of the classical scholars. We do not find that they utilised the Arabic term *"fakkaka"* (to dismantle) when discussing the issue of ruling by other than what Allāh has revealed.

"Signing On With The Apostate Leaders"

He uses this to discredit the scholars, but mainly the scholars of Saudi who are popular with the youth. By extension, Faisal thus impugns the scholars with *kufr* and as being apostates as he said about some of the senior scholars, which will be highlighted in this treatise. He also uses this mode of expression to encourage the youth through suspicion against the scholars for receiving finances and support from countries such as Saudi Arabia mainly. Yet when Faisal studied at *Imām Muhammad bin Saud University* in Riyadh, the capital of Saudi Arabia, the students also receive a stipend and other financial benefits when studying there, as is well known. It is interesting that Faisal never admits, acknowledges or refers to this at all within his tirades against the *Salafī* scholars of Saudi!

"Saudi Salafi"

This derogative alliteration helps Faisal to convey the distorted message that the *Salafis* are in some way attached at the hip to everything 'Saudi'. However, the reality is that Salafiyyah is neither confined to a particular place nor to specific geographical boundaries. The scholars of the *Salafis* hail from all lands across the globe, but the majority of the major scholars reside in Saudi. His use of this term is the best indicator of his hatred of not only Salafiyyah but also of the Kingdom of Saudi Arabia. As for his hatred of Saudi Arabia then not only does this indicate the fallacy of the claim that Saudi Arabia has in some way been responsible for spreading extremism in the UK (as most of the actual UK-based Takfiri idealodues detest Saudi Arabia), but also demonstrates his two-faced nature vis-a-vis Saudi Arabia. As Faisal not only allegedly studied in Riyadh but also lived there and benefitted from its hospitality.

He uses the term 'Saudi Salafi' in a rather odd sense, so for example he does not refer to Safar, Salmān and Ā'id, who Faisal made much reference to throughout his lectures in the 1990s, as being 'Saudi Salafis'. Furthermore, they have apparently freed themselves from *takfeer*, *ghulū*, bombings and ideas of the likes of Faisal! Currently these scholars also share platforms and podiums with Sufis and Shi'a, and have even been openly praised by the rulers! So it looks as if Faisal's own scholars have totally changed from their previous views, so much for Faisal's hasty support of them!

Faisal also applied this term to attempt to mock and slander the Salafis, which is the same as the claim that the Salafis unjustly and purposefully informed the police to arrest certain individuals. In an Online video in 2008, Faisal had a discussion with a Nigerian Salafi and mentioned that Dr. Abdul-Haqq Baker (from Brixton Mosque) had incited the arrest of Muslims by informing about them and this is false.[1]

---

[1] It must be noted here that Dr. Abdul-Haqq Baker warned against the beliefs, views and ideas of well-known extremist takfiri preachers and individuals. He neither incited the arrest of anyone nor promoted informing on the average Muslim who may merely disagree with him on some things! It has been simplistically asserted by the *takfiris* and their sympathisers that Dr. Abdul-Haqq Baker was some sort of 'police informer', 'grass'or 'snitch'. Yet it must be stressed that it is not possible for a Muslim to merely inform without any evidence or on the basis that one does not like the views of another. Rather, the main callers have to be warned about what they call to and if any Muslim is sure that a terrorist incident is going to take place wherein innocent people, women and children will be killed unjustly then they have to warn and inform the authorities about that, as the Salafi scholars have clearly mentioned. This in itself is based on principles of Usūl, which assess the benefits and harms of an action.

As for merely running to the police or the media when one happens to not agree with the particular views of another Muslim and then conjure up a premise that necessitates running to the police - then this is nothing but a farce which even the police would discredit for wasting their time! Furthermore, it must be said that in any case it is very hard for any Muslim to know the full whereabouts, movements, actions, beliefs and plans of others as they are not with them all the time to know. As happened in the case of 'AbdurRaheem Richard Reid for example, the so-called 'shoe-bomber' – for he disappeared from Brixton for years unbeknown to the Muslim community and the *Salafis* of Brixton. In any case, Dr. Abdul-Haqq Baker gave evidence for the defence of Zacarias Moussaoui during his trial so that he would not achieve any martyrdom status and also he would not become a scapegoat for 9/11 in the US merely on account of his erroneous beliefs which he gained from the extremists. Refer to Dr. Abdul-Haqq Baker here on BBC radio 4's *Today* programme on Thursday 4th May 2006 (0810 – regarding the trial of Zacarias Moussaoui):

"Dodgy Scholar"

Another abusive term that he uses to incite the youth against the scholars and to drive a wedge between the youth and the senior scholars. In doing so, Faisal attempts to put himself forward as one who does not "water down" Islām and as one who "speaks the truth" even though Faisal speaks *bātil*, extremism and falsehood. None of this however should be regarded as being "a brave stance in speaking the truth" rather it is better for the likes of Faisal to remain silent as he has only contributed to *fitna*, controversy and incitement.

"Kāfir" and "Kāfirs"

Even though these words are totally legislated in the *deen*, Faisal is extreme in referring to these words and articulates these words in a vile manner within his lectures, and this is well known to the people!

The term "kāfir", as far as Faisal is concerned, only carries the meaning of the absolute kāfir; the kāfir concerning Allāh. However, the Sharī'ah recognises another type of kāfir, who is oblivious to Islām and has not rejected Islām in its true form, but he remains a kāfir because he has not accepted the message

---

http://www.bbc.co.uk/radio4/today/listenagain/ram/today3_911_20060420.ram
In any case, many of the London-based extremist *takfiri* preachers were arrested and imprisoned because of their own foolish statements and views not on account of anyone informing on them!

of Muhammad ﷺ. Thus, due to Faisal's wilful denial of this type of kāfir, he has fostered an unhealthy melancholy mood towards all non-Muslims. Once upon a time, Faisal was once a kāfir himself, which makes one wonder how responsive he would have been to Islām if he had met a Muslim in the form of himself?!

In the first lecture which will be analysed Faisal states: **"Kāfirs will always be kāfirs, every kāfir will always find a time to make you feel ashamed of your religion, every kāfir! Kāfirs will always be Kāfirs"**!! All of this in one small sentence! Not to mention the fact that ("el") Faisal himself used to be a "kāfir"!

Faisal al-Jamaykī stated after one hour and 13 minutes into the audio entitled *'Luqman the Wise (2)'*, which is supposedly a 'tafseer' (!?) of Sūrah Luqman:

"He (Mūsā) blew it! That was his last chance, Mūsā flunked the course! It's like you go to university and you flunk the course, you've failed! Mūsā failed!"

This is in keeping with the creed of Sayyid Qutb, 'Abdullāh El-Faisal's ideological predecessor, in more ways than one! This shocking statement just captures so much about Faisal. How can we expect him to observe any level of decency and honour for other Muslims when he does not even have the required amount of respect and humility towards the Prophets and Mighty Messengers of Allāh, the most perfect of humanity? The Prophets are infallible in conveying their messages and they are to be respected as Allāh has granted them virtue, nobility and lofty status. Their honour is preserved by Allāh to the extent that the earth does not devour their bodies,[1] so who are we to devour their honour and nobility? This statement from Faisal is clear mockery, Mūsā ﷺ in no way "failed" in his da'wah and preaching and the ruling on suggesting such is kufr. Allāh says:

---

[1] Hadeeth in Sunan an-Nasā'ī and Ibn Mājah, authenticated by Imām al-Albānī.

﴿ وَوَهَبْنَا لَهُ إِسْحَقَ وَيَعْقُوبَ كُلاًّ هَدَيْنَا وَنُوحًا هَدَيْنَا مِن قَبْلُ وَمِن ذُرِّيَّتِهِ دَاوُدَ وَسُلَيْمَنَ وَأَيُّوبَ وَيُوسُفَ وَمُوسَىٰ وَهَرُونَ وَكَذَلِكَ نَجْزِى ٱلْمُحْسِنِينَ . وَزَكَرِيَّا وَيَحْيَىٰ وَعِيسَىٰ وَإِلْيَاسَ كُلٌّ مِّنَ ٱلصَّلِحِينَ . وَإِسْمَعِيلَ وَٱلْيَسَعَ وَيُونُسَ وَلُوطًا وَكُلاًّ فَضَّلْنَا عَلَى ٱلْعَلَمِينَ . وَمِنْ ءَابَآئِهِمْ وَذُرِّيَّتِهِمْ وَإِخْوَنِهِمْ وَٱجْتَبَيْنَهُمْ وَهَدَيْنَهُمْ إِلَىٰ صِرَطٍ مُّسْتَقِيمٍ ﴾

"And We gave to Abraham, Isaac and Jacob - all [of them] We guided. And Noah, We guided before; and among his descendants, David and Solomon and Job and Joseph and Moses and Aaron. Thus do We reward the doers of good. And Zechariah and John and Jesus and Elias – and all were of the righteous. And Ishmael and Elisha and Jonah and Lot - and all [of them] We preferred over the worlds. And [some] among their fathers and their descendants and their brothers - and We chose them and We guided them to a straight path." *{al-An'ām (6): 84-87}*

Here Allāh mentions that Mūsā عليه السلام was among those who:

- was guided
- was a doer of good
- was of the righteous
- was preferred over the worlds
- was chosen and guided to a straight path.

So how on earth can it be said that Mūsā عليه السلام *"failed"*, *"blew it"* and *"flunked it"*? The Prophet ﷺ stated, as reported in the Saheeh from the hadeeth of Ibn

'Abbās ﷺ, *"A Prophet will come on the Day of Judgement and he will have a man or two with him. Then another Prophet will come with a group of men with him, while another Prophet will come with a small group of followers. Then another Prophet will come with no followers with him whatsoever."* This is a Prophet! Allāh chose him to have this great status and yet with that he will come with no one with him; his *da'wah* is still successful without doubt because he is Prophet.

Faisal made this statement in regards to the verse in the Qur'ān wherein Khidr عليه السلام said to Mūsā:

﴿ قَالَ هَٰذَا فِرَاقُ بَيۡنِى وَبَيۡنِكَ ۚ سَأُنَبِّئُكَ بِتَأۡوِيلِ مَا لَمۡ تَسۡتَطِع عَّلَيۡهِ صَبۡرًا ﴾

"[Al-Khidhr] said, "This is parting between me and you. I will inform you of the interpretation of that about which you could not have patience." *{al-Kahf (18): 78}*

Ibn Katheer says in his tafseer of the noble ayah:
Meaning: because you (Mūsā) said after the boy was killed that if you asked me anything after that, you would not accompany me any further. So this is the parting of the ways between me and you.

Nothing from Ibn Katheer about Mūsā *"failing"* or *"blowing it"* or *"flunking it"* – such language from Faisal indicates his loose tongue leads him to even make statements of mockery of Allāh's Messengers. Indeed, Faisal himself stated eight minutes into his "tafseer" of Sūrah Yūsuf: **"People at times behave**

disrespectful to the Prophets of Allāh." Indeed Faisal! He seems to have forgotten this himself though!

El Faisal's Views On The Illustrious Companion 'Abdullah Ibn 'Abbas ﷺ

Like other new-age *takfīrī* activists, Faisal al-Jamaykī has even stooped to the level of denigrating the illustrious Sahābī 'Abdullāh Ibn 'Abbās ﷺ and describing him as "having many mistakes"!?[1] What is also strange is that Faisal's new-found supporters in America, headed by the ignoramus Yousuf al-Khattab (aka Joey Cohen)[2], see nothing wrong in this? As for Yousuf "al-Khattab" Cohen's support for 'Abdullāh Faisal then this in itself is ironic, Faisal has a lecture entitled *'Jewish Traits in the Ummah'* and referred to his enemies as being *"Jews of the Ummah"*; only for 'Abdullāh Faisal to take as a co-ordinator of his affairs in the West an ex-Hasidic Jew?! Irony in its most vivid form! After 29 minutes into the video which was a recording of a "debate" between the decrepit 'Abdullāh Faisal and a Salafi brother in Nigeria, which can be found Online, Faisal exclaims that:

---

[1] This was also asserted by Abū Hamza al-Misrī (former usurper of Finsbury Park Mosque in North London) in his paper entitled *Ruling by Man-Made Laws is Kufr Akbar*. We find on page 15 of the document that Abū Hamza al-Misrī makes the same conclusions about Ibn 'Abbās ﷺ as Faisal did in his video debate with the brother in Nigeria. Therefore, all Faisal has done is follow the folly of Abū Hamza al-Misrī. The 'paper' by Abū Hamza al-Misrī is obviously poor in its academic standard and clearly has not emanated from one who even has a mustard seed of Islamic scholarship.

[2] Refer to: http://www.salafimanhaj.com/pdf/SalafiManhaj_YusufKhattaab.pdf

"First of all, we do not worship Ibn 'Abbās and if he said that dismantling the Sharee'ah is kufr dūna kufr, it's a mistake and Ibn 'Abbās is known for making mistakes...so Ibn 'Abbās is known for making many many mistakes. So if he said that to dismantle the Sharee'ah is minor kufr we dismiss it as one of the mistakes of Ibn 'Abbās. Because he was a young Sahābah and we stick to the fatwa of Ibn Katheer and Ibn Taymiyyah"

Another of the glaring proofs of his crazed Khārijiyyah which, incidentally, his followers find nothing wrong with?! Ironically, the fatwahs of both Ibn Taymiyyah and Ibn Katheer completely contradict El-Faisal's counterfeit creed. Shaykh ul-Islām Ibn Taymiyyah does not even mention the term 'dismantle'; rather, this is a word forged in the furnaces of Faisal's revolutionary imagination, which he conveniently inserted into his translation of Ibn Taymiyyah's words to bolster his position. More on this will be mentioned later within our critique of sample lecture no.18.

The Status of the Illustrious Companion 'Abdullāh Bin 'Abbās ﷺ[1]

From 'Abdullāh ibn 'Abbās ﷺ: I was in the house of Maymūnah bin al-Hārith and I prepared some water for the Messenger of Allāh ﷺ to make tahārah with. The Messenger of Allāh ﷺ said: *"Who prepared this?"* Maymūnah said:

---

[1] From Shaykh Abū Usāmah Saleem bin 'Īid al-Hilālī, *Qurrat ul-'Uyūn: Fī Tas-heeh Tafseer 'Abdullāh Ibn 'Abbās ﷺ li-Qawlihi ta'ala "wa man lam yahkum bimā anzala Allāh fa ūlaika hum al-Kafirūn"* ('Ajmān, UAE: Maktabat ul-Furqān, 1422 AH/2001 CE), pp.36-38.

"Abdullāh did." The Prophet ﷺ said: *"O Allāh, grant him understanding of the deen and teach him the interpretation."*[1]

Via 'Amru bin Dīnār from Kurayb from Ibn 'Abbās that he said: "I went to the Messenger of Allāh ﷺ and he supplicated for me that I be increased in knowledge and understanding."[2]

Al-Hāfidh Ibn Hajar stated in *al-Fath* (vol.1, p.170):

---

[1] Reported by Ibn Abī Shaybah, *al-Musannaf* (vol.12, pp.111-112, no.12273); Ahmad in *al-Musnad* (vol.1, pp.266, 314, 328 and 335) and in *Fadā'il us-Sahābah*, vol.2, pp.955-956, no.1856, p.956, no.1858, pp.963-964, no.1882; Ibn Sa'd, *at-Tabaqāt ul-Kubrā*, vol.2, p.365; al-Fasawī, *al-Ma'rifah wa't-Tārīkh*, vol.1, pp.493-494; at-Tabarī, *Tadheeb ul-Āthār*, p.168, no.262, p.169, no.263 – Musnad Ibn 'Abbās; at-Tabarānī, *al-Mu'jam al-Kabeer*, vol.10, p.238, no.10587; Ibn Hibbān, *Saheeh*, vol.15, p.531, no.7055; Ibn Abī 'Āsim, *al-Āhād wa'l-Mathānī*, vol.1, p.287, no.380; al-Hākim, vol.3, p.534; al-Bayhaqī, *Dalā'il un-Nubuwwah*, vol.6, pp.192-193 via 'Abdullāh ibn 'Uthmān bin Khuthaym. Also reported via Dāwood bin Abī Hind by at-Tabarānee: in *al-Mu'jam al-Kabeer*, vol.10, p.263, no.10614 and in *al-Mu'jam as-Sagheer*, vol.1, p.197. And via Sulaymān al-Ahwal as reported by: at-Tabarānī in *al-Mujam al-Kabeer*, vol.12, p.55, no.12506 and in *al-Muj'am al-Awsat*, vol.3, p.345, no.3356; and Abū Tāhir adh-Dhuhalī in *Fawā'id* as in *al-Isābah*, vol.2, p.331. The third narration is from Sa'eed bin Jubayr from Ibn 'Abbās. I say: its chain of transmission is *Saheeh* and its narrators are *thiqāt* (trustworthy). Al-Bukhārī reported in his *Saheeh*, vol.1, p.169, no.75 and vol.7, p.100, no.3756, vol.13, p.245, no.7270 – via Khālid al-Hidhā from 'Ikrimah from Ibn 'Abbās C – in a *marfu'* form[1]: *"O Allāh grant him knowledge of the Book"* and in another narration: "wisdom." Bukhārī reported in his *Saheeh*, vol.1, p.244, no.143 as did Muslim in his *Saheeh* along with others – via 'Ubaydullāh bin Abī Ziyād from Ibn 'Abbās in *marfu'* form: *"O Allāh grant him understanding of the deen"*, Muslim however did not mention the word *"deen"*.
[2] Reported by: Ahmad, *Fadā'il us-Sahābah*, vol.2, p.956, no.1857; al-Fasawī, *al-Ma'rifah wa't-Tāreekh*, vol.1, p.518; at-Tabarī, *Tahdheeb ul-Āthār*, p.169, no.264, Musnad Ibn 'Abbās; Abū Nu'aym, *al-Hilyah*, vol.1, pp.314-315; Abu'l-Fadl az-Zuhrī, *Hadeeth*, vol.1, p.394, no.393. The wording of Abu'l-Fadl az-Zuhrī is: *"O Allāh grant him knowledge of ta'weel"* but the wording of the majority is the most authentic.

This supplication was assured to be responded to on account of what the Prophet supplicated for as he knew the condition of Ibn 'Abbās in gaining understanding of tafseer and fiqh of the deen, radi Allāhu 'anhu.

Al-Hāfidh Ibn Katheer stated in *Tafseer ul-Qur'ān al-'Adheem*, vol.1, p.4, when mentioning who to be referred back to in regards to tafseer of the Qur'ān:

And from them are: al-Habr al-Bahr (the scholar and vast ocean), 'Abdullāh bin 'Abbās, the cousin of the Messenger of Allāh (sallallāhu 'alayhi wassallam) and the Commentator of the Qur'ān based on the blessed supplication of the Messenger of Allāh ﷺ for him, wherein he stated: *"O Allāh grant him understanding of the deen and of ta'weel."*

'Abdullāh bin Mas'ūd ﷺ: "If Ibn 'Abbās comprehended our (more senior) generation then then men from us would not be able to compete with him (in knowledge)."[1] Ibn Mas'ūd also stated: "What a blessed commentator of the Qur'ān is Ibn 'Abbās."[2]

---

[1] It is Saheeh and documented in: *Tārīkh Ya'qūb bin Sufyān*; *Fath ul-Bārī*, vol.7, p.100 and *al-Isābah*, vol.4, p.92.

[2] This was reported by: Ibn Abī Shaybah, *al-Musannaf*, vol.12, pp.110-111, nos.12268, 12269; Ahmad, *Fadā'il us-Sahābah*, vol.2, p.957, nos.1860, 1861 and 1863; Abū Khuthaymah,[2] *al-'Ilm*, p.120, no.48; Ibn Sa'd, *at-Tabaqāt al-Kubrā*, vol.2, p.366; at-Tabarī, *Tahdheeb ul-Āthār*, p.172, no.268, p.173, nos.269, 270, 271 – Musnad Ibn 'Abbās; at-Tabarī, *Jāmi' ul-Bayān*, vol.1, p.31; al-Fasawī, *al-Ma'rifah wa't-Tārīkh*, vol.1, pp.494-495; al-Ājurrī, *ash-Sharee'ah*, vol.5, p.2271, no.1755 (Dār ul-Watan edition); al-Hākim, vol.3, p.537; al-Bayhaqī, *Dalā'il un-Nubuwwah*, vol.6, p.193; al-Khateeb al-Baghdādī, *Tārīkh Baghdād*, vol.1, p.174. Others also reported this narration via al-'Amash from Uslim bin Sabeeh Abi'd-Duhā from Masrūq from Ibn Mas'ūd. The chain

Mujāhid bin Jabar al-Makkī the successor and Imām ﷺ,[1] stated: "Ibn 'Abbās ﷺ was called 'al-Bahr' ('the ocean') due to his vast knowledge (vast like an ocean)."[2]

of transmission is Saheeh according to the conditions of Shaykhayn as mentioned by al-Hākim and adh-Dhahabī. Al-Hāfidh Ibn Katheer stated in *Tafseer ul-Qur'ān il-Kareem*, vol.1, p.5: *"This chain of transmission is authentic up to Ibn Mas'ūd that he used this expression for Ibn 'Abbās."* Al-Hāfidh Ibn Hajar stated in *Fath ul-Bārī*, vol.7, p.100: *"Ya'qūb bin Sufyān narrated in his Tārīkh with an authentic chain of transmission from Ibn Mas'ūd that..."* - then he mentioned the narration. Al-Mizzī also verified this narration in *Tahdheeb ul-Kamāl*, vol.15, p.155.

[1] He is Mujāhid bin Jabar al-Makkī, the freed slave of as-Sā'ib bin Abī as-Sā'ib al-Makhzūmī. He was born in 21 AH and learned the *tafseer* of the Qur'ān from Ibn 'Abbās ﷺ. Ibn Ishāq reported from him that he said: "I reviewed the entire *mus-haf* – from its beginning to its end – with Ibn 'Abbās on three separate occasions, stopping at each *ayah* and asking him about it." Sufyān Ath-Thawrī said: "If the interpretation (of an ayah) comes to you from Mujāhid, then it is sufficient for you." Ash-Shāfi'ī relied on his *tafseer* (of the Qur'ān), as did al-Bukhārī who quoted often from him in his Saheeh. In the last part of his biography of him, adh-Dhahabī said: "The ummah is in unanimous agreement that Mujāhid is an Imām and that his *tafseer* is to be relied on as proof." He died in Makkah while in the state of prostration in the year 104 AH at the age of 83.
See: http://www.al-ibaanah.com/articles.php?ArtID=117

[2] This was reported by: Ahmad in *Fadā'il us-Sahābah*, vol.2, p.975, no.1920; Ibn Sa'd, *at-Tabaqāt ul-Kubrā*, vol.2, p.366; al-Fasawī, *al-Ma'rifah wa't-Tārīkh*, vol.1, p.496; at-Tabarī, *Tahdheeb ul-Āthār*, p.176, no.276 – Musnad Ibn 'Abbās; Abū Nu'aym, *Ma'rifat us-Sahābah*, vol.3, p.1700, no.4251 and in *Hilyat ul-Awliyā'*, vol.1, p.316; al-Hākim, vol.3, p.535 and al-Khateeb al-Baghdādī, vol.1, p.174. The chain of transmission is Saheeh from al-'A'mash from Mujāhid. He also said: *"I did not see a gathering like the gatherings of Ibn 'Abbās, the day he died a great scholar of the Ummah died."* Reported by: 'Abbās ad-Dūrī in *Tāreekh*, vol.2, p.316, no.377; ad-Dinawarī, *al-Majālisah*, vol.4, p.62, no.1125 and al-Hākim, vol.3, p.535 – via Sufyān bin 'Uyaynah from Ibn Abī Najeeh from Mujāhid. The chain of transmission is Saheeh.

Muhammad bin al-Hanafiyyah stated when Ibn 'Abbās died: *"Today an 'Ālim Rabbānī of this Ummah has died."*[1]

Abū Nu'aym al-Asbahānī stated in *Ma'rifat us-Sahābah*, vol.3, pp.1699-1700:
He was named 'al-Habr al-Bahr' due to his vast amount of knowledge and his sharp understanding, he was the scholar and faqeeh of the Ummah...du'a was made for him by the tongue of the message for him to be granted fiqh of the religion, knowledge of interpretation and commentating on the Qur'ān...

Imām adh-Dhahabī stated in *Ma'rifat ul-Qurā' al-Kubrā'*, vol.1, p.46:
The merits of Ibn 'Abbās are plentiful, his knowledge is vast and there was none on the face of the earth during his time more knowledgeable than him.

The Prophet ﷺ threatened the one who undermines, mocks or insults companions. He said:

من سب أصحابي فعليه لعنة الله والملائكة والناس أجمعين

"Whoever insults my companions, the curse of Allāh, the angels and the whole of mankind will be upon him."[2]

---

[1] This was reported by: Ahmad, *Fadā'il us-Sahābah*, vol.2, p.951, no.1842; 'Abbās ad-Dūrī, *Tārīkh*, vol.2, pp.315-316; al-Hākim, vol.3, p.535 and others with an authentic chain of transmission.
[2] *As-Silsilah As-Sahīhah*, p. 2340.

The Prophet ﷺ said:

لا تسبوا أصحابي ، فوالذي نفسي بيده لو أنفق أحدكم مثل أحد ذهباً ما بلغ مد

أحدهم ولا نصيفه

"Do not insult any of my companions, for by Him in Whose hand is my soul,
if one of you were to spend the equivalent of Uhud in gold, it would not
amount to a mudd, or even half of it."

Imām at-Tahāwī said when explaining the belief of Ahlu as-Sunnah wa al-Jamā'ah:

ونحب أصحاب رسول الله صلى الله عليه وعلى آله وسلم ، ولا نفرط في حب أحد

منهم ، ولا نتبرأ من أحد منهم ، ونبغض من يبغضهم ، وبغير الخير يذكرهم ، ولا

نذكرهم إلا بخير ، وحبهم دين وإيمان وإحسان ، وبغضهم كفر ونفاق وطغيان.

We love the Companions of Allāh's Messenger ﷺ, and we do not neglect
to love anyone of them. We do not disassociate from any of them, and
we hate those who hate them and criticise them and we only mention
them in good terms. Loving of them is a part of the deen, īmān and
ihsān, and hating them is kufr, nifāq and tughyān.

Imām Ahmad ؓ said:

89

وقال الإمام أحمد : إذا رأيت الرجل يذكر أحداً من أصحاب رسول الله صلى الله عليه وسلم بسوء : فاتهمه على الإسلام.

"If you see a man mentioning one of the Companions of Allāh's Messenger ﷺ in a bad way, then call into question his Islām."

Shaykh al-Islām Ibn Taymiyyah said:

وأما من سبهم سباً لا يقدح في عدالتهم ولا في دينهم مثل وصف بعضهم بالبخل أو الجبن أو قلة العلم أو عدم الزهد ونحو ذلك ، فهذا هو الذي يستحق التأديب والتعزير ، ولا نحكم بكفره بمجرد ذلك ، وعلى هذا يحمل كلام من لم يكفرهم من أهل العلم

If a person slanders them in a way that does not impugn their good character or religious commitment, such as describing one of them as being stingy or cowardly or lacking in knowledge or not being an ascetic and so on, then he deserves to be rebuked and disciplined, but we do not rule him to be a kāfir because of that. This is how the words of those who were not regarded as kāfir by the scholars are to be understood.[1]

---

[1] *As-Sārim al-Maslūl ʿalā Shātim ar-Rasūl*, p. 590.

Sample Lecture Number One:
'Al-Wala Wal-Bara'[1]

Faisal states just four minutes within the lecture, referring to and meaning himself first:

"Any shaykh, maulana, muftī who seeks to revive this concept[2] in the ummah of the Prophet ﷺ such a person would be slandered viciously. He will be called derogatory names "extremist", "khawārij" and people will warn others to stay away from that person, "that person has deviated, he has now become a khawārij", why? Because you are embedding in the Muslims, you are teaching the Muslims the importance of loving and hating for the sake of Allāh."

Faisal then states about eighteen minutes into the lecture;

"...Most Muslims[3] find it extremely difficult to reject faith in the tāghūt! Look how many of you believe in democracy, look how many of

---

[1] www.archive.org/stream/alwala1/alwala.rmvb
[2] i.e. *al-walā wa'l-barā*
[3] Herein Faisal states *"most Muslims"*, not even "a few", "some" or "a small number" but rather "most Muslims" find it difficult to reject faith in *Tāghūt*!! So what do "most Muslims" believe in then??!

91

you believe in socialism, look how many of you[1] believe in capitalism...we believe in some false deity whether it is socialism, capitalism, democracy, which is the greatest shirk..."[2]

Hereby describing Muslims with having major *shirk*, and not even minor *shirk*. Faisal says that *"most Muslims"* believe in what he considers to be, whilst not one of all the scholars of the past or present concurs with this, the greatest *shirk*!! What exactly does he intend by the words "many of you believe in"? Does he mean that Muslims believe democracy is better than Allāh's legislation? On the other hand, could it perhaps mean that they believe in abiding by these democratic laws installed in non-Muslim countries as long as they do not violate Allāh's laws so as not to cause a greater evil by shunning them?! Has he established an absolute truth in any one of these variables before making blanket *takfeer* like this? Indeed Faisal even accused his own audience of *juhāl* of believing in *tawāgheet*! Allāh says:

$$\text{﴿ أَمۡ نَجۡعَلُ ٱلَّذِينَ ءَامَنُواْ وَعَمِلُواْ ٱلصَّٰلِحَٰتِ كَٱلۡمُفۡسِدِينَ فِى ٱلۡأَرۡضِ أَمۡ نَجۡعَلُ ٱلۡمُتَّقِينَ كَٱلۡفُجَّارِ ﴾}$$

"Or should We treat those who believe and do righteous deeds like corrupters in the land? Or should We treat those who fear Allāh like the wicked? *{Sād (38): 28}*

---

[1] This is another common method of Faisal, he talks as if he is talking directly to his audience and uses terms such as *"you..."* and this technique is to pressurise the audience and listeners into believing whatever Faisal tells them in the name of Islām.

[2] See the lecture here: www.archive.org/stream/alwala1/alwala.rmvb

Allāh also says:

$$\text{﴿ أَفَنَجْعَلُ ٱلْمُسْلِمِينَ كَٱلْمُجْرِمِينَ ۝ ﴾}$$

"Then will We treat the Muslims like the criminals?"

{al-Qalam (68): 35}

Allāh also says,

$$\text{﴿ هَلْ يَسْتَوِيَانِ مَثَلاً ۚ أَفَلَا تَذَكَّرُونَ ۝ ﴾}$$

"Are they equal in comparison? Then, will you not remember?"

{Hūd (11): 24}

Then twenty-five minutes into the lecture he states:

"The tāghūt of today they even control what you learn about Islām..."

Firstly, this is a new-age usage of monolithic and distorted terms (i.e. 'homophobe', 'Islamist', 'tāghūt' etc), which are pre-loaded terms within any calibre of definition. Such terms are then discharged against anyone or anything that falls under its broad and politically orientated definition. Cue the 'gung ho' Takfīrī Muslims and their unbridled abuse of the word "Tāghūt", which they have unshackled from its legislated definition, and use with impunity and indiscrimination.

Secondly, seeking to promote himself as a credible source from which Islām can be acquired. Because with this statement he has discredited many of the scholars, he continues:

93

"You don't know an ayah of the Qur'ān or a hadeeth or an aspect of Islamic history "unless we give our scholars the permission to preach that on the minbar. When we give them the permission to preach that on the minbar then you learn about it. But if we don't give them the permission...so what we don't want you to learn of Islām you will not learn of Islām" so the tāghūt of today[1], even the very Islamic education they have monitored and they have controlled."

So does this also refer to Faisal, who himself studied in a Saudi university? Did he learn in a "*tāghūt institution*" which is controlled? If so, then that means that his own credentials are in question according to his own views!! What is clear is that we have a Faisal 'then' and a Faisal 'now'. What produced the latter version of Faisal was not an epiphany of truth, but rather his personal altercations with the Salafis. He continues:

"And they didn't stop there, they set-up bookshops all over, all over the world and they have their hypocritical scholars writing books and when they talk about the seven conditions of shahādah it is watered down; and when they talk about *al-walā al-barā'* it is watered down; when they talk about shirk it is watered down. They will never mention shirk al-Hākimiyyah, the shirk of dismantling the Sharī'ah and they water down, they water down, they water down, every single book of theirs is watered

---

[1] Making *takfeer* here of Muslim governments, and in Faisal context he insinuates Saudi primarily above any other country.

down, but people rush to buy it because the cover is glossy, a glossy cover."

Clear extremism is observable here. As for the claim that what is in the books has been changed and watered down, this is absolute nonsense as in the last few years certain disbelieving elements have tried to get Saudi, for example, to take things out and really water things down. There are even neo-con and Christian-Zionist think-tanks, organisations, websites and blogs that have been established in order to present Saudi Arabia as a haven of intolerance, hatred and extremism based on what is found within the Saudi national Islamic Studies curriculum.

So Faisal is just trying to hoodwink the listener with his spurious calls to '*shirk al-hākimiyyāh*', which Faisal drones on about like a broken record, but which scholar or Imām from the *Salaf* mentioned it? We never mention '*shirk al-hākimiyyāh*', because as a benign technical term, it does not exist in the books of the Salaf. Rather, this term is a new-age weapon, forged in the furnaces of the neo-Takfīrīs and then un-sheathed against the rulers and all those in opposition to the Takfīrī ideology. We are still waiting for those influenced by Sayyid Qutb to produce the *daleel*! Let's see what the scholars of Riyadh, where Faisal himself studied, have to say on the issue. Shaykh Sālih as-Sadlān said:

Whoever makes Hākimiyyah a fourth category from the categories of Tawheed, then he is either an ignoramus or an innovator taking an opinion from the opinions of the philosophers. These are opinions that

95

are not known in the Creed or the Sharī'ah. He could also be a person who is relating things and he does not know what he is relating.[1]

Shaykh Nāsir al-'Aql stated:

Likewise is the claim that Hākimiyyah is the most important characteristic from the characteristics of Ulūhiyyah: there is no basis for this. It is an innovated claim.[2]

Not only is the term *'Shirk al-Hākimiyyah'* an innovated term, but it is also a term which is exercised for corrupt means, which violates a well-known principle among the *Fuqahā* and the *Usūliyūn*. Ibn Qayyim ﷽ said:

There is no restriction in using technical terminologies as long as they do not include any corruption.[3]

Technical terms and categorisations should only serve a purpose to facilitate comprehension of al-Islām, particularly in latter days when familiarity of the Arabic language and Sciences of Islām have declined and the Arabic tongue has become infused with other foreign languages. Therefore, the term *'Shirk al-Hākimiyyah'* is not only an innovated term, which has no reference that stems back to the Salaf, but it is also a term which was not designed for the purpose of alleviating the masses from ignorance. Rather it is an innovated term brought

---

[1] *Al-Muslimūn* newspaper, issue no. 639
[2] Ibid.
[3] *Madārij as-Sālikeen,* vol.3, p.306.

into existence solely to serve a small minority in their war against the Muslim rulers.

Ironically, if anyone has 'watered down' anything, it is Faisal himself. Faisal is the one who has perpetrated the crime of disemboweling Tawheed by removing one of its organs (i.e. *Hākimiyyah*) from one of its catergories so that he can persuade the youth that the most important component (and not even category) of Tawheed is *al-Hākimiyyah*. Faisal then states around forty-five minutes into the lecture that:

> **"This drives home to you the importance of the Islamic Sharī'ah, the importance of hating the tāghūt, the importance of hating those who dismantle the Sharī'ah, the importance of condemning the system, the importance of killing the tāghūt ..."**

Abu'l-Hasan al-Ash'arī 🕮 stated:

> As for the sword, then all of the khawārij speak of it and hold it, except the Ibādiyyah…they emphasise removing the tyrannical leaders.[1]

So if Faisal has already described certain Muslim governments as being *"tāghūt governments"* what is the logical deduction to be made from this, if not to incite and endorse assassinations of Muslim governments or others who Faisal defines as being "a tāghūt"? Ibn Taymiyyah stated:

---

[1] Abu'l-Hasan al-'Asha'rī, *Maqālāt ul-Islamiyyeen*, vol.1, p.204

The khawārij are the most apparent of the people of innovation and fighting against the rulers.[1]

The term '*tāghūt*' has become a figurative bogeyman, sensationalised by the neo-Takfīrīs. This type of scare mongering is nothing new amongst the ranks of the people of innovation. The Ash'arī-Sūfī Hamza Yūsuf (pre - 9/11 of course!) characterised a whole system with the term 'Dajjāl system' despite there being no reference for such an expression leading back to the Qur'ān or Sunnah. Layth, Abū 'Ubaydah, al-Kasā'ī and most of the Arabic linguists and grammarians stated: at-Tāghūt is all that is worshipped other than Allāh. Al-Jawharī said:

"At-Tāghūt, al-Kāhin, ash-Shaytān and every head of misguidance."[2]

Ibn ul-Qayyim stated:
"at-Tāghūt is whatever the servant transgresses his bounds in regards to what is worshipped, followed or obeyed."

The Tāghūt is everyone who refers judgment to other than Allāh and His Messenger, or worships a person other than Allāh or follows another person

[1] *Majmū' al-Fatāwā*, vol.7, p.217
[2] Abū Yūsuf Madahat bin al-Hasan Āl Farrāj, *Fatāwā al-A'immah Hawl Qadayā al-Ummah al-Maseeriyyah min Shaykh ul-Islām Muhammad bin 'AbdulWahhāb ilā Samāhat ish-Shaykh 'Abdul'Azeez bin 'Abdullāh bin Bāz* [The Rulings of the Imāms Around Ongoing Issues of the Ummah: From Shaykh ul-Islām Muhammad bin 'AbdulWahhāb Upto the Eminent Shaykh 'Abdul'Azeez bin 'Abdullāh bin Bāz]. Riyadh, KSA: Maktabat ur-Rushd, 1428 AH/2007 CE, 2nd Edn., vol.1, p.325. Introduction by Shaykh Ibn Jibreen.

without guidance from Āllāh or obeying other than Allāh.[1] Imām 'Uthaymeen ﷻ stated:

"At-Tāghūt is all who oppose the rule of Allāh and His Messenger, because whatever opposes the rule of Allāh and His Messenger is tughyān and transgression..."[2]

Lajnah ad-Dā'imah stated (no. 8008):
The general meaning of at-Tāghūt is: all that is worshipped other than Allāh absolutely, gaining nearness to it via prayer, fasting, vows, slaughtering, travelling to it, in that which should only be done for Allāh, in order to lift harm or gain benefit, or to rule by it as a substitute for Allāh's Book and the Messenger's Sunnah; and the like. The meaning of at-Tāghūt in the ayah (Nisā: 60) is: all who avert from Allāh's Book and His Messenger's Sunnah to defer judgement to: (political) systems, man-made laws, or traditions, inherited customs, or tribal leaders so as to divide them by that, or based on what the leader of the jama'ah views, or a fortune-teller. This makes clear that: a system which is put in place so as to refer judgment to it, emulating Allāh's legislation, is included within the meaning of at-Tāghūt.[3]

Abū Yūsuf Madahat Āl Farrāj states:

---

[1] Ibid., vol., p.328
[2] *Majmū' al-Fatāwā wa Rasā'il Shaykh Ibn 'Uthaymeen*, vol.1, p.39
[3] Abū Yūsuf Madahat bin al-Hasan Āl Farrāj, *op.cit.*, vol.1, p.332.

99

"At-Tāghūt is of three types: Tāghūt of hukm, Tāghūt of 'Ibādah, Tāghūt of obedience and following..."[1]

So we understand from all of this that while a system can be referred to as being a "tāghūt" so can a misguided preacher and deviant propagator, this definition seems to have slipped the neo-Takfīrī dialectic, probably because it applies to their own ideologues! Faisal continues, in his injustice:

"And if you are living in this country and a person approaches you and ask you {sic} "what do you think about the system" and you say to yourself, or you say to the person, 'Alhamdulillāh, it's not a bad system, it's a good system, even though my name is Muhammad I'm allowed to sign on and on top of that I live in the Royal Borough of Kensington and Chelsea, I can't complain.' Now you are in this system and you can't see anything wrong with the system you say "it's okay"! Just to give that answer "it's okay" you become a kāfir!" (!!!)

Reflect on this *khawārij manhaj* and look at the ease in which one can become a disbeliever within the corrupt Usūl of Faisal. Where are conditions or preventive means in Faisal's DIY handbook of takfeer? Ibn Taymiyyah ﷺ said about the *khawārij*:

They have two well-known qualities which they separate the unity of the Muslims and their leaders with. One of them is that they leave out the

---

[1] Ibid., vol.1, p.337.

Sunnah and declare evil that which is not evil or they declare good that which is not good.[1]

Faisal then goes on to say that it is due to one not having perfected rejection of the *tāghūt*, yet in another lecture Faisal himself encourages his blind followers to take welfare state benefits and British government hand-outs, as occurs in the lecture *Challenges Facing the Youth*!!? Furthermore, Shaykh ul-Islām Ibn Taymiyyah notes that:

> Civilisation is rooted in justice, and the consequences of oppression are devastating. Therefore, it is said that Allāh aids the just state even if it is non-Muslim, yet withholds His help from the oppressive state even if it is Muslim.[2]

So this statement of Ibn Taymiyyah highlights Faisal's phobia of being unable to recognise justice or equity that can be witnessed, to some extent, in the lands of non-Muslims. Faisal suffers from an acute bout of intolerance, which has convinced him that all non-Muslims lack the capacity to perform any act of good. Do you think that Faisal's mentality could accommodate the notion that not only can a non-Muslim state be just, but it can also be aided by Allāh, as mentioned by Ibn Taymiyyah? Ibn Taymiyyah also noted that some Christians are equitable, just and 'okay', as it were, he said ﷺ:

---

[1] Ibn Taymiyyah, *Majmū' al-Fatāwā*, vol.19, p.27
[2] *Ibn Taymiyyah Letters from Prison,* (Middlesex, UK: Message of Islam, 1419 AH/ 1998 CE), p.7.

What is clear is that, all those who have done good towards the Muslims and leaned towards them, were never harmed by the Muslims. Indeed, the result of such work is good and a lasting relationship repaying the extent of the service received.[1]

Faisal also states:

> "Kāfirs will always be kāfirs, every kāfir will always find a time to make you feel ashamed of your religion, every kāfir!...Kāfirs will always be Kāfirs!"

What a pathetic piece of hyperbole from one who used to be "a kāfir" himself! Indeed, from one who used to be in the Christian Salvation Army!? What is Faisal trying to insinuate here? He makes no distinction whatsoever here and this is an example of his blanket generalisations, which are filled with error and injustice. The Book of Allāh – the same Book that is meant to govern the beliefs and behaviour of Faisal – makes a clear distinction between those disbelievers towards whom we may show good gesture and those against whom we are stern. Allāh says:

﴾ لَّا يَنْهَىٰكُمُ ٱللَّهُ عَنِ ٱلَّذِينَ لَمْ يُقَـٰتِلُوكُمْ فِى ٱلدِّينِ وَلَمْ يُخْرِجُوكُم مِّن دِيَـٰرِكُمْ أَن تَبَرُّوهُمْ وَتُقْسِطُوٓاْ إِلَيْهِمْ ۚ إِنَّ ٱللَّهَ يُحِبُّ ٱلْمُقْسِطِينَ ﴾

---

[1] Ibid. p.55

"Allāh does not forbid you to deal justly and kindly with those who fought not against you on account of religion and did not drive you out of your homes. Verily, Allāh loves those who deal with equity."

{al-Mumtahanah (60): 8}

Perhaps Faisal in his selective readings skipped this verse and homed in on the verse that can be used to back his agenda. Allāh says:

﴿ إِنَّمَا يَنْهَىٰكُمُ ٱللَّهُ عَنِ ٱلَّذِينَ قَٰتَلُوكُمْ فِى ٱلدِّينِ وَأَخْرَجُوكُم مِّن دِيَٰرِكُمْ وَظَٰهَرُواْ عَلَىٰ إِخْرَاجِكُمْ أَن تَوَلَّوْهُمْ وَمَن يَتَوَلَّهُمْ فَأُوْلَٰئِكَ هُمُ ٱلظَّٰلِمُونَ ﴾

"It is only as regards those who fought against you on account of religion, and have driven you out of your homes, and helped to drive you out, that Allāh forbids you to befriend them. And whosoever will befriend them, then such are the Zalimun (wrong-doers those who disobey Allāh)." *{al-Mumtahanah (60): 9}*

Even if Faisal were to refer to this verse to bolster his Takfīrī temper tantrums, the particle *innamā* (only), which initiates this verse, puts a stop to that and restricts applying it absolutely.

In the question and answer session, about an hour and twenty-nine minutes into the lecture, Faisal is asked if Omar Bakri Muhammad al-Fostok (Fustuq),[1]

---

[1] For more on him refer to Abū Ameenah 'AbdurRahmān as-Salafī and 'AbdulHaq al-Ashantī, *A Critical Study of the Multiple Identites and Disguises of "al-Muhajiroun"* (London: Jamiah Media, 1430 AH/2009 CE).

another deviant, should be killed!! Observe here how his takfeer- thirsty crowd is not satisfied with just asking if he is misguided or a real Muslim, but also if his blood should be shed! This just drums home the mentality of these people who give ear and heart to Faisal's vicious teachings. Incidentally, this was due to Bakri being involved in a documentary about himself entitled *'The Tottenham Ayatollah'* which was aired on Tuesday 8 April 1997 CE on *Channel 4* in the UK.[1]

Sample Lecture Number Two: 'Exposing The Hypocrites'[2]

Faisal states in the lecture entitle *'Exposing the Hypocrites'*, which is a lecture based on the works of 'Ā'id al-Qarnī (!!):

"Another sign of the hypocrite is that he's very pessimistic, so he says... 'how can we fight America, it's impossible let us throw our towel in the ring and give-up, we'll never fight America. We don't have the ability to build submarines and planes and tanks, tomahawk cruise missiles and patriot missiles and so on and so on. It doesn't make sense that we declare war on these people, we don't have the weapons' <u>this is a</u> <u>hypocrite speaking.</u> He's very pessimistic and he spreads this da'wah around to convince the other Muslims to give up jihād 'don't fight the

---

[1] The documentary is available on *Google Videos*, accessed Wednesday 10 November 2010.
[2] www.pureislam.co.za

enemy because you don't have the technology they have' this is a real hypocrite, very pessimistic. Then he (the hypocrite) has another point which is called Irjā'."

So just because a Muslim says that armed *jihād* should not be fought at a particular time necessitates that Muslim being a hypocrite according Faisal's ruined analysis! It is no coincidence that those who propogate the same sullied da'wah seem to always say the same thing. Compare this statement with a statement of another neo-Takfīrī, Anwar al-Awlakī,[1] who says:

These people can come in the form of Shuyūkh and they will tell you that it is not the time for Jihād fi Sabeelillah, and because they are scholars you would listen to them. Allāh says: "And there would have been some among you who would have listened to them." Why would they listen to these people? Because of the status they have. They are leaders in their community, they're scholars, they're people who know how to speak. They discourage a Muslim from doing Jihād fi Sabeelillah and they are Munāfiqoon; whoever discourages a Muslim from doing Jihād fi Sabeelillah is a Munafiq since this ayah is referring to the Munafiqoon. A Muslim who has become a Mujahid since this ayah is these people; he doesn't care about their status, "how good you are at speaking or how scholarly you claim to be. This is what Allāh wants from me and I'm gonna do it". And this is one of the most, I would say today, serious fitnas

---

[1] See http://www.salafimanhaj.com/pdf/SalafiManhaj_Awlaki.pdf

today that the young brothers face. That their scholars are not encouraging them instead they are discouraging them, that Islamic movements are preparing but rather holding them back.

Let's us refer to what Muslim scholars actually say on the very important issues that Faisal ignorantly delved into. Imām Muhammad bin Sālih al-'Uthaymeen ﷻ said in response to a question which was put to him:

ولهذا لو قال لنا قائل : الآن لماذا لا نحارب أمريكا وروسيا وفرنسا وانجلترا ؟؟!!!!

لماذا؟؟ لعدم القدرة الأسلحة التي قد ذهب عصرها عندهم هي التي في أيدينا وهي

عند أسلحتهم بمنزلة سكاكين الموقد عند الصواريخ ما تفيد شيئاً فكيف يمكن أن

نقاتل هؤلاء ؟ ولهذا أقول: إنه من الحمق أن يقول قائل :أنه يجب علينا أن نقاتل

أمريكا وفرنسا وانجلترا وروسيا كيف نقاتل هذا تأباه حكمة الله عز وجل ويأباه

شرعه لكن الواجب علينا أن نفعل ما أمر الله به عز وجل

For this reason, if it is said to us: 'Today, why don't we wage war against America, Russia, France and England??!!'[1] Why not? Due to the lack of military power which time has passed by all for them. The weapons that are in our hands are kitchen utensils like kitchen knives against rockets; this would not benefit a thing! So how is it even possible for us to fight those? For this reason I say: 'It is from foolishness to say that it is

---

[1] Just as Faisal has stated!

obligatory for us to fight America, France, England and Russia, how can we fight those when we disobey the wisdom of Allāh and shun His Divine Legislation.' What is rather obligatory for us to do is do what Allāh has instructed us to do:

$$﴿ وَأَعِدُّواْ لَهُم مَّا ٱسْتَطَعْتُم مِّن قُوَّةٍ ﴾$$

'And prepare against them what you are able to from power...'

{al-Anfāl (8): 60}

هذا الواجب علينا أن نعد لهم ما استطعنا من قوة، وأهم قوة نعدها هو الإيمان والتقوى ...ا.هـ

This is obligatory for us, to prepare ourselves what we are able to from power and the most important form of power is īmān and taqwā.[1]

Shaykh 'Abdul'Azeez bin Rayyis ar-Rayyis notes that from the particular affairs in comprehending the condition of the Muslims is that if they are weak due to their numbers, or due to their lack of preparation in relation to their enemies, it is not correct for them to tread the path of armed jihād against the enemy due to their condition of weakness. What makes this apparent is the fact that Allāh did not instruct His Messenger ﷺ and the Companions ﴾ to fight the *kuffār* when they were in Makkah due to their weakness in number and readiness in comparison to their enemies. Ibn Taymiyyah ﴾ said:

---

[1] See http://www.salafimanhaj.com/pdf/SalafiManhaj_TakfeerAndBombing.pdf

وكان مأموراً بالكف عن قتالهم لعجزه وعجز المسلمين عن ذلك، ثم لما هاجر إلى المدينة وصار له بها أعوان أذن له في الجهاد، ثم لما قووا كتب عليهم القتال ولم يكتب عليهم قتال من سالمهم؛ لأنهم لم يكونوا يطيقون قتال جميع الكفار . فلما فتح الله مكة وانقطع قتال قريش وملوك العرب، ووفدت إليه وفود العرب بالإسلام أمره الله - تعالى - بقتال الكفار كلهم إلا من كان له عهد مؤقت، وأمره بنبذ العهود المطلقة، فكان الذي رفعه ونسخه ترك القتال ١.هـ

It was instructed to abstain from fighting them due to his inability and the inability of the Muslims, then when they migrated to Madeenah and gained assistance, Allāh permitted him ﷺ to make armed jihād and then when they grew in strength Allāh prescribed for them fighting and did not prescribe fighting for them for their own safety as they were not able to fight all of the kuffār. But when Allāh opened up Makkah for them and halted fighting against the Quraysh and the kings of the Arabs and a delegation of Arabs came into Islām, Allāh instructed the Prophet ﷺ to fight all of the kuffār except those who had a temporary bond of agreement. Allāh then instructed him to annul those absolute agreements and that which annulled it was leaving fighting.[1]

Ibn Taymiyyah also said:

---

[1] *Al-Jawāb as-Saheeh*, vol.1, p.237

وسبب ذلك أن المخالفة لهم لا تكون إلا مع ظهور الدين وعلوه كالجهاد، وإلزامهم

بالجزية والصغار، فلما كان المسلمون في أول الأمر ضعفاء لم تشرع المخالفة لهم، فلما

كمل الدين وظهر وعلا، شرع ذلك ا.هــ—

The reason for that tax upon them is only when the deen is manifest and raised such as jihād and their adherence to paying the jizya and subjugation. So when the Muslims were in a state of weakness in the beginning the duty (which the non-Muslims pay to the Muslim state) was not Divinely Legislated, only after the deen had been completed and manifest was that Divinely Legislated.[1]

Then Ibn Taymiyyah said:

فكان ذلك عاقبة الصبر والتقوى اللذين أمر الله بهما في أول الأمر، وكان إذ ذاك لا

يؤخذ من أحد من اليهود الذين بالمدينة ولا غيرهم جزية، وصارت تلك الآيات في

حق كل مؤمن مستضعف لا يمكنه نصر الله ورسوله بيده ولا بلسانه، فينتصر بما يقدر

عليه من القلب ونحوه، وصارت آية الصغار على المعاهدين في حق كل مؤمن قوي

يقدر على نصر الله ورسوله بيده أو لسانه، وبهذه الآية ونحوها كان المسلمون يعملون

آخر عُمُر رسول الله ﷺ وعلى عهد خلفائه الراشدين، وكذلك هو إلى قيام الساعة،

---

[1] *Iqtidā' as-Sirāt ul-Mustaqeem*, vol.1, p.420

لا تزال طائفة من هذه الأمة قائمين على الحق ينصرون الله ورسوله النصر التام، فمن

كان من المؤمنين بأرض هو فيها مستضعف أو في وقت هو فيه مستضعف فليعمل بآية

الصبر والصفح عمن يؤذي الله ورسوله من الذين أوتوا الكتاب والمشركين، وأما أهل

القوة فإنما يعملون بآية قتال أئمة الكفر الذين يطعنون في الدين، وبآية قتال الذين

أوتوا الكتاب حتى يعطوا الجزية عن يد وهم صاغرون ا.هـ

This was the result of patience and consciousness of Allāh which Allāh
instructed (the Muslims to have) at the very beginning of Islām and
during that time the jizya was not taken from any of the Jewish
community, or other non-Muslim communities, who were living in
Madeenah. Those verses then became applicable to every Muslim in a
state of weakness who is not able to aid Allāh and His Messenger with his
hand or via his tongue (i.e. by speaking), but could help by using what
he was able to by his heart and the likes. The verses about subduing those
non-Muslims who have contracts with Muslims are applicable to every
strong believer who is able to help the deen of Allāh and His Messenger
with his hand and tongue (i.e. via speaking). The Muslims were applying
these verses during the last epoch of the Messenger of Allāh ﷺ and
during the epoch of his rightly guided caliphs. And thus it will be until
the Day of Judgement as there will never cease to be a group from this
ummah who are well established on the truth who help Allāh and His
Messenger ﷺ with complete help. So whoever from the believers is weak

in the earth, or is weak in the time in which he is living, must apply those verses of the Qur'ān which mention patience and forgiveness against those who were given the scriptures prior and also from the polytheists that are seeking to harm Allāh and His Messenger from those. As for those people who are in a state of strength then they are to apply the verses regarding fighting the leaders of kufr who slander the deen. They are also to apply the Qur'ānic verses regarding fighting those who were given the scriptures prior until they pay the jizya and are subjugated.[1]

Imām 'AbdurRahmān as-Sa'dī ﷺ said:

هذه الآيات تتضمن الأمر بالقتال في سبيل الله، وهذا كان بعد الهجرة إلى المدينة، لما قوي المسلمون للقتال أمرهم الله به، بعدما كانوا مأمورين بكف أيديهم ا.هـ —

These verses include the order to fight in the way of Allāh and this was after the hijra to Madeenah. So when the Muslims became strong Allāh instructed them to fight, after they were instructed to abstain from it.[2]

Imām as-Sa'dī then said:

---

[1] *As-Sārim al-Maslūl*, vol.2, p.413
[2] *Tafseer*, p.89

—: ومنها: أنه لو فرض عليهم القتال — مع قلة عددهم وعددهم، وكثرة أعدائهم —

لأدى ذلك إلى اضمحلال الإسلام، فروعي جانب المصلحة العظمى على ما دوها،

ولغير ذلك من الحكم. وكان بعض المؤمنين يودون أن لو فرض عليهم القتال في

تلك الحال غير اللائق فيها ذلك، وإنما اللائق فيها القيام بما أمروا به في ذلك الوقت

من التوحيد والصلاة والزكاة ونحو ذلك، كما قال تعالى

And from it: is that if fighting was obligated upon them, with their small numbers and many enemies, that would have led to Islām disappearing. Some of the believers held that fighting during that condition was improper. What is actually suitable in such a period of weakness is to establish what Allāh has instructed from *Tawheed*, prayer, giving charity (*zakah*) etc. As Allāh said:

﴿ وَلَوْ أَنَّهُمْ فَعَلُواْ مَا يُوعَظُونَ بِهِۦ لَكَانَ خَيْرًا لَّهُمْ وَأَشَدَّ تَثْبِيتًا ﴾

'... But if they had done what they had been instructed to do it would have been better for them and would have strengthened (their faith).' *{an-Nisā (4): 66}*

فلما هاجروا إلى المدينة ، وقوي الإسلام ، كتب عليهم القتال في وقته المناسب

لذلك ا.هـ

So when they migrated to Madeenah and Islām became powerful, Allāh prescribed fighting for them at the suitable time.[1]

Imām Muhammad bin Sālih al-'Uthaymeen ﷺ said:

لابد فيه من شرط وهو أن يكون عند المسلمين قدرة وقوة يستطيعون بها القتال، فإن لم يكن لديهم قدرة فإن إقحام أنفسهم في القتال إلقاء بأنفسهم إلى التهلكة ، ولهذا لم يوجب الله سبحانه وتعالى على المسلمين القتال وهم في مكة ، لأنهم عاجزون ضعفاء فلما هاجروا إلى المدينة وكونوا الدولة الإسلامية وصار لهم شوكة أمروا بالقتال، وعلى هذا فلابد من هذا الشرط ، وإلا سقط عنهم كسائر الواجبات لأن جميع الواجبات يشترط فيها القدرة لقوله تعالى

There is a necessary condition within this which is that: the Muslims have the ability and power that enables them to fight. If they do not possess the power yet put themselves forward to fight, they will be destroyed.[2] For this reason, Allāh did not obligate the Muslims to fight whilst they were in Makkah as they were unable to, due to their

---

[1] *Tafseer*, p.188

[2] This is what has taken place in the West, with London being an excellent example of where the efforts of the so-called 'leaders of *jihād*' have not materialized whatsoever. Their calls have been totally quashed, squashed, crushed, quelled and destroyed and their ideologues have been thrown into the prisons of the *kuffār*, with no positive effects of their *da'wah* for the Muslims or societies whatsoever. Indeed, some of them have even freed themselves from terrorism and agitation due to their realising the negative effects.

condition of weakness. But when they migrated to Madeenah and established the Islamic state they assumed power and were instructed to fight. Based upon this there is no escape from this condition and if not, the remaining obligations would be redundant as all of the obligations have the condition of ability based on Allāh's saying:

$$ \text{﴿ فَٱتَّقُواْ ٱللَّهَ مَا ٱسۡتَطَعۡتُمۡ ﴾} $$

'Fear Allāh as much as you can...' {Taghābun (64): 16}

وقوله

And Allāh's saying:

$$ \text{﴿ لَا يُكَلِّفُ ٱللَّهُ نَفۡسًا إِلَّا وُسۡعَهَا ﴾} $$

'Allāh does not burden a soul more than it can bear...'
{Baqarah (2): 286}.[1]

Then Imām al-'Uthaymeen 🙰 said in response to a question related to the Islamic society's need for *jihād* in the path of Allāh which asked:

فضل الجهاد ومنزلته العظيمة في الشرع الإسلامي ليكون الدين كله لله، وأضاف

هل يجب القتال أو يجوز مع عدم الاستعداد له؟

The virtue of jihād and its lofty status in the Divine Legislation of Islām is in order for the deen to be entirely for Allāh. In addition to this I ask is fighting obligated or permissible without being prepared for it?

---

[1] *Sharh ul-Mumti'*, vol.8, p.9

The answer from Imām al-'Uthaymeen ﷺ:

لا يجب ولا يجوز ونحن غير مستعدين له، والله لم يفرض على نبيه وهو في مكة أن

يقاتل المشركين ، وأن الله أذن لنبيه في صلح الحديبية أن يعاهد المشركين ذلك العهد

الذي إذا تلاه الإنسان ظن أن فيه خذلاناً للمسلمين . كثير منكم يعرف كيف كان

صلح الحديبية حتى قال عمر بن الخطاب: يا رسول الله ألسنا على الحق وعدونا

على الباطل ؟. قال: بلى. قال: فلم نعطي الدنية في ديننا ؟، فظن أن هذا خذلان،

ولكن الرسول صلى الله عليه وسلم ما في شك أنه أفقه من عمر، وأن الله تعالى أذن

له في ذلك وقال: إني رسول الله ولست عاصيه وهو ناصري ... وإن كان ظاهر

الصلح خذلاناً للمسلمين ، وهذا يدلنا يا إخواني على مسألة مهمة وهو قوة ثقة

المؤمن بربه .. المهم أنه يجب على المسلمين الجهاد حتى تكون كلمة الله هي العليا

ويكون الدين كله لله، لكن الآن ليس بأيدي المسلمين ما يستطيعون به جهاد الكفار

حتى ولو جهاد مدافعة وجهاد المهاجمة ما في شك الآن غير ممكن حتى يأتي الله بأمة

واعية تستعد إيمانياً ونفسياً ، ثم عسكرياً ، أما نحن على هذا الوضع فلا يمكن أن

نجاهد ا.هـ ــ

It is neither obligatory nor permissible without being prepared for it. Allāh did not obligate on His Prophet ﷺ whilst he was in Makkah to fight the Mushrikeen and permitted His Prophet ﷺ in the Treaty of Hudaybiyah to make an agreement with the Mushrikeen.[1] This was an agreement which if a person read would think that within it was a

---

[1] The *Hudaybiyah Treaty* was made between the Muslims and the polytheists of Quraysh. The *mushrikeen* of Quraysh witnessed the determination of the Muslims to risk their lives, properties, wealth and families for their faith in order to spread it peacefully. Therefore, a treaty of reconciliation and peace was made between the Quraysh and the Muslims. The clauses of the treaty were:

The Muslims would return and come back in the following year (7 AH) but they would not stay in Makkah for more than three days and without arms except those concealed.

War activities were to be suspended for ten years, during which time both sides would live in security with neither side waging war against the other.

Whoever wished to join Muhammad ﷺ was free to do so and likewise whoever wished to join the *mushrikeen* of the Quraysh was also free to do so.

If anyone from the Quraysh joined Muhammad ﷺ without his parent's or guardian's permission, he should be sent back to the Quraysh, but should any of Muhammad's followers return to the Quraysh, they were not to be sent back. (See Safiur-Rahman al-Mubarakpuri, *The Sealed Nectar (ar-Raheequl-Makhtum)* Darusalam, 2002, p.403.)

The treaty was significant in that the Quraysh began to recognise the Muslims' legitimate existence and began to deal with them on equal terms. Safiur-Rahman al-Mubarakpuri notes in his biography of the Prophet Muhammad *(sallallāhu alayhi wassallam)* pp.407-408: "The Muslims did not have in mind to seize people's property or kill them through bloody wars, nor did they ever think of using any compulsive approaches in their efforts to propagate Islam, on the contrary their sole target was to provide an atmosphere of freedom in ideology or religion. '...Then whosoever wills, let him believe, and whosoever wills, let him disbelieve.' {al-Kahf (18): 29}" The Muslims on the other hand had the opportunity to spread Islām over areas not then explored. When there was the peace agreement, war was suspended, and men met and consulted each other, none talked about Islām intelligently without entering it; within two years following the conclusion of the treaty, twice as many people entered Islām than ever before. This is supported by the fact that the Prophet *(sallallāhu alayhi wassallam)* went out to al-Hudaybiyah with only 1400 men, but when he set out to liberate Makkah, two years later, he had 10,000 men with him.

setback for the Muslims. Many of you know how the Treaty of Hudaybiyah was to the extent that 'Umar ibn al-Khattāb ﷺ said 'O Messenger of Allāh! Are we not upon the truth and our enemies upon bātil?'The Messenger of Allāh ﷺ said '*Yes.*' 'Umar said 'Then why should we accept such difficult terms in the affairs of our deen?' 'Umar thought that there was a setback for the Muslims within the treaty. However, there is no doubt that the Messenger of Allāh ﷺ had more understanding than 'Umar and Allāh permitted the Messenger to do that. The Messenger of Allāh ﷺ said '*Indeed, I am the Messenger of Allāh and I would not disobey Him and He will help me.*' So if it was clear that the treaty was a setback for the Muslims then this indicates to us brothers an important issue which is the strength of a believer's trust in his Lord. So what is important is that it is obligatory upon Muslims to wage jihād in order to make the word of Allāh the most high and so that the deen will be entirely for Allāh. However, currently we do not possess, as Muslims, that which can enable us to wage *jihād* against the *kuffār*, even if is defensive. As for offensive jihād then there is no doubt that this is not possible right now until Allāh brings consciousness to the *ummah* which prepare the ummah in terms of *eemān*, personally and militarily. As for us today in this regard we are not able to wage *jihād*.[1]

Al-'Allāmah Sālih al-Fawzān ibn 'Abdullāh *(hafidhahullāh)* was asked:

---

[1] *Liqā'* (open session) 33, Thursday 1 Safar 1414 AH/July 20 1993 CE

There are those who see the hadeeth of the Prophet ﷺ: *'Jihād is continuous until the Last Hour is established'*[1] and then say 'why do the scholars say that the ummah is not able to make offensive jihād during our present era and that this time resembles the first Makkan period? And the Prophet ﷺ said that *'Jihād is continuous until the Last Hour is established.'*?

Answer from al-'Allāmah Sālih al-Fawzān:

Yes, Jihād is continuous if the conditions and basics have been fulfilled then it is continuous. As for when the conditions and basics have not been fulfilled then it is to be awaited for until power, capability and readiness returns to the Muslims, so then they can fight their enemies. So for example, if you have a sword or a gun, can you face airplanes, bombs and rockets? No, because what they have prepared against us will lead to severe harm. But if you have that which is ready to face what they have

---

[1] Shaykh Muhammad ibn Fahd al-Husayn says in his commentary and editing of Shaykh Sālih al-Fawzān's treatise on *jihād*, with regards to this *hadeeth*: "I did not find this *hadeeth* with this wording and what Abū Dāwūd transmitted with the wording *'Jihād is continuous from the time Allāh sent me until the last part of this ummah fight the Dajjāl'* has within the chain of transmission Yazeed ibn Abī Tushbah, about whom Ibn Hajar said in *at-Taqreeb 'majhūl.'"* For this reason, he stated in *Fath al-Bārī* (vol.6, p.67) that in its chain of transmission is weakness. The wording that the scholars mention in the books of creed is as at-Tahāwī ﷺ said *"Hajj and jihād are both continuous with the leader of the Muslims, good or evil, until the Hour is established. They are not annulled at all or diminished." Sharh 'Aqeedah Tahawiyyah*, 387. See: Muhammad bin Fahd al-Husayn (ed.), Shaykh, Dr. Sālih bin Fawzān al-Fawzān, *al-Jihād wa Dawābituhu ash-Sharī'ah* (Riyadh: Maktabah ar-Rushd, 1424 AH/2003 CE), p.48.

118

prepared, or the likes of it, then face them. As for you not having anything to face them, then Allāh says:

$$\text{﴾ وَلَا تُلْقُوا بِأَيْدِيكُمْ إِلَى التَّهْلُكَةِ ﴿}$$

"...and do not throw (yourselves) with your own hands into destruction." *{Baqarah (2): 195}*

And this will harm the Muslims more than benefiting them, if indeed there is any benefit in it at all.

So look at the huge gaping difference between the scholars and the likes of Faisal and those like him, such as Anwar al-'Awlaki![1] Then Faisal says:

"The 'Murjif is the person who spreads negativity in the ranks of the believers for them to give up the jihād. So if you are going on the battlefield you're marching forward with your Kalashnikov on your shoulder to fight listen to the hypocrite in your rank: 'O the sun is too hot my shoes is[2] *{sic}* squeezing me *{sic}* the journey is too far we're gonna faint and die before we reach there' and then another person will say 'Yeah it's true I think it's true you know'."

---

[1] For more on him refer to: http://www.salafimanhaj.com/pdf/SalafiManhaj_Awlaki

[2] This is not a typo error! We have reproduced the words of Faisal here word for word. So he says: "my shoes is" here when the correct English grammar is actually "my shoes are" as the following word is a plural noun. 'Is' on the other hand is associated with singular nouns.

Firstly, this statement is the archetypal trait of the *Khawārij Qa'diyyah*. Where has Faisal himself fought and on which battlefield has he ever been? He mentions all of this as if he has some kind of experience, when the reality is he himself has never been on any kind of 'military expedition' for him to have knowledge of this whatsoever! He is merely trying to encourage the youth to something based on ignorance.

Secondly, Faisal also incorrectly describes the characteristics of the Murjifūn, or at least does not give their full description. The word 'Murjif' is derived from the verb 'Rajafa' which means: 'to shake, tremble, shudder', and the Murjif is thus the one who seeks to shake and disturb the peace. Allāh says:

$$﴿ وَٱلْمُرْجِفُونَ فِى ٱلْمَدِينَةِ ﴾$$

"...and those who spread rumors in al-Madīnah..." *{al-Ahzāb (33): 60}*

Ibn Katheer in his tafseer states about that this *ayah*:

> Means: those who say that the enemy has come and war has started, which is a lie and a fabrication.

The Murjifūn are those who spread false rumours, agitate, stir-up and provoke problems, indeed, the correct definition could actually apply to El-Faisal himself! Then Faisal says:

"Who told you that jihād is a simple thing? There's difficulty in jihād, so if you're marching forward and you're tired and weary but that

120

doesn't give you the right to spread negativity in the ranks of the believers (and say) 'Oh the journey's too far' or 'Oh I'm hungry where's the food?'."

Observe the subtle deception here. Can you see how his examples are all examples, which have been brought after the rulings and conditions of Jihād have been fulfilled and that the Muslims are actually marching to war? However, in his initial condemnation of Muslims who harbour doubts, nothing of the rulings and conditions of Jihād were established. His criticisms were purely directed at a realistic glance on our spiritual and military impotence. What we have here are two completely different scenarios jumbled together for a corrupted purpose. Then he says in a statement, which applies more to Faisal than anyone else and thus demonstrating his contradictions:

"Another sign of the hypocrite is that he likes to slander pious Muslims. In this country today (i.e. UK) don't think that those who are working for Islām, that the kāfirs are their greatest enemies, the hypocrites are their greatest enemies! People who are giving da'wah to the correct fikra,[1] their greatest enemies are not the kāfirs, they are not being slandered by kāfirs, the deviant groups, are our greatest enemies. So Ahmad Ibn Hanbal was called a khawārij in his time, Ibn Taymiyyah was called a khawārij in his time, Muhammad ibn 'AbdulWahhāb was

---

[1] For Faisal the only people who are "giving da'wah to the correct fikra" as he calls it, all have to be imprisoned or on the run!

called a khawārij in his time and today we, the members of Ahl us-Sunnah wa'l-Jamā'ah, are called khawārij in our time by the hypocrites of our time!"

Indeed, it was Faisal himself, who called Salafis: **"the real khawārij of the era"**! So if we remain faithful to his above statement concerning Salafis, and follow faithfully his line of thought, does this inadvertently imply that Salafis are also the people of the truth? Since everyone else mentioned above who was labelled with the title of Khawārij, Faisal himself deems as being from the righteous! What about calling other Muslims **"Jews of the ummah"**, **"the worst *Salafis*"**, **"major hypocrites"** and that **"there is no difference between them and the followers of Musaylimah al-Kadhab"**?? All of which Faisal said about the Salafis at *Masjid Ibn Taymiyyah (Brixton Mosque)* in his lecture *'The Devil's Deception of the Saudi Salafis'*, if slander is one of the signs of the hypocrites as ("el") Faisal said, then what about all of the slander he made in that particular lecture?! Then Faisal says in praise of Ā'id al-Qarnī:

"Ā'id al-Qarnī himself was viciously slandered and the policy of the Saudi government is that whenever there is a scholar who is famous they kill his character or throw him in prison..."

Is it indeed? So what about 'Ā'id al-Qarnī, who now who appears on Saudi TV on the podiums with the rulers and they praise him openly; is this also their policy according to Faisal? If it is their policy, al-Qarnī does not seem to be currently suffering at all and on the contrary, he is on more Arabic TV channels than the actual senior scholars! So 'Ā'id al-Qarnī is currently being promoted, so much for the policy being to throw them in prison! Not to mention the fact that Ā'id al-Qarnī has also retracted from many of his extreme views from the past and has gone through many ups and downs and changes of opinion.[1] Faisal then says:

> "Every kāfir is a hypocrite and every hypocrite is a kāfir!"

This is what he says with his own words, so when he thus described the Salafis in the lecture 'Saudi Salafis' as being "major hypocrites" it is clear then that within Faisal's corrupted extremist khārijī mentality, he considered Salafis to be kuffār! Indeed, one of the signs from al-Qarnī's book, which Faisal did not elaborate upon at all, was that "the hypocrite has no knowledge of the deen of Islām" yet Faisal conveniently and quickly skipped over this and did not explain it at all! Regarding jihād, Faisal says that the Salafis (who he describes as being 'Madkhalis' and 'Jāmīs' of Brixton Mosque) hate jihād!? He then says that Salafis say: "there is no jihād unless there is a caliph." This is false, and it is interesting that Faisal within all of this does not refer at all to what the scholars have stated regarding jihād. First of all, for Jihād ud-Dafʿa many 'Ulama have stated that the permission of the leader, let alone a Caliph, is not necessary,

---

[1] For more on this, and for a thorough critique of Ā'id al-Qarnī refer to the following critique of him by Shaykh 'Abdul'Azeez bin Rayyis ar-Rayyis which has been translated here: http://www.salafimanhaj.com/pdf/SalafiManhaj_AlQarni.pdf

even though otherwise it is one of the main conditions for Jihād.[1] Shaykh ul-Islām Ibn Taymiyyah ﷺ stated that when the enemy encroach into Muslim lands then the Muslims of that land defend their land, and those nearby help, without the permission of the leader or the parents. This is also mentioned by Imām Abu'l-Qāsim 'Umar bin Husayn al-Khirqī in his *Mukhtasar* that:

...if the enemy surprise them and it is not possible to seek the permission of the Ameer because if the enemy come to them Jihād would become Fard 'Ayn upon all of the Muslims and no one would be allowed to refrain from it.[2]

Thirdy, practical examples of this can be seen within the life of Shaykh ul-Islām Ibn Taymiyyah when the Mongols attacked Damascus and Ibn Taymiyyah and his students went out to face them without the permission of the leader.[3] In addition more recently, when the Muslims defeated the Soviet Communists in Afghanistan the Mujāhideen organised themselves without there being one sole leader co-ordinating the fighting. The same occurred during the Jihād in Bosnia wherein groups organised themselves and co-operated with each other against the ethnic cleansers of the former Yugoslavia, without there being an overall

---

[1] Shaykh ul-Islām Ibn Taymiyyah, *Majmū' al-Fatāwā* (Tarteeb of 'AbduRahmān bin Muhammad Qāsim and his son Muhammad, 1398 AH, 2ⁿᵈ Edn.), vol.28, p.358.

[2] 'Abdullāh bin Ahmad Ibn Qudāmah al-Maqdisī, *al-Mughnī* (Beirut: Dār ul-Fikr, 1405 AH, 1ˢᵗ Edn.), vol., pp.389-390.

[3] Ibn 'AbdulHādī, *al-Intisār fī Dhikr Ahwāl Qāmi' il-Mubtadi'een wa Ākhar ul-Mujtahideen Taqiuddeen Abi'l-'Abbās Ahmad bin Taymiyyah* (Cairo: Wizārat ul-Awqāf-Markāz as-Seerah wa's-Sunnah, 1ˢᵗ Edn., 1423 AH/2003 CE), p.56

Amīr of it, let alone a Caliph. However, if a given leader viewed that there was a *Shari' maslahah* (benefit) in withholding from a defensive Jihād such as, for example, in order to outline a better plan and strategy and organise troops, and this does not bring about more harm – then at this point the leader of the Muslims can withhold from any defensive action.[1]

Fourthly, Salafis do not say that there has to be a Caliph but there does have to be an *Amīr*. The Caliph or the Amīr, or Imām at least, is for *Jihād ut-Talab* and there are texts in this regard as highlighted by our Shaykh Mashhūr Hasan Āl Salmān.[2] In fact, these texts are mainly from the Hanbali scholars! This is the view mentioned by Ibn Qudāmah al-Maqdisī in *al-Mughnī*.[3] Which is the madhhab which ("el") Faisal claims to adhere to?! Therefore, we can summarise the following points:

✓ There is a differentiation between *Jihād ut-Talab* and *Jihād ud-Dafa* in regards to the issue of seeking the permission of the leader of the Muslims, whether this is the Caliph, Sultān, Imām or Ameer.

✓ Most of the 'Ulama view the permission of the leader is only a condition in *Jihād ut-Talab* but not for *Jihād ud-Dafa*.

---

[1] Refer to Hasan bin 'AbdurRahmān bin Husayn Wahdān, Shaykh Abū 'Ubaydah Mashhūr Hasan Āl Salmān (intro and notes), *Ahkām ul-Jihād 'inda Ibn Taymiyyah: Tatbeeqāt ul-Mu'āsirah* ('Ammān, Jordan: Dār ul-Athariyyah, 1428 AH/2007 CE), p.95.
[2] Ibid., p.95, ftn.4
[3] Ibn Qudāmah al-Maqdisī, *al-Mughnī*, vol., pp.368, 389-390.

✓ *Jihād ud-Daf'a* is based on the *maslahah* and looking at the results and consequences. Therefore, it can be said here that for *Jihād ud-Daf'a*, if the permission of the leader is not a condition, then at the very least the people of knowledge are to be referred to.

Faisal, in his over-simplification and much needed distortion of the issue leaves out any mention of all of these conditions. Faisal says in the 'question and answer' session that he was involved in in a debate with some members of Hizb ut-Tahreer and that this debate was recorded but *"not released because we are not of those who blackmail people"*. Yet Faisal in the lecture entitled *'21ˢᵗ Century House Niggas'* secretly recorded a discussion that he had with Idrees Palmer and produced this in the lecture for all to listen to! So what kind of double-standard is this?! Also within the session he states that Salafis *"reject the Islamic state which the Tālibān established"* and this again is false and either a blatant lie or Faisal is pure ignorant. This is because Salafis accept *any ruler* who comes about and acquires power and control via any means, as long as the affair is in his control. This is like the *Hākim al-Mutaghallib* who is the ruler who seized control even though the means in which he came into power may have not been entirely in line with the *Sunnah*. Al-Hāfidh Ibn Hajar al-'Asqalānī transmitted this in *Fath al-Bārī* from Imām Ibn Battāl, who has an explanation of *Saheeh Bukhārī* which has been published:

The fuquhā (Islamic jurists) have reached consensus that obedience must be made to the leader who becomes dominant (mutaghallib)[1] and making jihād with him and that obeying him is better than revolting against him due to the bloodshed in that, and this would not be permissible unless there was clear kufr from the leader.[2]

---

[1] Shaykh 'Alī Hasan al-Halabī *(hafidhahullāh)* stated in a lesson at the *Imām Albānī Centre* ('Ammān, Jordan) in March 2006 CE: "Here we must stop at this word **'mutaghallib (the one who overpowers and becomes dominant)'** for a while. In the next session, it will be made apparent to us that the paths for a ruler acquiring power are numerous and from the paths are in the case of a ruler who becomes dominant and overpowers others (al-Mutaghallib). It is when a person opposes the Divine Legislation and revolts against the Muslim leader and thus becomes dominant, and this has happened in Islamic history and the scholars noted that this opposes the Divine Legislation. However, the one who revolted against the Muslim ruler has established and settled security and command now and is able to control the Muslim lands as he obviously is a Muslim yet has opposed the consensus of the Muslims by revolting in the first place yet has seized the reins of power from the first bearers of it. The scholars have reached agreement that the leader who overpowers the reins of authority from another leader is to be obeyed and this is Divinely Legislated. Why? Because it is feared that revolting against this one again will only cause a worse tribulation. For that reason, the greatest intents of the Divine Legislation is that preventing the harms takes precedence over enforcing the benefit."

[2] As now, the leader would have been expelled from the condition of being a Muslim due to falling into clear *kufr*. For this reason, the Prophet ﷺ said: *"Until you see clear (buwāhan) kufr, for which you have with you evidence from Allāh."* Pay attention here: *"you have with you ('indakum)"* meaning that this evidence is firmly settled in you hearts and is clear in front of your eyes, not any type of *kufr* rather it must be clear, explicit and apparent!

127

However, at the same time this does not mean that the *Islamic beliefs* of the Tālibān cannot be questioned,[1] especially in the case of those who claim to be doing things in line with Islām.

Sample Lecture Number Three: 'Challenges Facing The Youth'

Faisal's states in the lecture:

> "If he is a supporter of kufr, a Saudi Salafi, you have to kill him and chop of his head..."!!

Not only are these words a cause for concern, but this also further demonstrates Faisal's vigilante-type attitude. This is within Faisal's model of an 'Islamic state'!! Use of the second person pronoun "you" implies that implementation of the punishment for murder is a right for anyone to exercise. Abu'l-Hasan al-Ash'arī 🙵 stated:

> As for the sword, then all of the khawārij speak of it and hold it, except the Ibādiyyah...they emphasise removing the tyrannical leaders.[2]

---

[1] See the distinction here 'their Islamic beliefs' not their sins, as if there are beliefs of *shirk* that are being taught and encouraged then these have to be condemned more so than a person's own personal sins that they may fall into.

[2] Abu'l-Hasan al-'Asha'rī, *Maqālāt ul-Islamiyyeen*, vol.1, p.204

So what is the Islamic position with regard to carrying out retaliatory punishments, like for apostasy, murder etc? Imām al-Qurtubī said:

لا خلاف أن القصاص في القتل لا يقيمه إلا أولو الأمر الذين فرض عليهم النهوض بالقصاص وإقامة الحدود وغير ذلك لأن الله سبحانه خاطب جميع المؤمنين بالقصاص ثم لا يتهيأ للمؤمنين جميعا أن يجتمعوا على القصاص فأقاموا السلطان مقام أنفسهم في إقامة القصاص وغيره من الحدود

There is no dispute (among the scholars) that *qisās* (retaliatory punishments) in matters of execution can only be carried out by those in positions of authority who are obliged to carry out the qisās and hadd punishments etc, because Allāh has addressed the command regarding qisās to all the Muslims, and it is not possible for all the Muslims to gather together to carry out the qisās, which is why they appointed a leader who may represent them in carrying out the qisās and other hadd punishments.[1]

Faisal's above statement is erroneous from three angles:
- ✓ he expels Muslims from the fold of Islām for matters that do not even amount to sin, let alone major kufr
- ✓ he makes and advocates takfir without applying its conditions and preventive measures

---

[1] *Tafsīr* al-Qurtubi, vol,22 pp.245-246.

✓ and not only does he advocate vigilante-type style executions, which contradict the ijmā of the 'Ulama, but he also promotes the killing of innocent Muslims in non-Muslim lands.

Faisal then states during the so-called 'question and answer session', displaying another definitive sign of his corrupted methodology:

"You're allowed to take all these benefits that these kāfirs offer you, because everything that the kāfir owns is yours. Every single thing that the kāfir owns is yours so you're allowed to take all the benefits that they offer you and you're even allowed to have four wives and put them on benefit, so hope that they give you a mansion in Hampstead Heath!"

With the audience of blind followers finding this funny, as if they are being amused by a comedian at comedy club!? Ibn Taymiyyah ﷺ said about the *khawārij*:

They have two well-known qualities which they separate the unity of the Muslims and their leaders with. One of them is that they leave out the Sunnah and declare evil that which is not evil or they declare good that which is not good.[1]

Is this the *jihād* that Faisal is waging? Then Faisal tries to say that it is permissible to sell alcohol to disbelievers as we are not in an Islamic state!?

---

[1] Ibn Taymiyyah, *Majmū' al-Fatāwā*, vol.19, p.27

Again, where is the evidence for this? He tries to bring an obscure statement attributed to Imām Abū Haneefah ﷺ supposedly in *al-Mugni* of Ibn Qudāmah al-Maqdisī yet does not mention the source. He blindly accepts this knowing that the listeners will utilise it as a proof even though it may be a weak and rejected view, if indeed it even is a view of Imām Abū Haneefah!

The proofs refuting Faisal's assertion that *"everything the kāfir owns is yours (i.e. belongs to Muslims)"* are many. In Saheeh ul-Bukhārī the long hadeeth of the treaty of Hudaybiyah mentions that al-Mugheerah ibn Shu'bah ﷺ knew some people during Jāhilliyah that used to make alcohol and get drunk, and Mugheerah killed them and took their money. Mugheerah was thinking about accepting Islām after he had taken the money from these people, then he went to the Messenger of Allāh informing him that he wanted to be a Muslim and that he had with him the money from those people. What did the Messenger of Allāh ﷺ say to him? He said ﷺ:

»أما الإسلام فأقبل، وأما المال فلست منه في شيء«

"As for your Islām, I accept it and as for the money then I have nothing to do with it."

Meaning: I accept your Islām but as for the money that you acquired from the people without right I have nothing to do with it. Also there was no jihād at that time so what do those people who make permissible robbing and stealing other people's money say? This was after the jihād and Allāh's Messenger ﷺ is not a Messenger of treachery. If such wealth was allowed to keep then Allāh's Messenger ﷺ would have accepted it with no problem. Ibn Hajar stated in regards to this hadeeth in *Fath ul-Bārī*:

»قوله: (وأما المال فلست منه في شيء) أي لا أتعرض له لكونه أخذه غدرا.

ويستفاد منه: أنه لا يحل أخذ أموال الكفار في حال الأمن غدراً؛ لأن الرفقة

يصطحبون على الأمانة، والأمانة تؤدى إلى أهلها مسلما كان أو كافرا، وأن أموال

الكفار إنما تحل بالمحاربة والمغالبة، ولعل النبي ﷺ ترك المال في يده، لإمكان أن يسلم

قومه فيرد إليهم أموالهم«.

His saying ﷺ: *"As for the wealth then I have nothing to do with it whatsoever"* it means: I have no part of it as it was taken via betrayal and treachery. The benefit from this it is not permissible to take wealth and property (Amwāl) from the kuffār treacherously when they have trusted you during a period of safety and security, and trusts should be fulfilled whether the person is a Muslim or a disbeliever. The wealth and property (Amwāl) of the kuffār is only permissible to take through warfare or combat. Maybe the Prophet ﷺ left the wealth that was in his (Mugheerah's hand) because of the possibility of his people embracing Islām and then their wealth would have to be returned to them.[1]

---

[1] Ibn Hajar al-'Asqalānī, *Fath ul-Bārī: Sharh Saheeh ul-Bukhārī* (Beirut: Dār ul-Kutub al-'Ilmiyyah, 3rd Edn., 1421 AH/2000 CE, ed. Muhammad Fu'ād 'AbdulBāqī), *Kitāb ush-Shurūt* [The Book of Conditions], vol.6, p.428.

Imām Abū Bakr Muhammad bin Ibrāheem Ibn ul-Mundhir an-Naysābūrī (d. 318 AH) stated in *al-Awsat fi's-Sunan wa'l-Ijmā' wa'l-Ikhtilāf* that Imāms ash-Shāfi'ī, al-Awzā'ī and Ahmad viewed it impermissible for a Muslim to betray the people of Dār ul-Harb when the Muslim enters their land with a covenant of safety and security.[1] Al-Awzā'ī used the hadeeth of al-Mugheerah as a proof for this view. Ibn ul-Mundhir stated:

»إذا دخل الرجل دار الحرب بأمان فهو آمن بأمانهم، وهم آمنون بأمانة، ولا يجوز له أن يغدر بهم، ولا يخوفهم، ولا يغتالهم، فإن أخذ منهم شيئاً، فعليه رده إليهم، فإن أخرج منه شيء إلى دار الإسلام وجب رد ذلك إليهم، وليس لمسلم أن يشتري ذلك ولا يتلفه، لأنه مال له أمان«

If a (Muslim) man enters Dār ul-Harb with a covenant of security then he is safe from them based on their agreement of security and they are also safe from him. Thus, it is not allowed for him to betray them, cause fear to them or kill them. If he takes anything from them he has to return it back to them and if he takes anything with him back to Dār ul-Islām he has to give it back. A Muslim should neither purchase such

---

[1] Ibn ul-Mundhir however relays, as does Ibn ul-Munāsif in *Kitāb ul-Injād fī Abwāb il-Jihād*, that Imām Abū Haneefah allowed betrayal, yet we have not come across this view within Hanafī fiqh books.

(taken) property nor destroy it because the wealth and property has a trust.[1]

Ibn Qudāmah ﷺ in *al-Mughnī*[2] stated:

«.. وأما خيانتهم فمحرمة؛ لأنهم إنما أعطوه الأمان مشروطاً بتركه خيانتهم، وأمنه

إياهم من نفسه، وإن لم يكن ذلك مذكوراً في اللفظ، فهو معلوم في المعنى، ولذلك

من جاءنا منهم بأمان فخاننا كان ناقضاً لعهده. فإذا ثبت هذا لم تحل خيانتهم لأنه

غدر ولا يصلح في ديننا الغدر. وقد قال النبي –صلى الله عليه وسلم–: «المسلمون

عند شروطهم»

...and as for betraying them, then it is harām (prohibited), because they gave him the covenant of safety and security on the condition that he will neither betray them nor harm them, and even if this was not written therein as it is known contextually. Thus, whoever gained a covenant of safety and security into our countries and betrayed us then it is as if he withdrew his covenant. And thus, if this was true, then it is prohibited to

---

[1] Imām Abū Bakr Muhammad bin Ibrāheem Ibn ul-Mundhir an-Naysābūrī, *al-Awsat fi's-Sunan wa'l-Ijmā' wa'l-Ikhtilāf* (Riyadh, KSA: Dār Tayyibah, 1420 AH/1999 CE, ed. Dr Abū Hammād Sagheer Ahmad bin Muhammad Haneef), vol.11, p.292.

[2] In *Kitāb ul-Jihād, Mas'alat Man Dakhala Ard ul-'Aduw bi-Amān* [The Issue of Entering the Land of the Enemy with an Agreement/Covenant of Safety and Security]. See Muwaffaquddeen Abī Muhammad 'Abdullāh bin Ahmad bin Muhammad bin Qudāmah al-Maqdisī, 'Abdullāh at-Turkī and 'AbdulFattāh al-Halu (eds.), *al-Mughnī* (Riyadh: Dār 'Ālim il-Kutub, 1417 AH/1997 CE, 3rd Edn.), vol.13, p.152.

betray them, because our religion prohibits betrayal. In this respect, the Prophet ﷺ said: '...the Muslims must stick to their conditions'[1]

Ibn Qudāmah here was himself commenting on what was stated by al-Khirqī al-Hanbalī ﷺ when al-Khirqī said:

«جاء في متن الخرقي الحنبلي «من دخل أرض العدو لم يخنهم»»

It is found in the text of al-Khirqī al-Hanbalī: 'Whoever enters the land of the enemy should not betray them (betray the covenant or agreement with them).'

Abu'l-Hasan 'Ali bin Abī Bakr bin 'AbdulJaleel al-Marghīyānī (511-593 AH/1118-1197 CE)[2] stated in *al-Hidāyah: Sharh ul-Bidāyah al-Mubtadi'*, p.134:

وإذا دخل المسلم دار الحرب تاجرا فلا يحل له أن يتعرض لشيء من أموالهم ولا من دمائهم لأنه ضمن أن لا يتعرض لهم بالاستئمان , فالتعرض بعد ذلك يكون غدرا ،

والغدر حرام

---

[1] *Hasan Saheeh*; reported by Abū Dāwūd (3594) from Abū Hurayrah; at-Tirmidhī (1352) from 'Amr Ibn 'Awf al-Muzanī; and our Shaykh classified Saheeh therein, while al-Bukhārī (in *Kitāb ul-Jizyah*) reported it *ta'leeqan* (without a chain of narrators), "and so in case one betrays them, steals from them, or borrows anything, then he should give back what he took." See a*l-Mughnī*, vol.10, p.507
[2] The great Hanafī jurist, was born at Marghiyān in the vicinity of Farghana in Present Day Uzbekistan. He studied with Najmudden Abū Hafs 'Umar an-Nasafi, his son Abu'l-Layth Ahmad bin 'Umar an-Nasafī and other eminent teachers, and excelled in Hadeeth, Tafseer, Fiqh and other studies.

If a Muslim enters Dār ul-Harb as a trader, then he is like a Muslim who is Musta'min in Dār ul-Harb, and it is, therefore, not permissible for him to dishonour them in anything in terms of their wealth and blood as he is within Isti'mān which necessitates he does not dishonour them. If he dishonours them after this then this is betrayal and betrayal is harām.[1]

Our Shaykh, Mashhūr Hasan *(hafidhahullāh)* thus states:

Based upon this, it becomes clear to us the accuracy of what has been acknowledged by the 'Ulama of our era in regards to the prohibition of wreaking havoc, hijacking airplanes and killing non-Muslims in their lands which is committed by some young Muslims who enter those lands with Amān (safe-passage and security),[2] in the form of entry visas. For this is an example of betrayal and treachery, the prohibition is intensified when it is ascribed to the Sharī'ah and considered as being from "Jihād", as they claim![3]

Faisal also states:

"Shaykh Bin Bāz died and did not take back his fatwa, so his entry into Paradise is in grave jeopardy."

---

[1] *Kitāb us-Siyar, Bāb ul-Musta'min*

[2] And if they are Mu'āhadeen then the opposition to the *Sharī'ah* would be from two angles, like a person who steals pork and eats it!

[3] From the edit of Shaykh Muhammad bin Zakariyyā Abū Ghāzī and our Shaykh Mashhūr Hasan Āl Salmān to Imām al-Mujtahid Abū 'Abdullāh Muhammad bin 'Īsā bin Muhammad bin Asbagh al-Azdī al-Qurtubī (aka Ibn Munāsif), *Kitāb ul-Injād fī Abwāb il-Jihād* (Beirut: Mu'assasah ar-Rayān, 1425 AH/2005 CE), vol.1, pp.63-81.

Firstly, Faisal here assumes to know the fate of a person, and not any person at that, but the final destination of an Imām of the Sunnah! How can Faisal even attempt to boldly assert who will or will not be placed in Paradise and who will have their entry "in grave jeopardy"? Faisal here has asserted to have knowledge of something that is only in Allāh's realm of knowledge.

﴿ قُل لَّا يَعْلَمُ مَن فِى ٱلسَّمَـٰوَٰتِ وَٱلْأَرْضِ ٱلْغَيْبَ إِلَّا ٱللَّهُ ﴾

"Say: 'None in the heavens and the earth knows the Ghaib (Unseen) except Allāh,'" {an-Naml (27):65}

Secondly, Faisal here demonstrates a rather odd understanding of ijtihaad and dealing with scholars opinions which are based on their ijtihaad. The Prophet ﷺ stated: *"If a judge rules and strives hard (to ascertain the correct view) and is correct (in his opinion) then he gets two rewards. If he judges and strives hard (to ascertain the correct view) and errs then he gets one reward."*[1] Thus, there is no difference of opinion among the scholars that if a Mujtahid, who has fulfilled the conditions of ijtihād, is correct in his ijtihād will have two rewards yet if he is mistaken he will have one reward. As for regarding a qualified scholar having his entry to Jannah placed "in grave jeopardy" merely for having an acceptable view which some do not agree with then - this is a concept which is not found within the scholarly works. As long as the issue is still within the realm of ijtihād,

---

[1] Saheeh Bukhārī and Muslim.

acceptable and not against the Usūl then there is no such threat as asserted by El-Faisal.

Thirdly, is the qualified and accepted Mujtahid, who errs and is mistaken, to be excused or not? Is he regarded as sinful or not? According to the Salaf from the Sahābah ﷺ, the Tābi'een and those that followed them in goodness – they do not make takfeer, tafseeq or regard as sinful the Mujtahid over academic and practical issues whether in the Usūl or the Furū'. This is in light of the following rules:

1. That the Mujtahid who has erred has *īmān* in Allāh and His Messenger ﷺ – excuses are made for people like this. If his eemaan is anticipated with certainty then this is not removed by doubt after the proof has been established.

2. That the Mujtahid has a truthful intention in striving for the true and correct view.

3. That the Mujtahid exerted himself in ascertaining the correct view, fearing Allāh has much as he is able in the process. If he does this and errs due to: the proofs not reaching him; the presence of a doubt; or an acceptable interpretation – then such a person is excused.[1]

---

[1] For more on this see Muhammad bin Husayn bin Hasan al-Jīzānī, *Ma'ālim Usūl ul-Fiqh 'inda Ahl is-Sunnah wa'l-Jama'ah* [Signposts of Islamic Legal Principles According to the People of Sunnah]. Dammām, KSA: Dār Ibn ul-Jawzī, 1428 AH/2007 CE, pp.482-483.

As for ijtihād and who is qualified to perform it, Imām ash-Shātibī ﷺ notes that:

الاجتهاد المعتبر هو الصادر عن أهله الذين اضطلعوا بمعرفة ما يفتقر إليه الاجتهاد

The ijtihād which the Shar' takes into consideration is: issued by those who are qualified to the extent that they understand the prerequisites of ijtihād.[1]

Ibn Taymiyyah ﷺ stated:

وأهل السنة لا يبتدعون قولاً ولا يكفِّرون من اجتهد فأخطأ، وإن كان مخالفًا لهم مستحلاً لدمائهم، كما لم تكفِّر الصحابة الخوارج مع تكفيرهم لعثمان وعلي ومن والاهما، واستحلالهم لدماء المسلمين المخالفين لهم

Ahl us-Sunnah do not innovate statements and they do not make takfeer of whoever makes ijtihād and errs, even if he (the opposer) is in opposition to them, makes takfeer of them and deems their blood as being permissible (to shed). Just as the Companions did not make takfeer of the Khawārij even though they (the Khawārij) made takfeer of 'Uthmān ﷺ, 'Ali and whoever allied with them, and they (the Khawārij) made lawful (to shed) the blood of the Muslims who opposed them.[2]

---

[1] Imām ash-Shātibī, *al-Muwāfaqāt* (Khobar, KSA: Dār Ibn 'Affān, 1417 AH, ed. Shaykh Abū 'Ubaydah Mashhūr bin Hasan Āl Salmān), vol.5, p.131.
[2] Ibid.

Ibn Taymiyyah also noted[1] that the scholars concur that any ijtihād which is not acceptable (due to going against a decisive concensus; emerging from one who is not a scholar; being based on something is not to be taken into consideration; opposing the statements of the Salaf or opposing the verified clear authentic evidences) is not to be followed. Yet this is for scholars to decipher and not for the likes of El-Faisal to indulge in assessing, as he does not possess the requisite tools to differentiate issues in ijtihād. It is possible for scholars to err as this is the habit of human beings as they are not infallible hence they are susceptible to slip-ups and errors. Thus, as Shareef Hātim bin 'Ārif al-'Awnī highlights:

> However, while we do not elevate people over the truth or the evidences, at the same time we do not forget that they take priority over us in knowing the evidences.[2]

Yet as al-'Awnī notes it is allowed to discuss with scholars the reasons for their views yet this has to be done with a sense of academia, investigation and etiquettes[3] – all of which would immediately barr the likes of El-Faisal from being able to participate in such scholarly discussion! Such scholarly debate and

---

[1] Ibn Taymiyyah, *Bayān ud-Daleel 'alā Butlān at-Tahleel*, (Dammām, KSA: Dār Ibn ul-Jawzī, 1425 AH, ed. Dr Ahmad Khaleel) p.155.

[2] Shareef Hātim bin 'Ārif al-'Awnī, *Ikhtilāf ul-Mufteen wa'l-Mawqif al-Matlūb bi Tijāhahu min 'Umūm il-Muslimūn: Muwwasslan min Adilat il-Wahyyayn* [Disagreements Among Those Who Issue Edicts and the Sought-after Position of the Generality of Muslims: Based on Revelatory Evidences]. Riyadh, KSA: Dār us-Sumay'ī, 1429 AH/2008 CE, p.165.

[3] Ibid., p.172.

discussion requires good manners, respect and good character – not *takfeer*, *tafseeq*, *tabdī'*, vile language and utter disrespect, all of which characterises El-Faisal's dialectic. Ibn Rajab al-Hanbalī stated in his treatise *al-Farq Bayna an-Naseehah wa't-Ta'yeer* [The Difference Between Advising and Shaming]:

وأما بيان خطأ من أخطأ من العلماء قبله إذا تأدب في الخطاب وأحسن في الرد والجواب فلا حرج عليه ولا لوم يتوجه إليه وإن صدر منه الاغترار بمقالته فلا حرج عليه

As for explaining the error of a scholar who erred beforehand, if the one explaining this error does so with manners in his address and is better in his responding and answering, then there is no problem in this and the one who does this is not to be deemed as blameworthy. Even if there is some boldness in his (the critic's) statements (about his own stance being the correct one) – there is no problem in this.[1]

Then Ibn Rajab states:

وأما إذا كان مرادُ الرادِّ بذلك إظهارَ عيب من ردَّ عليه وتنقصَه وتبيينَ جهله وقصوره في العلم ونحو ذلك كان محرماً سواء كان ردُّه لذلك كان في وجه من ردِّ عليه أو في غيبته وسواء كان في حياته أو بعد موته وهذا داخل فيما ذمَّه الله تعالى في

---

[1] Ibn Rajab al-Hanbalī, *al-Farq Bayna an-Naseehah wa't-Ta'yeer* [The Difference Between Advising and Shaming] within *Majmū' ar-Risālah* (Cairo: al-Fārūq al-Hadeethah, 1423 AH, ed. Tal'at bin Fu'ād al-Hulwānī), vol.2, pp.406-407.

كتابه وتوعد عليه في الهمز "يا معشر من آمن بلسانه ولم يؤمن بقلبه لا تؤذوا

المسلمين ولا تتبعوا عوراقم ، فإنه من يتبع عوراقم يتبع الله عورته ، ومن يتبع الله

عورته يفضحه ولو في جوف بيته"

As for his (the critic's) intent in refuting being just to manifest the faults of the one being refuted, belittle him, show his ignorance, his deficiency in knowledge and the likes – then this is harām. This is whether the refutation is in the man's face or behind his back, whether it is during his (the one being refuted) lifetime or after his death. This is within what Allāh has censured in His Book and He has placed a threat for those who fall into backbiting (hamz) and derision (lamz). Also included in this is the Prophet's statement ﷺ: "O gathering of those who believe with the tongue but do not believe (fully) in heart: do not harm the Muslims and do not expose their faults. For whoever exposes the faults of the Muslims Allāh will expose his faults, and if Allāh exposes his faults Allāh will shame him even if he is within the depths of his own house."[1]

Then Ibn Rajab states:

---

[1] Reported by Abū Dāwud from the hadeeth of Sa'eed bin'Abdullaah bin Jurayj, the freed slave of Abū Barzah, from his master Abū Barzah ﷺ in marfū' form. The chain of transmission is *hasan*. Also reported by at-Tirmidhī and within his chain of transmission is some discussion as highlighted by ad-Dāraqutnī in *al-'Ilal*, vol.6, pp.309-310 – yet the observations do not weaken the hadeeth.

وهذا كله في حق العلماء المقتدى بهم في الدين فأما أهل البدع والضلالة ومن تشبه

بالعلماء وليس منهم فيجوز بيان جهلهم وإظهار عيوبهم تحذيراً من الاقتداء بهم.

All of this is in regards to the 'Ulama who are trusted and followed in the deen; as for Ahl ul-Bida' wa'd-Dalālah [the people of innovation and misguidance], and those who try to resemble the 'Ulama while he is not from them – then it is permissible to clarify his ignorance and manifest his faults as a warning against following them.[1]

Hence, the folly of the likes of El-Faisal trying to rise to the occasion to "correct", condemn and throw doubts on mountains of knowledge such as Imām Bin Bāz and hence our refutation on El-Faisal.

Sample Lecture Number Four: 'Enjoining The Good And Forbidding The Evil'

Within this lecture, Faisal states:

"Now I am saying that the'aqeedah that says that to enjoin the right and forbid the wrong is 'the job of scholars, maulanas, muftis and sheikhs and not for us' is a dodgy 'aqeedah, a false 'aqeedah and it was Shaytān who handed them this 'aqeedah on a silver platter…"

---

[1] Ibn Rajab al-Hanbalī, *al-Farq Bayna an-Naseehah wa't-Ta'yeer*, within *Majmū' ar-Risālah* (Cairo: al-Fārūq al-Hadeethah, 1423 AH, ed. Tal'at bin Fu'ād al-Hulwānī), vol.2, pp.406-407.

Actually, the only thing 'dodgy' is the statement itself! Salafis are essentially free from such allegations, because Salafis believes that the ruling of enjoining the good and forbidding the evil is *Fard al-Kifāyah* (a collective duty). However, in order to enjoin the good and forbid the evil correctly, certain characteristics must accompany the one who exercises this principle, namely: knowledge, kindness and patience. Shaykh ul-Islām Ibn Taymiyah said:

> These three are essential: knowledge, kindness and patience: knowledge before enjoining or forbidding, kindness when doing so and patience afterwards, as it was narrated that one of the Salaf said: No one can enjoin what is good or forbid what is evil unless he understands what he is enjoining or forbidding, and is kind in enjoining and kind in forbidding, and is patient and forbearing when enjoining and when forbidding.[1]

Faisal's allegations also encourage scorn, mockery and disregard of the scholars within the common masses of Muslims, which is a salient feature of Faisal's lectures so beware! It is a common and regular pattern for ("El") Faisal to do this. Let us see what the qualified senior Islamic scholars say on this matter, not the likes of Faisal. Al-'Allāmah Sālih al-Fawzān stated:

---

[1] *Majmū' al-Fatāwā*, vol.28, p.137.

It is obligatory for the jāhil (ignoramus) to not speak and to keep quiet and fear Allāh, The Exalted and Majestic, and to not speak without knowledge, Allāh says:

$$\text{﴿ قُلْ إِنَّمَا حَرَّمَ رَبِّيَ ٱلْفَوَٰحِشَ مَا ظَهَرَ مِنْهَا وَمَا بَطَنَ وَٱلْإِثْمَ وَٱلْبَغْيَ بِغَيْرِ ٱلْحَقِّ وَأَن تُشْرِكُوا۟ بِٱللَّهِ مَا لَمْ يُنَزِّلْ بِهِۦ سُلْطَٰنًا وَأَن تَقُولُوا۟ عَلَى ٱللَّهِ مَا لَا تَعْلَمُونَ ﴾}$$

'Say, My Lord has only forbidden immoralities – what is apparent of them and what is concealed – and sin,[1] and oppression without right, and that you associate with Allāh that for which He has not sent down authority, and that you say about Allāh that which you do not know.' {al'A'rāf (7): 33}

So it is not permissible for the jāhil (ignoramus) to speak in issues of knowledge especially in regards to major issues such as takfeer, jihād and al-walā wa'l-barā'. As for slander and backbiting in regards to the honour of the people in authority and the honour of the scholars, then this is the most severe type of backbiting and as a result is not permissible. As for current events which have passed or are taking place then these are affairs for the people in authority to research and seek counsel over and it is for the scholars to explain its Divinely Legislated ruling. As for the general

---

[1] Any unlawful action

and common people and beginning students it is not their issue. Allāh says:

﴿ وَإِذَا جَآءَهُمْ أَمْرٌ مِّنَ ٱلْأَمْنِ أَوِ ٱلْخَوْفِ أَذَاعُواْ بِهِ ۖ وَلَوْ رَدُّوهُ إِلَى ٱلرَّسُولِ وَإِلَىٰٓ أُوْلِى ٱلْأَمْرِ مِنْهُمْ لَعَلِمَهُ ٱلَّذِينَ يَسْتَنۢبِطُونَهُ مِنْهُمْ ۗ وَلَوْلَا فَضْلُ ٱللَّهِ عَلَيْكُمْ وَرَحْمَتُهُ لَٱتَّبَعْتُمُ ٱلشَّيْطَٰنَ إِلَّا قَلِيلًا ﴾

'And when there comes to them something (i.e. information) about (public) security or fear, they spread it around. But if they had only referred it back to the Messenger or to those in authority among them, then the ones who can draw correct conclusions from it would have known about it. And if not for the favour of Allāh upon you and His mercy, you would have followed Satan, except for a few.' {an-Nisā (4): 83}

So it is incumbent to refrain the tongue in speaking about the likes of such issues, especially takfeer, allegiance and disavowal. And humans are mostly ignorant of its application and can apply it incorrectly and thus judge a person with misguidance and kufr, and the ruling could thus return upon the claimant. So if a person says to his brother "O kāfir, O fāsiq" and the man is not like that (i.e. neither a kāfir nor a fāsiq) the ruling can return upon the one who said it, and Allāh's refuge is sought. This is a very dangerous issue, so it is upon the one who fears Allāh to refrain his tongue except if he is from those who are entrusted to deal with such issues, from the people in authority or the scholars.

It is these who look into issues and find a solution to it, as for one who is from the common people or from the junior students (of Islamic knowledge) they do not have the right to issue rulings on people and slander the honour of people while he is an ignoramus (jāhil) who backbites and speaks about issues regarding takfeer, tafseeq and other matters, this only harms the one who does this. So it is for the Muslim to withhold his tongue and not get involved in what does not concern him. Such a person should make dua' for the Muslims for them to be victorious and make dua against the kuffār for them to be punished, this is obligatory. As for discussing rulings of the Divine Legislation, falling into error and speaking about the honour of people in authority and the scholars and judging them with kufr or misguidance this is very dangerous for you O speaker. Those you speak about will not be harmed by your speech, and Allāh knows best.[1]

Then Faisal states:

"The language that the kāfir respects does not come from your mouth, it comes from your Kalashnikov! That's the only language kāfirs respect, this is why the Prophet said jihād is compulsory until Yawm ul-Qiyāmah."

---

[1] Shaykh, Dr Sālih bin Fawzān al-Fawzān, Muhammad bin Fahd al-Husayn (editor and compiler), *al-Ijabāt al-Muhimmah fi'l-Mashākil al-Mumilah* (Riyadh: Matābi' al-Humaydī, 1425 AH/2004 CE, Second Edition), pp.56-58

Hereby making no distinction whatsoever and merely mentioning this for show, and the ignorant audience laugh as if Faisal is some kind of comedian as opposed to someone who has a connection to Islamic knowledge. The actual Islamic scholars however have stated that *kuffār* are not to be categorised into one simplistic category as Faisal has suggested here. Shaykh Sālih Āl ush-Shaykh (*hafidhahullāh*) noted in his lecture on the subject of *Rights in the Sharī'ah (Human Rights)*[1] that:

أقسام غير المسلمين في الأرض هذه الأربعة أقسام:

- أن يكون ذمياً.
- أن يكون معاهَداً.
- أن يكون مستأمَنا.
- أن يكون حربياً.

و النبي صلى الله عليه وسلم أمر بأداء الحقوق لهؤلاء؛ بل أمر الله جل وعلا بأداء

الحقوق لغير المسلمين في كتابه إذا لم يكونوا حربيين إذا لم يكونوا مظهرين العدواة،

فقال جل وعلا

The non-Muslims of the earth can be divided into four categories, they can either be a *dhimmi* (non-Muslim living under Muslim rule); a *mu'āhid* (one with whose country the Muslims have a peace deal); a *musta'man* (one who is granted security in a Muslim land) or a harbī (non-Muslim combatant of war). And the Prophet ﷺ instructed each one

---

[1]   The   Arabic   text   version   is   available   here: http://islamport.com/w/amm/Web/1058/5718.htm

be given their due rights. Rather, Allāh instructed non-Muslims be given rights in His Book, if they are not at war (with Muslims) and do not manifest enmity (against the Muslims). Allāh says:

﴿ لَّا يَنْهَىٰكُمُ ٱللَّهُ عَنِ ٱلَّذِينَ لَمْ يُقَٰتِلُوكُمْ فِى ٱلدِّينِ وَلَمْ يُخْرِجُوكُم مِّن دِيَٰرِكُمْ أَن تَبَرُّوهُمْ وَتُقْسِطُوٓا۟ إِلَيْهِمْ إِنَّ ٱللَّهَ يُحِبُّ ٱلْمُقْسِطِينَ . إِنَّمَا يَنْهَىٰكُمُ ٱللَّهُ عَنِ ٱلَّذِينَ قَٰتَلُوكُمْ فِى ٱلدِّينِ وَأَخْرَجُوكُم مِّن دِيَٰرِكُمْ وَظَٰهَرُوا۟ عَلَىٰٓ إِخْرَاجِكُمْ أَن تَوَلَّوْهُمْ وَمَن يَتَوَلَّهُمْ فَأُو۟لَٰٓئِكَ هُمُ ٱلظَّٰلِمُونَ ﴾

'Allāh does not forbid you from those who do not fight you because of religion and do not expel you from your homes – from being righteous toward them[1] and acting justly toward them.[2] Indeed, Allāh loves those who act justly.[3] Allāh only forbids you from those

---

[1] Ibn Katheer ﷺ says about this: "to be gentle with them."

[2] Ibn Katheer ﷺ says about this: "to be fair with them."

[3] Ibn Katheer ﷺ transmits in regards to this in the *ayah*: Imām Ahmad recorded that Asmā' bint Abū Bakr ﷺ said, "My mother, who was an idolatress at the time, came to me during the Treaty of Peace, the Prophet conducted with the Quraysh. I came to the Prophet and said, *'O Allāh's Messenger! My mother came visiting, desiring something from me, should I treat her with good relations.'* The Prophet ﷺ said, **'Yes. Keep good relations with your mother.'** The Two Saheehs recorded this hadeeth. Imām Ahmad recorded that 'Abdullah bin Zubayr ﷺ said, "Qutaylah came visiting her daughter, Asmā' bint Abī Bakr ﷺ, with some gifts, such as Dibab, cheese and clarified (cooking) butter, and she was an idolatress at that time. Asmā' ﷺ refused to accept her mother's gifts and did not let her enter her house. 'Ā'ishah ﷺ asked the Prophet about his verdict and Allāh sent down the ayah, **"Allāh does not forbid you with those who fought not against you on account of religion..."** {al-Mumtahanah (60): 8} until the end of the ayah. Allāh's Messenger ﷺ ordered Asmā' ﷺ to accept her mother's gifts and to let her enter her house." Allāh's statement, **"......Indeed Allāh loves those who act**

who fight you because of religion and expel you from your homes and aid in your expulsion – (forbids) that you make allies of them.[1] And whoever makes allies of them, then it is those who are the wrongdoers.' *{al-Mumtahinah (60): 8-9}*

فإذن الحق الذي للذمي ثابت في الشريعة، فلا يعني كونه كافراً أن نهضمه حــق الإنسانية، هو حق جعله الله جل وعلا له، قال عليه الصلاة والسلام: «مــن آذى ذمياً فقد آذاني» أو كما جاء في الحديث، وصحَّ عنه عليه الصلاة والسلام أنه قال: من قتل معاهداً لم يرح رائحة الجنة، لماذا؟ لأن المسلمين يسعى بذمتهم أدناهم، هذا قد جاء بعهد، وجاء بأمان، وكان في بلاد الإسلام بأمان وعهد، فالواجب ألا يُعتدى عليه في نفسه، وألا يعتدى عليه في دمه، وألا يعتدى عليه في عرضه، وألا يعتـدى عليه في ماله، فالحقوق واجبة له شرعاً.

والنصوص في أداء حق أهل الذمة وحق المعاهَدين وحق المستأمَنين متعددة، وكلام العلماء في ذلك كثير. أما الحربيون فهم الذين بيننا وبينهم حرب، فهــؤلاء بيننـا

---

justly." *{al-Mumtahanah (60): 8}* And we can clearly see the contrary of this being applied from those who abandon their non-Muslims parents for fifteen years!

[1] Ibn Katheer ﷽ states about this part of the verse: "Allāh forbids you from being kind and befriending with the disbelievers who are openly hostile to you, those who fought against you, expelled you and helped to expel you. Allāh the Exalted forbids you from being their friends and orders you to be their enemy."

وبينهم حرب، فيه أحكام كثيرة تتعلق بهم، وحتى لو تمكنا منهم، فإنهم إذا كــانوا

أسارى فإنهم يكرمون، وإذا   تُمِكن منهم فإنه لا يقتل الوليد، ولا يقتل الطفل، ولا

تقتل المرأة، ولا يتقل منهم الشيخ العجوز ونحو ذلك من الأمثلة. مع أن في شرائع

أخرى يقتل الجميع كما ذكر أن في شريعة موسى عليه الصلاة والسلام أن الجميع

يقتلون في حال الحرب.أما شريعة الإسلام فالله جل وعلا حباها لما في ذلــك مــن

المصلحة لامتداد الشريعة إلى قيام الساعة بألا يقتل من المحاربين إلا المقاتلة فقـــط،

وإذا أسر فإن للأسرى أحكاما كثيرة. الذمي في دار الإسلام له حقوق، إذا كان في

بيته فانه يمارس ما شاء، لكن ليس له أن يُعلن في شارع المسلمين أو أن يظهر شيئاً

من المحرمات، إما أن يظهر دينه ليس له ذلك يعني في..... هذا في المعاهد والمستأمن.

أما الذمي ففيه تفصيل الكلام، كما إذا كان في أرض قد فتحت، وفيها الكنــائس

والبيع كما في بلاد الشام وفي مصر والعراق ونحو ذلك

Therefore, the right of the dhimmi is well-established in the Divine
Legislation. Not rights from people, but rights that Allāh has set for the
dhimmi. The Prophet ﷺ stated 'Whoever harms a dhimmi has harmed
me'[1] or as is stated in the hadeeth. It is also authenticated from him ﷺ
that he said 'Whoever kills a mu'āhad will not smell the fragrance of

---

[1] Saheeh Muslim

Paradise, the smell of which can be smelt for the distance of forty years.[1] Why? Because the Muslims honour their lives as they came with an agreement, they came with a trust and are, therefore, not to be transgressed against with regards to their life, blood, honour and money. Rights are therefore obligatory to them in the Divine Legislation. The texts regarding the rights of the enemies, the rights of the people of dhimma, the rights of the people of agreement (mu'āhadeen), the rights of the people with whom there is a trust, are various and the statements of the people of knowledge regarding the field are abundant. As for the harbī'ūn, they are the ones whom between us and them is war and there are many regulations in regards to them and if we gain empowerment over them, they are respected if they are Christians and none of their children, women or elderly are killed. Whereas, within other legislations everyone is to be killed, as is mentioned within the Divine Legislation of Mūsā ﷺ that all are to be killed during war. As for the Divine Legislation of Islām, Allāh allowed for only the fighter to be killed during battle, due to the benefits in the Divine Legislation for this. The dhimmi in an abode of Islām has rights and within his home can do as he wills yet is not allowed to advertise what he does or anything from the prohibited actions. He is also not allowed to manifest his deen, this is for the mu'āhad and for the musta'min, as for the dhimmi there is some

---

[1] Saheeh Bukhārī in *Kitāb ul-Jizyah* under the chapter *'The sin of the one who kills a mu'āhad who has not committed any crime.'*

explanation required for this speech in relation to those countries which were conquered yet there were already churches there like in Shām, Egypt, 'Irāq and the likes of these countries.

Faisal continues:

"There are many kāfirs who realise Islām is the truth but why they don't take shahādah? Because they don't see no {sic} showkah, no power. But if you should have a strong army with planes and tanks, and can you imagine that you have an army with five million men? And your taking over countries after countries, you capture Saudi Arabia, Pakistan, Afghānistān, 'Irāq and you have all the oil wealth in your hands can you imagine how many kāfirs would rush into Islām? Because they see showkah! But if they don't see no {sic} showkah, no power, they will say 'you're all talk, where's your Islamic state?'"[1]

Subhān'Allāh! A very impressive figment of Faisal's imagination! Firstly, is Faisal serious? Do you notice that all of the countries that he mentions here are all Muslim countries which Faisal envisages to be conquered and waged war against?!! So beware! In any case how on earth can the Muslims gather all of these when the majority of the Muslims do not even know how to pray?! Then Faisal says, in utter ignorance of actual events and the situation:

---

[1] So Faisal thinks that kuffār are only interested in *"where's your Islamic state"*!? Nothing about *tawheed, adab, akhlāq* and *deen*, only a political view!

153

"Everything which I was teaching you here is on the cassette (of Shaykh 'Ali al-Hudhayfī) in a nutshell, everything which I was saying here Shaykh Hudhayfī in Madeenah says on the cassette. So this is why they lock him up {sic} and throw away the key..."

This is false as Imām al-Hudhayfī was not locked up at all, let alone the key being thrown away, as he is still currently leading the prayer in *Masjid un-Nabawī* in Madeenah to this day while the likes of Faisal actually have been imprisoned due to foolish statements! In this lecture he again reiterates that it is okay to sell alcohol to non-Muslims, despite the seller of alcohol being mentioned as one of those whom Allāh curses! Abū Dāwūd and Ibn Mājah both reported that Ibn 'Umar ♦ said that Allāh's Messenger ♦ said: *"Allāh has cursed alcohol (all intoxicating beverages), and (He has cursed): the one who drinks it; the one who pours it; the one who sells it; the one to whom it is sold; the one who squeezes it (i.e. grapes); the one for whom it is squeezed; the one who transports it and the one for whom it is transported."*[1] With regards to the evils of alcohol that is within some Muslim countries and warning against it, he says that such warning against alcohol is "lop-sided" as it diagnoses the problem yet provides no cure. The cure according to Faisal: to overthrow the leaders who 'allow' alcohol into their countries?!

---

[1] Imām al-Albānī has graded it as authentic.

Sample Lecture number five:
'Fiqh ul-Waqi'[1]

This is one of the lectures in which Faisal's hatred of the scholars is again demonstrated. In this topic Faisal himself shows that he has no idea whatsoever of the *fiqh* of current affairs himself and thus concocts his usual poison against the Salafi scholars in particular. This is a common trait of Faisal; we will see that in most, if not all, of his lectures the Salafi scholars are the ones who bear the brunt of criticisms and this is a despicable aim. He states:

"Brothers and sisters our situation is very pathetic and it is because our scholars are jāhil. It's a very bold statement and the reason is that...they are not aware of the surroundings."

Indeed, it is a very bold statement – not only bold, but also simplistic, delusional and devoid of any responsibility. Why are the scholars to blame for our "pathetic situation"? Oh, yes, because "they are not aware of our surroundings"! That same old chestnut; the one that yawns on about the scholars being ignorant regarding *fiqh ul-wāqi'*.

---

[1] www.clickislam.org

Sample Lecture Number Six:
'Fiqh ul-Waqi'

He says:

"Because many of the scholars are jāhil and do not know the fiqh ul-wāqi' they pass ridiculous fatwas."

Indeed, this more applies to Faisal himself in any case, who says horrific and outrageous things under the pretext of him being a 'Shaykh' which he called himself. The term 'ridiculous' applies more to him because not only does he have no right to be delivering *fatāwā*, but when he does give his "fatāwā", they are truly ridiculous, as proven on multiple occasions.

Faisal continues:

"For example, there are scholars and there is a scholar who says that we should leave occupied Palestine and give it to the Jews. Who passed that fatwa? Albānī! The ijmā of the ummah says if the kāfirs are approaching the Muslim country to take it...jihād becomes fard al-'ayn on all the Muslims to fight and repel the kāfirs. From the ijmā'... so the Jews are now occupying Palestine and there you have Albānī going against the ijmā of the ummah telling the Muslims in Palestine to leave the land in Palestine to the Jews. Salāuddeen al-Ayyūbī who did he fight against? The crusaders. Richard the Lion-heart where did he come from? England, and why was he called 'the lion-heart' because he killed

Muslims. So England and Italy and Germany all these people are Christian crusaders. Now what would you think about a person if a Jew, a Rabbi passed a fatwa allowing the Muslims to come and take Israel, to have a military base inside of Israel and that military base should be used to kill Jews? Would a Rabbi do that? No Rabbi would do that![1] So if a Jewish Rabbi would never pass a fatwa to allow Muslims to come inside of Israel and set up a military base to be used to kill Jews. How then can Shaykh Bin Bāz pass a fatwa to let the Dajjāl, the army of the Dajjāl, America, England and the rest of the world, to set up a military base inside the holy land? And that military base is used as an operation centre to kill Muslims! This is the ultimate treachery! So the holy land has been colonised by kāfirs, the scum of the earth and it was a Shaykh, a so-called Shaykh who gave legitimacy, who made it halāl for them to come into the holy land and set up a military base and operation centre to massacre the believers.[2] From that military base 200,000 Iraqis were

---

[1] Hereby seeking to compare the Muslims to *kuffār*, *again*, rather Allāh says, "Then is one who was a believer like one who was defiantly disobedient? They are not equal." *{as-Sajdah (32): 18}* Allāh also says, "Then will We treat the Muslims like the criminals?" *{al-Qalam (68): 35}* Allāh also says, "Are they equal in comparison? Then, will you not remember?" *{Hūd (11): 24*

[2] They were not allowed into Makkah and Madeenah, which some scholars define as being the *Jazeerat ul-'Arab* (Arabian Peninsula); while some scholars define the Arabian Peninsula to be Makkah, Madeenah and al-Yamāmah; some scholars define the Arabian Peninsula as being Makkah, Madeenah, al-Yamāmah and Yemen. See Shaykh 'Abdul'Azeez ar-Rayyis, *al-Burhān al-Muneer* [The Clear Proofs for Refuting the Doubts of the People of Takfeer and Bombing], pp.60-68: http://www.salafimanhaj.com/pdf/SalafiManhaj_TakfeerAndBombing.pdf

slaughtered, from that military base! A scholar passed a fatwa today that peace with the Jews is halāl, not Albānī, but Bin Bāz."

So here again Faisal unleashes that destructive piece of flesh, which sends many to the fire, against the people of knowledge and his speech revolves around political discussion with no reference whatsoever to what Allāh or His Messenger ﷺ said, so beware! Let us deal with Faisal's statement here:

"The ijmā of the ummah says if the kāfirs are approaching the Muslim country to take it...jihād becomes fard al-'ayn on all the Muslims to fight and repel the kāfirs."

This is an over-simplification, as there are some precise details to this matter. Scholars have noted, as relayed by Shaykh, Dr Muhammad bin 'Umar Bāzmūl in his book *al-Muhkam wa'l-Mutashābihah fi't-Takfeer wa'l-Jihād*, that there are two instances when defensive jihād become Fard 'Ayn:

One: when the Muslim land comes under a surprise attack from enemies and their land is surrounded. At this point it becomes an individual obligation to repel the invaders. The conditions which are made for offensive jihād are not applicable in this case.

Two: when the enemy becomes established in the land of the Muslims and the Muslims do not have the ability to either repel or expel the invading forces then the conditions which apply to offensive jihād apply in this case.

So according to the 'Ulama defensive jihād only becomes Fard 'Ayn in two cases:

1. When the Muslim land is surrounded by the invading forces
2. When the Muslims come under a surprise attack.

Anything other than this is not included in regards to when defensive jihād becomes Fard 'Ayn. These details are discreetly swept under the carpet by some due to emotion, politics and chaos. The view of some 'Ulama who say that "defensive jihād does not have the same conditions as offensive" is not to be taken in the absolute sense. Their intent is when the defence is to be immediate against the aggressor as in the two instances mentioned above. Ibn Taymiyyah stated:

> As for defensive fighting then it is of the most sever forms of repelling the aggressor from the sanctities and deen, it is obligatory according to consensus as when the immediate aggressing enemy corrupts the deen and dunya there is nothing else to do after īmān except repel him. There are no conditions to be set for this rather the aggressor is to be repelled according to whatever is possible. 'Ulama from our companions, and others, have documented this, it is necessary to differentiate between averting the immediate aggressing disbelieving oppressive enemy and seeking him out in his own land.[1]

---

[1] Ibn Taymiyyah, *al-Ikhtiyārāt al-Fiqhiyyah*, p.532; *al-Fatāwā al-Kubrā*, vol.5, p.538.

Ibn Taymiyyah also stated:

As for if the enemies attack the Muslims then to repel them becomes obligatory upon those who are intended with the attack and on those who are not intended for attack so as to help them.[1]

Ibn Taymiyyah further stated:

If the enemies enter a land of Islām then there is no doubt that it is obligatory to repel them on those who are the nearest and the next nearest, as all lands of Islām have the level of one land.

Shaykh Muhammad Bāzmūl therefore highlights that this ruling is not on all Muslims, rather Ibn Taymiyyah said: *the nearest and then the next nearest"* not that all Muslims in all countries participate merely to repel an attack or siege by the kuffār, of a Muslim land.[2] Moreover, even in this case, there still has to be the necessary ability to provide the support and aid to those Muslims and if not then Muslims can enter into agreements and treaties with the invaders.[3]

Ibn Taymiyyah stated:

[1] Ibn Taymiyyah, *as-Siyāsah as-Sharī'ah*, p.171.
[2] Shaykh, Dr Muhammad bin 'Umar bin Sālim Bāzmūl (Professor at College of Da'wah and Usūluddeen, Book and Sunnah Department, Umm ul-Qurā' University, Makkah), *al-Muhkam wa'l-Mutashābih fi't-Takfeer wa'l-Jihād* [The Clear and Unclear in Takfeer and Jihād]. Cairo: Dār ul-Istiqāmah, 1429 AH/2008 CE, p.256.
[3] Ibid., pp.308, 369-370.

وإذا دخل العدو بلاد الإسلام فلا ريب أنه يجب دفعه على الأقرب فالأقرب ؛ إذ بلاد

الإسلام كلها بمنزلة البلدة الواحدة ، وأنه يجب النفير إليه بلا إذن والد ولا غريم

If the enemies enter the lands of Islām then there is no doubt that it is obligatory, on the nearest and then the next nearest, to repel them. As the lands of Islām are all like one land and it is obligatory to repel them with neither the permission of the parent nor of the adversary.[1]

Not only does Faisal greatly simplify the words of Imām Albānī ﷺ but he also distorts the intended meanings of the scholars to make it look as if the scholars sanctioned the killing of Muslims directly and this is false. For example, Faisal states:

"So the Jews are now occupying Palestine and there you have Albānī going against the ijmā of the ummah telling the Muslims in Palestine to leave the land in Palestine to the Jews."

Here, Faisal cleverly neglects to mention, either purposefully or out of ignorance, but knowing Faisal's methods it was no doubt purposefully, that Imām al-Albānī rejected *jihād* as being *fard al-'ayn* completely. The reality of the matter furthermore is that during the 1980s Afghān *jihād* for example,

---

[1] Muhammad bin 'Ali al-Ba'lī, *al-Ikhtiyārāt al-Fiqhiyyah min Fatāwā Shaykh ul-Islām Ibn Taymiyyah* (Dār ul-Fikr, n.d.), p.311; Muhammad Rawwās Qal'ah Jī, *al-Mawsū'ah Fiqh Ibn Taymiyyah* (Beirut: Dār un-Nafā'is, First Edn., 1419 AH/1998 CE,), vol.1, p.50.

Imām Albānī said that it was *fard al-'ayn* as is well known, so where is the justice of the likes of Faisal? Here again is another one of Faisal's tricks to throw doubt, scorn, suspicion and distrust of the scholars of the *Sunnah* of this era. The fact also, that in 1948 Imām al-Albānī himself took his weapon and went to defend Palestine against the Zionist forces, seems to have escaped him! So before "el" Faisal was even born in Jamaica, Imām al-Albānī had already put his life on the line for Allāh in order to defend the Muslims of Palestine. Imām al-Albānī documented this in a book entitled *Rihlati ila Najd* [My Journey to Najd] which was copied out by the Imām's grand-daughter. It is mentioned that Imām al-Albānī prayed at Masjid ul-Aqsa yet he and other Mujāhideen were turned back from participating in fighting. This is mentioned by Shaykh Mashhūr Hasan Āl Salmān in the book *as-Salafiyūn wa Qadiyat Filisteen* [The Salafis and the Palestinian Issue].

As for Faisal claiming that 200,000 Iraqis were killed from a base that was in Saudi then from which base is this exactly? He gives no details of this and merely expects the listeners to uncritically follow him. He furnishes this serious claim with absolutely no proof whatsoever and claims without substance are rejected until evidence is produced which proves otherwise. It actually indicates that Faisal himself has no understanding of *fiqh ul-wāqi'* as he does not give any details about this whatsoever. As for him naming the *kuffār* armies as being "the armies of the Dajjāl" then this is also false as the Dajjāl is not yet here!? So how can Faisal assign to the Dajjāl an army when the Dajjāl is not even present! Furthermore, those who Faisal thinks will be the followers of the Dajjaal are mentioned in the Prophetic sources. The majority of the Dajjāl's followers will be from the Jews, Persians and Turks, and a mixture of other people mostly of the Bedouin Arabs and women.

روى الإمام مسلم في صحيحه برقم 5237 عن أنس بن مالك رضي الله عنه : أن

رسول الله صلى الله عليه وسلم قال : " يَتْبَعُ الدَّجَّالَ مِنْ يَهُودِ أَصْبَهَانَ سَبْعُونَ أَلْفًا

عَلَيْهِمْ الطَّيَالِسَةُ " والطيالسة : كساء غليظ مخطط

Imām Muslim narrated in his *Sahīh* (5237) from Anas Ibn Mālik who said that Allāh's Messenger said: "*Seventy-thousand Jews from Asfahan, wearing heavy striped garments.*" And in the aforementioned *hadith* of Abu Bakr it sates: "*A people will follow him with faces like burnished shields.*" (At-Tirmidhī, hadeeth no. 2136)

Also:

يَنْزِلُ الدَّجَّالُ في هَذِهِ السَّبْخَةِ بِمَرِّقَنَاةَ – وادٍ بالمدينة – فَيَكُونُ أَكْثَرَ مَنْ يَخْرُجُ إِلَيْهِ

النِّسَاءُ، حَتَّى إِنَّ الرَّجُلَ لَيَرْجِعُ إِلَى حَمِيمِهِ وَإِلَى أُمِّهِ وَابْنَتِهِ وَأُخْتِهِ وَعَمَّتِهِ فَيُوثِقُهَا

رِبَاطًا مَخَافَةَ أَنْ تَخْرُجَ إِلَيْهِ

"*The Dajjāl will come to this pond at Marriqanāh (a valley in Madeenah), and the majority of those who will go out to him will be women, until a man will come to his mother-in-law, his mother, his daughter, his aunty and tie them up tightly for fear that they will go out to him.*" (Musnad Ahmad, hadeeth no. 5099)

163

Faisal also has an issue with his definition of 'the holy land', and here he is merely blindly following the likes of Salmān and Safar in their opinions of this in the past. It is important then for us to assess the definition of the 'Arabian peninsula' as some scholars define as being the *Jazeerat ul-'Arab* (Arabian Peninsula) just Makkah and Madeenah; while some scholars define the Arabian Peninsula to be Makkah, Madeenah and al-Yamāmah; some scholars define the Arabian Peninsula as being Makkah, Madeenah, al-Yamāmah and Yemen. See Shaykh 'Abdul'Azeez ar-Rayyis, *al-Burhān al-Muneer* [The Clear Proofs for Refuting the Doubts of the People of Takfeer and Bombing!], pp.60-68.[1] Yet Faisal, as occurs an hour into the lecture of the *Devil's Deception of the Saudi Salafis* says that the Arabian Peninsula is:

"Saudi Arabia, Kuwait, Qatar, Oman, Bahrain and Yemen, all these are the Arabian Peninsula."

From Faisal's other errors are his saying:

"A peace treaty can only be for a year, two years or three years if you make it forever you abrogate jihād and if you abrogate jihād you have done kufr!"

This is idiotic and within all of this Faisal did not at all refer to the *Treaty of Hudaybiyah* and did not outline this detailed matter based on what the *Fuqahā*

---

[1] http://www.salafimanhaj.com/pdf/SalafiManhaj_TakfeerAndBombing.pdf

had stated, another indication of his doubtful knowledge. Firstly, Imām Ibn ul-Munāsif states in his *magnum opus* on Jihād entitled *Kitāb ul-Injād fī Abwāb il-Jihād*[1] that:

The scholars also differed in regards to Muhādanah (making treaties) and if it is allowed to make them unlimited? It has been said that: it is permissible and this is what is apparent in the madhhab of Mālik.[2] It has also been said: it is not permissible to make a treaty except for a (restricted) period[3] because making a treaty without setting a period necessitates holding off from them always and this is not permissible. For fighting them whenever one is able is obligatory. Or alternatively they are to pay the jizyah if they qualify as people who should pay it, this is the view of ash-Shāfi'ī.[4] Then the scholars differ in regards to the length of time for the treaty it has been said: it depends on the necessity of a benefit for the people of Islām.

---

[1] From the edit of Shaykh Muhammad bin Zakariyyā Abū Ghāzī and our Shaykh Mashhūr Hasan Āl Salmān to Imām al-Mujtahid Abū 'Abdullāh Muhammad bin 'Īsā bin Muhammad bin Asbagh al-Azdī al-Qurtubī (aka Ibn Munāsif), *Kitāb ul-Injād fī Abwāb il-Jihād* (Beirut: Mu'assasah ar-Rayān, 1425 AH/2005 CE), vol.2, p.329.

[2] The period of time according to the Mālikī scholars is not specified rather it is based on the *ijtihād* of the Imām and what he views as being more beneficial and in the greater interest at the time of making the treaty and whether it should be lengthy or not.

[3] Refer to Ibn ul-Mundhir, *al-Iqnā'*, vol.2, p.498. This is the *madhhab* of the majority of 'Ulama except for the Mālikī scholars as Ibn ul-Munāsif has stated here.

[4] Refer to Imām ash-Shāfi'ī, *al-Umm*, vol.4, p.200-201; *al-Muhadhhab*, vol.2, pp.259-260; *al-Iqnā'*, p.177; *al-Bayān*, vol.12, p.306; *Minhāj ut-Tālibeen*, vol.3, p.304; *Rawdat ut-Tālibeen*, vol.10, p.335 and *Mughnī al-Muhtāj*, vol.4, p.261.

According to Shaykh ul-Islām Ibn Taymiyyah ﷺ there are two categories of treaty:

First: the Hudnah Mu'aqqatah, temporary treaty – wherein the time has to be adhered to and honoured by both sides.

Second: the Hudnah Mutlaqah, the absolute, unrestricted treaty that the Imām can make if there is a *maslahah* (general benefit) in this, Ibn Taymiyyah stated when clarifying these two types:

As for Allāh's saying:

$$\text{﴿ بَرَآءَةٌ مِّنَ ٱللَّهِ وَرَسُولِهِۦٓ إِلَى ٱلَّذِينَ عَٰهَدتُّم مِّنَ ٱلْمُشْرِكِينَ ﴾}$$

"[This is a declaration of] disassociation, from Allāh and His Messenger, to those with whom you had made a treaty among the polytheists." *{at-Tawbah (9): 1}*

Then these agreements are allowed and not compulsory, for they are unrestricted and there is a choice over whether to implement it or annul it, like *wakālah* and its like. The *Fuqahā* from our companions and others who say: "the treaty is inaccurate unless it is temporary" even though this opposes the Usūl of Ahmad, is refuted by the Qur'ān and Sunnah of the Messenger of Allāh ﷺ in regards to most of the Mu'āhadeen and a time was not restricted with them.[1]

---

[1] Ibn Taymiyyah, *Majmū' al-Fatāwā* (Tarteeb of 'AbdurRahmān bin Muhammad Qāsim and his son Muhammad, 1398 AH, 2nd Edn.), vol.29, p.140.

So regarding the Hudnah the following can be concluded from Shaykh ul-Islām Ibn Taymiyyah:

1. A Hudnah is based on the *maslahah Sharī'ah* as the Muslim ruler views and sees fit and the benefits can be of different types. Because at times it may be more beneficial in the *Sharī'ah* to fight; at times it may be more beneficial to make a treaty and at times it may be more beneficial to withhold and get prepared without making a treaty.[1]

2. It is permitted to make an agreement, be it a pact of safety or a treaty, with non-Muslims.[2]

3. Agreements which are specified to certain times cannot be broken, Allāh says:

$$﴿ وَإِمَّا تَخَافَنَّ مِن قَوْمٍ خِيَانَةً فَٱنۢبِذْ إِلَيْهِمْ عَلَىٰ سَوَآءٍ إِنَّ ٱللَّهَ لَا يُحِبُّ ٱلْخَآئِنِينَ ﴾$$

"If you [have reason to] fear from a people betrayal, throw [their treaty] back to them, [putting you] on equal terms..."

{Anfāl (8): 58}

Ibn Taymiyyah says: *"It is only allowed to terminate the treaty when treachery is apparent because the termination of it came from them firstly."*

4. Shaykh ul-Islām Ibn Taymiyyah permits giving agreements of safety and security to whoever abandons fighting before their land has been

---

[1] Ibid., vol.15, p.174
[2] Ibid., vol.28, p.414

conquered, in order to secure his own self and wealth. *"For abandoning fighting includes safety and within it is a benefit for Muslims."*[1]

5. Ibn Taymiyyah ﷺ does not permit the leader of the Muslims to make an armistice with Mushrikeen without them having to pay the Jizyah or Kharāj without a necessity. As the Prophet ﷺ did at al-Hudaybiyah. Ibn Taymiyyah states: *"If we conquer a land and make a truce with it while the people are Mushrikeen and they are not people of Jizyah, then this is not permitted to recognise them without them giving Jizyah based on the ijmā' of the Muslims."*[2]

Also refer to the similar views of Ibn Taymiyyah's student Ibn ul-Qayyim in the second volume of his book *Ahkām Ahl udh-Dhimmah*. Many *Fuqahā* did not stress a limit on a treaty for ten years, let alone the maximum three years that 'Abdullāh Faisal gives in his quote! In fact, some of the *Fuqahā* stated that a Muslim ruler can renew a ten-year treaty indefintey and that permanent absolute peace treaties are allowed. This was noted by:

✓ Ibn Muflih[3]

✓ Imām an-Nawawī[4]

✓ As-Sarakhasī[5]

---

[1] Ibid., vol.29, pp.213-214

[2] Ibid., vol.29, p.209

[3] *Al-Mubdi' fī Sharh il-Muqnī* (Beirut: al-Maktab al-Islami, 1973 CE), vol.3, p.398-399.

[4] *Rawdat ut-Tālibeen*, vol.10, pp.334-335

[5] *Sharh*, vol.3, p.46-47

- ✓ Ar-Ramlī[1]

- ✓ Al-Marwadī[2]

- ✓ Ibn Qudāmah al-Maqdisī and other Fuqahā.[3]

Then Faisal says in total contradiction of what he said on a previous lecture, which we have quoted that:

"The kāfirs use DSS[4] to buy you out, poverty leads to kufr."

Yet it was Faisal himself who told his blind followers (in the lecture *Challenges Facing the Youth*) to take welfare state benefits and Faisal even told his listeners to take all benefits and money from *kuffār*! So beware of this man's gross contradictions and distortions.

Sample Lecture Number Seven: 'Ideological Warfare'

This lecture was conducted in New York (Imām Sirāj Wahhāj was also present at this *khawārij* lecture!?), herein Faisal states:

---

[1] *Nihāyat ul-Muhtāj*, Vol.8, p.107

[2] *Al-Hāwī al-Kabeer* (Beirut: Dār ul-Kutub al-'Ilmiyyah, 1414 AH/1994 CE), vol.14, p.352-353. Eds. 'Ali Muhammad Mu'awwad & 'Adil Ahmad 'AbdulMawjūd. There is also a *tahqeeq* by Dr. Mahmud Mathraji, (Beirut: Dār al-Fikr,1994 CE). And a critical edit (*tahqeeq*) by Ghazi Taha Salih al-Khusayfan (Riyadh: Maktabat al-Rushd, 2000).

[3] *Al-Mughnī*, vol.8, p.460-61

[4] This refers to the British welfare state benefits department, which gives people state 'hand-outs' depending on the employment, disability or age of an individual.

"Another strategy of the colonial powers is to control the Muslim governments, then they control the scholars. First of all they big up a scholar, highlight him, elevate him, praise him 'this is the Muftī of this country anything you want to learn about Islām go to him'[1] they big up the scholar, they elevate him. Secondly, they put him on their pay-roll[2] and control him, then they use this scholar to control the Muslims. So when they asked 'who is it will enable us to get into the gulf and kill ten thousand...' O I'm sorry '...100,000 Irāqī Muslims, men, women and children?'[3] What was their answer? Does anybody know what their answer was? Their answer was 'We control the Muslims by controlling their scholars.' When you are on the pay-roll of a kāfir government, a corrupted government you have absolutely no use to Muslims.....[4]So think about these people who have ten years of Islamic studies, twenty years of Islamic studies and they see the most shameful deeds taking place underneath their nose and they didn't speak out against it... So for you to see an evil act and you didn't stop it nor condemn it with

---

[1] Here Faisal intends Saudi Arabia and thus attempts to inculcate into his blind followers disrespect for Imām Bin Bāz and the other senior scholars of Saudi.

[2] When Faisal allegedly studied at *Imām Muhammad bin Saud University* in Riyadh, the capital of Saudi Arabia, the students also received a stipend and other financial benefits when studying there, as is well-known. It is interesting that Faisal never at all admits, acknowledges or refers to this within his tirade against the *Salafī* scholars of Saudi.

[3] Here indicates that Faisal himself is not even sure of the figures that he is throwing about!

[4] Does Faisal include his own self within this simplistic rubric, considering the fact that he also received finances, stipends and support from Saudi during his studies at *Imām Muhammad bin Saud University*?

your tongue nor hate it in your heart you are in the category of these Jews who were turned into apes!"

Honestly, there is enough conspiracy theory in this short passage to give the conspiracies surrounding the JFK Assassination a run for their money! We mean, seriously, what scholar from amongst the Salafi scholars are the "colonial powers" going to elevate and praise?! This again is another example of Faisal spending most of his time undermining the scholars and trying to defame, slander and attack them - indeed Faisal again tries to compare the scholars to Jews. You have to understand here the subtle form of sorcery that is forged by his use of words in order to be privy to the deceptive arts he is employing here. The sinister art manifested here by ("El") Faisal is to speak with generalities but at the same time paint precise, mental images of these silhouetted scholars. The reason why he has to employ this deceptive art is because he cannot provide specific examples to show how exactly these "colonial powers" control the scholars. To be honest the reality is the opposite. One only needs to be familiar with a small amount of legal opinions given by the Scholars to see their open opposition to anything that threatens the sancity of Islam. Then he says:

"The only reason that they have these scholars in prison (Safar, Salmān etc) is because they said 'we want the Sharī'ah' so whenever a scholar doesn't tow the line they make his life hell."

So what about now, considering Safar, Salmān and 'Ā'id have all been released and they now all openly praise the Saudi government! Do they no longer "want the Sharī'ah"?? Furthermore, the likes of Safar, Salmān and Ā'id are currently work hand-in-hand with the Saudi government. In fact, in November 2003 CE Ā'id al-Qarnī interviewed Ali al-Khudayr and al-Khudayr also freed himself from many of his past erroneous views and rulings![1] Therefore, if Faisal so passionately loves these individuals Faisal and his blind followers would follow their example and not agitate against the Saudi government! The whole fiasco

[1] See: http://news.bbc.co.uk/1/hi/world/middle_east/3280715.stm
Also in an article by Muhammad al-Harbi in the Arab News (dated 24 Ramadān 1424/Tuesday 18 November 2003 CE) entitled 'Khudair Repents Supporting Terror Attacks':
"DAMMAM, 18 November 2003 — Shaykh Ali Al-Khudair, a well-known Saudi scholar who was arrested in Madinah for supporting terrorist attacks, has repented.
He also denounced the terrorist attacks in Makkah and Riyadh.
In an interview with Saudi television, the scholar said the militants carried out the explosions because of their ignorance of Islamic teachings. 'The life and property of non-Muslims in the Kingdom are under state protection and must not be attacked,' he added. Al-Khudair said the bombing of the Al-Muhaya Compound in Riyadh which killed at least 18 people including women and children had tarnished the image of Islam and harmed da'wah work. He expressed his deep sorrow for issuing fatwas that incited terror attacks. He also withdrew fatwas he had issued declaring infidel, Saudi thinkers Turki Al-Hamad, Mansour Al-Naqeedan and Abdullah Abusamh. Al-Khudair's statement signals a major turnabout in the attitude of scholars supporting Al-Qaeda, and observers expect other scholars to follow suit. News of the interview with Al-Khudair, conducted by Shaykh Āid Al-Qarni, spread quickly throughout the Kingdom. Al-Khudair had earlier issued edicts declaring attacks against Saudi security forces halal or permissible. He had also praised the 19 terror suspects wanted by Saudi security authorities and acknowledged his relation with some of them. In the interview, Al-Khudair declared only rulers were in a position to declare jihād. 'It is not allowed to rise up against rulers unless they commit flagrant violations against Shariah,' he said." See:
http://www.arabnews.com/?page=1&section=0&article=35266&d=18&m=11&y=2003

shows the foolish insight of Faisal, he so passionately supported and praised Safar, Salmān and Ā'id for their imprisonment and yet now all three have retracted from the mistakes that the likes of Faisal followed them in![1] Indeed, like many of the hasty and partisan *takfīrī* activists of London, Faisal promoted Safar al-Hawālī and Salman al-'Awda and the folly of this promotion was not only evident then in the 1990s but even more so now! For the latter is an openly reformed preacher who praises the Shi'a, the modernist preacher 'Amr Khaled and the Sufi 'Ali Jifrī; while the former has had a number of peculiar outlooks which have included writing a letter to George Bush Jnr on 15 October 2001 saying:

> We Muslims desired to see you elected and we have proof that the votes which gave you victory were our votes, and I personally advised Muslims to vote for you.[2] (!!?)

So much for ruling by what Allāh has revealed and *barā'* from the kuffār! So much for "Fiqh ul-Wāqi'"! The shuyūkh of 'Abdullāh ("el") Faisal and the *takfīrī* activists seemingly need to take their own advice! So, does Faisal still look up to them or do his own vain desires take over? Indeed, in this lecture Faisal described them as being *"the most prominent scholars in Saudi Arabia"* and in actual fact, Faisal describes one of them as being the *"Ibn Taymiyyah of the era"*

---

[1] Even though Salmān, Safar and Ā'id now have other errors related to their adoption of an approach which is now more similar to that of the *Ikhwān ul-Muslimeen* [Muslim Brotherhood].

[2] http://www.Sunnahonline.com/ilm/contemporary/0025.htm

so does Faisal now accept that they have retracted from much of their *khurūj*, *khārijiyyah*, *ghulū* and *tatarruf*? In the foolish lecture Faisal also says that such 'scholars' have to be *"liberated, as they are on death row"!!* Well, they all look perfectly well to the masses of people now as Salmān and Ā'id are on more Arabic satellite channels than even the senior scholars![1] He is looking very relaxed talking and sipping tea with a non-Muslim journalist, this is the so-called "oppressed shaykh" of 'Abdullāh Faisal. Then he says, which again highlights his pure *khārijī manhaj*:

> "So we have to liberate the scholars, liberate Makkah, liberate Madeenah, liberate Masjid al-'Aqsā and we say to hell with the Saudi government because you can't kill the scholars of Islām! You may kill the scholars but you may not kill Islām!"

To which the audience scream "Allāhu Akbar!" in total opposition to the *Sunnah*. So what has Faisal contributed to liberating? He has not liberated anything! Merely a mouthpiece of action yet has done absolutely nothing! So after this 'impressive' (not) statement, Faisal has landed his own self into jail and has not brought about or witnessed any of this nonsense that he and his *khawārij* followers screamed for.

---

[1] Indeed, take a look at this picture of Salmān in December 2004, looking very cosy while sipping tea with a Western journalist:
http://www.rainmedia.net/images/photo_isoaq_3.jpg

174

Sample Lecture Number Eight: 'Jewish Traits In The Ummah'

The very title of this lecture shows Faisal's horrific ideas. There has not been one single Muslim scholar who authored a book with this title, who has preceded Faisal! He commences by showing his *khawārij* methods of making *takfeer* of other Muslims and branding them as being *kuffār*. He says at the beginning of the lecture:

"The reasons why we have not been able to defeat them is *{sic}* because we are equal to the Jews in sins...so I'm here today to prove to you that we are similar to the Jews in behaviour, we are equal to them in sins like a carbon copy."

Hereby seeking to compare the Muslims to *kuffār*, rather Allāh says:

﴿ أَفَمَن كَانَ مُؤْمِنًا كَمَن كَانَ فَاسِقًا لَّا يَسْتَوُۥنَ ۩ ﴾

"Then is one who was a believer like one who was defiantly disobedient?
They are not equal." *{as-Sajdah (32): 18}*

Allāh also says:

﴿ أَفَنَجْعَلُ ٱلْمُسْلِمِينَ كَٱلْمُجْرِمِينَ ۩ ﴾

"Then will We treat the Muslims like the criminals?" *{al-Qalam (68): 35}*

See the difference between the words of Allāh and the words of Faisal! Then Faisal states:

> "I have in front of me approximately 50 Jewish traits and how they have found their way into the ranks of the believers." (!!)

Then he immediately contradicts himself, as he mentions a 'trait' which Faisal himself has and does! He says:

> "Today, unfortunately, there are many Muslims who create fitna amongst the ranks of the believers. If they know that 'Abdullāh doesn't like Zayd or Khadeejah doesn't like 'Ā'ishah they spread news backward and forward... So the same way that the Jews create fitna and they love people to be at each other's throats there are many Muslims today who spread news backward and forward for Muslims to fight and kill each other..."

O really? So then according to Faisal's own definition he himself is the first to have this 'Jewish trait' after his labelling the people of *Sunnah* as being *"Jews of the ummah"*, *"the same as the followers of Musaylimah"*, *"House-niggas"*, *"kuffār"* and more! There has not been anyone who has unleashed their vile tongue against the Muslims more than Faisal, the only other contenders being other varieties of extremists, who are found to attack others in the name of Islām and the *Sunnah*. Faisal also in the lecture *The Devil's Deception of the Saudi Salafis* makes mention that: *"When I was in Riyadh the only people that were punished were Pakistanis."* Trying to make out that there is some sort of discrimination against Pakistani Muslims and thus trying to create enmity against Saudi from the Pakistani-derived Muslim community in the UK, which incidentally makes up the majority of Muslims in the UK.

The reality is that non-Muslim gangsters are also executed for crimes. Therefore, it would be inaccurate to assert that Saudi Arabia has a systematic policy of only punishing non-Saudis while their own citizens walk away scot-free from serious crimes. Famous cases include three Saudi security officers who were executed by firing squad for abducting and raping a Filipino man in the 1990s. Yet like any country there are bound to be shortcomings in regards to human rights and Saudi Arabia would in no way be the only country to fall short in that regard. In any case, the figures of those executed for committing serious crimes are small in comparison to those killed in the West due to crime and disorder, or the numbers killed as 'collateral damage'. Just for the record, this is not to say that racism does not occur against Pakistanis or any other ethnic groups in Saudi. Then Faisal states: *"There are many Muslims whose hearts are hard like the Jews."* We agree that there are Muslims who are hard-hearted, in terms of distortion and denial of Allāh's words, but Salafis remain disciplined and do not fall into pronouncing *takfeer*. We are actually prepared to go a step further and say that Faisal is actually one of these culprits. Another questionable statement is this:

"Take for instance those Muslims who do not believe in Tawheed al-Hākimiyyah.[1] That Allāh is the only law-giver, if you open the Qur'ān and show him the verse in sūrah eighteen where Allāh says: 'I do not allow anyone to share with Me in My Legislation' do you think he will believe in *Tawheed al-Hākimiyyah*?"

Which Muslim in a state of sobriety would deny Allāh's right of sovereignty over His creation? Perhaps what Faisal is intentionally concealing here is the innovated belief of a fourth category of *Tawheed*, which was forged in the factories of the people of innovation. So after decoding the encrypted speech of this man we believe that what Faisal is actually saying is: 'if you do not partake in separating and accepting al-Hākimiyyah as a fourth distinct category, then this is indicative of your disbelief in His Sovereignty'.

One does not need to invest much brain power to recognize the errors of his innovated conclusions. Firstly, even if al-Hākimiyyah was a separate, distinct category, how would denial of the existence of an extra category, not actually what it contains, place your Islam in jeopardy? Faisal constantly blabs on about the Salafis "denial" of *al-Hākimiyyah* as a separate category of *Tawheed* and

---

[1] This is another one of Faisal's emotional ploys to garner support from the audience. By saying this Faisal hopes to instill into the audience that whoever rejects the innovated concept of *'Tawheed Hākimiyyah'* is 'hard-hearted' when the reality is that *'tawheed hākimiyyah'* is a modern concept, which has its roots in the works of the journalist Sayyid Qutb, rather than from the works of Islamic scholars, let alone the *Salaf us-Sālih*!

178

links it somehow, to being a nullifier of Islam. But this linkage here is deceptive because Faisal cannot prove that Salafis deny the contents of the alleged category. So to summerise Faisal's logic: because Salafis reject the separate category of 'al-Hākimiyyah' this must mean that the Salafis also reject the belief that Allāh is the Law-Giver. Does this man have some fast-track *takfeer* system inbuilt in him? Secondly and more importantly, who concurs with him from among our righteous forefathers that al-Hākimiyyah is actually a fourth category?

"I debated with many Salafis and showed them in black and white in the Qur'ān, sūrah eighteen verse twenty six[1] where Allāh says that He doesn't allow anyone to share with Him in his legislation and still they say *'Tawheed Hākimiyyah* is bida'""

His purposely, concocted choice of words would have you believe that we as Salafis somehow believe that maintaining Allāh's right of sovereignty over his creation is an innovated concept! The 'sleight of hand' tactic deployed here is crafty, because when you omit the term 'category' it gives the impression that we are denying the reality of *Hākimiyyah* and not that we deny it as being an independant catergory, external of Allāh's *Rubūbiyyah* or *Ulūhiyyah*. Then he states:

"How many types of Tawheed are there? Four! Allāh is the only creator,

---

[1] Faisal rarely refers to the actual names of the Sūrahs he quotes, instead choosing to quote the Sūrah number as opposed to the name of the Sūrah itself? This again demonstrates his poor citation and referencing skills.

Allāh alone deserves to be worshipped, Allāh has ninety-nine Names and Attributes and Allāh is the only Law-Giver. *Tawheed ur-Rubūbiyyah, 'Ulūhiyyah, Asmā' wa's-Sifāt* and *al-Hākimiyyah.* If I, Faisal, look at you and say 'come to my house I will challenge you to a debate in regards to *Tawheed ar-Rubūbiyyah*' I become a kāfir. True or false? Do you understand the question? I am denying *Tawheed ar-Rubūbiyyah* that Allāh is the only creator and I says *{sic}* to you 'I am gonna check out my books and you come with your books and we'll have a debate with regards to *Tawheed ar-Rubūbiyyah*' if I challenge you to a debate I become a kāfir. Likewise, if I challenge you and the *Salafis* we have given them this challenge then they runaway and hide."[1]

Remaining loyal to his sinister arts, we witness once again his attempts to fabricate the belief that we as Salafis deny a fundamental aspect of *Tawheed.* The trick is the same as before, keep the term 'category' at bay and make it seem as if we are denying not just a 'title' or a 'concept' but the actual contents which are represented by this title. The example he brings of *Rubūbiyyah* proves this. Therefore, we say to Faisal: we do not want to come to your house and debate with you regarding the realities of *Rubūbiyyah* or *Hākimiyyah*, rather our challenge lies in you showing us that *Hākimiyyah* is a fourth category. Basically

---

[1] Indeed, if they do "runaway and hide" it is to be safe from Faisal's *khawārij manhaj* and beliefs of innovation! However, in many cases it was Faisal who "ran away to hide"!!

he has distorted our criticism and made it appear as if we are denying a substance part of *Tawheed*. Then he states:

"If a Salafi should open his mouth and challenge saying 'I'm going to have a debate, a public debate, in regards to *Tawheed al-Hākimiyyah*' if he (i.e. the Salafi) throws that challenge out to you that person becomes a kāfir! Are you convinced or you're not convinced? This is known of Islām by necessity that Allāh is the only Law-Giver... so why do the people reject it? Because their hearts are hard just like the Jews!"

The badgering of the audience is astonishing. It is obvious by his choice of words that he is trying to force a plotted conclusion from his audience here. His fascination and psychotic obsession with *takfeer* has become so dominant over him that it drives him to elicit from his audience a congregational, harmonious pronouncement of *takfeer* - such is his need and addiction for this verbal narcotic. The most concerning part is that he demands the *takfir* of the Salafi because he rightfully denies *Hākimiyyah* as a fourth category whilst maintaining complete *īmān* and *tasdeeq* in its contents. Then Faisal says: *"The reason why they say "kufr dūna kufr" because they want to protect their kāfir paymasters."* So Ibn 'Abbās, who was the author of this statement, had kuffār paymasters?! This is one of Faisal's major attempts to hoodwink the people and hide what Muslim scholars have actually said on the narration of *"kufr less than kufr."* Here is a clear example of Faisal's deception and pouring scorn onto the Muslim scholars of the *Sunnah* as well. Many scholars refer to the narration of *"kufr less than kufr"*[1] and utilise it as a narration which is verified and authenticated, such as with Imām Abū 'Ubayd al-Qāsim ibn as-Sallām[2], al-Marwazī in *Ta'dheem Qadr us-Salāh*[3] and Abī Madhfar as-Sama'anī when he stated:

> Ibn 'Abbās said 'The verse is about the Muslims and intends kufr less than kufr and I know that the Khawārij make deductions from these verses and say that: "whoever does not rule by what Allāh has revealed is a disbeliever" but the people of Sunnah say: "he is not to be considered a disbeliever due to leaving off judgement.'"[4]

Other scholars who also verify *"kufr less than kufr"* are: al-Baghawī in his *tafseer*[5], Ibn 'Arabī al-Mālikī[6], Shaykh ul-Islām Ibn Taymiyyah[7], Ibn ul-Qayyim[8], Imām Muhammad Nāsirrudeen al-Albānī[9], Imām 'Abdul'Azeez bin 'Abdullāh bin Bāz[10] and finally Imām Muhammad bin Sālih al-'Uthaymeen wherein he said:

---

[1] For example, in his Saheeh, al-Imam al-Bukhari titled chapter 26 in the Book of Iman as: 'Chapter: ungratefulness to one's husband and *kufr less than kufr* (*kufr doona kufr*)'! See al-Fath (2/113) of Ibn Hajr and al-Fath (1/142) of Ibn Rajab. Should we then suppose, as Faisal would like, that Imam al-Bukhari had a "dodgy aqeedah" too?!

[2] *Kitāb ul-Īmān*, p.45

[3] ibid Vol.2, p.250

[4] *Tafseer ul-Qur'ān*, vol.2, p.42

[5] ibid. Vol.3, p.61

[6] *Ahkām ul-Qur'ān*, vol.2, pp.624-625

[7] *Majmū' al-Fatāwā*, vol.7, pp.315 and 522.

[8] *Madārij us-Sālikeen*, vol.1, p.335

[9] *Silsilat as-Saheehah*, vol.6, pp.109-116

[10] *Majmū' Fatāwā wa Maqālāt*, vol.2, pp.326-330

However, due to this narration those who have been tested with takfeer have not been pleased and begin to say 'this narration is unacceptable! It is not authentically relayed from Ibn 'Abbās!' So it can be said to them: 'How can it not be authentic when those who are more virtuous and greater in knowledge than you in hadeeth have accepted the narration?!' In relation to the narration of Ibn 'Abbās, then it is sufficient for us that the noteworthy scholars such as Sheikh ul-Islām Ibn Taymiyyah, Ibn ul-Qayyim and others have all received the narration with acceptance and relay it as being an authentic narration.[1]

So did all of these scholars mention the narration of *"kufr dūna kufr"* because *"they wanted to protect their kāfir paymasters"*?[2] So beware of the tricks of the *Ruwaybidah*! Faisal continues:

"Do you know that it is impossible to find a Salafi book on the market, a book on Tawheed and they mention Tawheed al-Hākimiyyah? Have you seen such a book? And if you can find it bring it to the halaqah…so Tawheed al-Hākimiyyah that whenever the leader dismantle {sic} the Sharī'ah you should fight him because the Prophet said when you see

---

[1] From his notes to the book *Tahdheer min Fitnat it-Takfeer*, pp.68-69, also see for additional info, *Qurrat ul-'Uyūn fī Tasheeh Tafseer 'Abdullāh Ibn 'Abbās 'alā Qawlihi Ta'ala "Wa man lam yahkum bi ma Anzala Allāh fa Ūlayika hum ul-Kāfirūn"*, pp.87-94 by Shaykh Saleem al-Hilālī.

[2] For a detailed refutation of Faisal and other new-age *takfiri* activists and their criticisms of the *tafseer* of 'Abdullāh Ibn 'Abbās: "kufr dūna kufr" refer to: http://www.salafimanhaj.com/pdf/SalafiManhaj_KufrDoonaKufr.pdf

clear kufr you should fight him. You will never find when they write their books...but they will never mention *Tawheed al-Hākimiyyah* because they do not want to offend their kāfir paymasters. So they love money more than Allāh, they love their salary more than Allāh.[1] They prefer to offend Allāh than to offend their kāfir paymasters who they sign off and on with."

There are many books which highight the *Tawheed* of Allāh's *Hākimiyyah* since *Hākimiyyah* is a prerequisite of *Rubūbiyyah* or *Ulūhiyyah*. What is not found in the Books of the Salafis or the Salaf is the innovated, politically induced concept of *Hākimiyyah* as an independant fourth category. Faisal says yet again:

"Another Jewish trait is that they kick people out...the Jews took sides with other people to kill their Jewish brothers and drove them out of their homes. Now how are we the Muslims similar to this? When Saddam Hussein misbehaved[2] what did the Saudis do? They brought America in who are the greatest enemies of Islām and took sides with America[3] to kill the Iraqis. So the same way how the Jews in Baqarah 84-85 took sides with the kuffār and drove their own people out of their

---

[1] Hereby Faisal insinuates that he can look into their hearts by stating these slanderous claims.

[2] This is an understatement to say the least! Saddam Hussein and his army of Ba'ath is noticeable underplayed within most of Faisal's vitriol and this is not adequate. Saddam entered al-Khafji, which was Saudi territory, after he had invaded Kuwait.

[3] To say "they took sides" is simplistic, Saudi had their own interests of protecting their borders and maintaining their religion from Ba'athism, while others had their interests.

homeland it is the same thing that happened in the gulf war when they brought the crusaders in. Those same crusaders the Saudis brought them in to occupy the holy land and kill the Muslims of 'Iraq. And they bombed 'Iraq at night, and they did not exactly see who they were bombing and they killed men, women and children and even animals without discretion, <u>so they took sides with the crusaders in massacring the Muslims</u> and they killed 300,000 thousand civilians, innocent civilians in 'Iraq…"[1]

First of all we can see that Faisal has mentioned yet another figure of the amount killed in 'Iraq?! He stated 200,000 in one talk we have mentioned, 10,000 in another talk only to correct himself and say "100,000" and within this audio recording he states "300,000"!! So how many is it and where is Faisal getting his stats from? He has mentioned four different numbers and he has not verified them whatsoever yet mentions them just to incite and hype-up his ignorant followers. So beware of such absence of verification. However, Faisal wants to make out that the Salafi scholars have no idea of the *"fiqh of current affairs"*! He continues unleashing his tongue against the Salafis:

---

[1] Faisal also claims that Yemenis who were resident in Saudi were expelled due to 'Ali 'Abdullāh Sālih agreeing with Saddam when he invaded Kuwait. Faisal says that the Yemenis were **"made homeless by the Saudis"** and this again is utter falsehood that Faisal states, as there was no mass expulsion whatsoever of the Yemenis from Saudi. Faisal also claims that Saudis took all money and wealth from them when the Yemenis returned to Yemen!?

"The Jews said: 'we are the people of paradise, we are God's chosen people, paradise is exclusive to us, everybody is going to the Hell Fire' there is a group in this country who is well known to everyone who claim that 'we are the saved sect and every other Muslim group is going to the Hell Fire.' Who is that group? And if I was to put that in an exam question no one would get it wrong... And we say to the Salafi if you claim that you are God's chosen people why don't you wish for death,[1] they will never wish for death they love life so much they say that there's no jihād anywhere in the world...and you have to be firmly grounded in knowledge before you can make jihād. The Jews used to seek knowledge to show off. There was a man who the Salafis used to big-up 'he's our Shaykh' and when he came from America and told them about *Tawheed al-Hākimiyyah* they classify him *{sic}* as a deviant (and say) 'he's not our Shaykh anymore he's now become a deviant'so they change their tune to suit them[2] and this is a sign of the hypocrites."

Words are powerful and when unleashed they can paint any picture one wishes to be visualised in people's minds. The above words would give anyone the impression that we, as Salafis, roam the streets telling everyone that we are the 'saved sect' and that everyone besides us is destined for the hell-fire. Such behaviour can be easily linked to arrogance and pride when scripted in a

---

[1] Where do Salafis say that they "are God's chosen people"??
[2] This isn't "changing the tune" it is rather rejecting what is in contradiction to the Qur'ān, Sunnah and *manhaj* of the *Salaf*, who or whatever that may be!

negative fashion. Is this the case concerning Salafis? The term 'saved sect' is not used when the Salafis are describing themselves, rather it is brought with the sole aim of identifying the characteristics that embody it. So by saying that you endeavour to follow the saved sect in matters of belief and action is tantamount to saying that you follow the Qur'ān and Sunnah as understood by the Sahābah. Who would have a problem with one saying or hearing this alternative? Imām 'Abdul'Azeez bin Bāz ﷺ stated:

> If there is a person or group which calls to the Book of Allāh and the Sunnah of His Messenger, and calls to the Tawheed of Allāh and following of His Sharī'ah – then they are the Jama'ah and from the Firqat un-Nājiyyah. As for whoever calls to other than the Book of Allāh, and to other than the Sunnah of His Messenger – then such a person is not from the Jama'ah, rather he is from the misguided destroyed sects. As for the Firqat un-Nājiyyah then they are the preachers to the Book of Allāh and the Sunnah, even if there are groups of them here and there (around the world) as long as the goal and 'aqeedah is one.[1]

Al-'Allāmah Sālih al-Fawzān was asked:

> Is 'Salafiyyah' a hizb (partisan group)? Is ascription to it censured? Who are their scholars?

Answer from al-'Allāmah Sālih al-Fawzān:

---

[1] *Majmū' al-Fatāwā Ibn Bāz*, vol.8, p.182

Salafiyyah is the Firqat un-Nājiyyah and they are Ahl us-Sunnah wa'l-Jama'ah, Salafiyyah is not a hizb (party) from among the range of (political) parties which are named as such today. Salafiyyah is the Hizb of Allāh and His soldiers they are a Jama'ah upon the Sunnah and deen... Salafiyyah is: what the madhhab of the Salaf was upon and what the Messenger of Allāh ﷺ and his companions were upon. It is not a party from among the range of contemporary (political) parties, rather it is an old Jama'ah from the time of the Messenger of Allāh ﷺ and is hereditary and continuous, for they will not cease to be upon the truth manifest up until the hour is established, as the Prophet ﷺ informed.[1]

Remove the twisted distorted fashion in which Faisal articulates his words and you will realise his criticism is fuelled by nothing but a deep hatred for the Salafis due to their rejection of him and his fanatical ways. Faisal is also insinuating 'Ali Timimi, who none of the Salafis, from what we know, ever proclaimed was a Shaykh to refer back to.

Sample Lecture Number Nine: 'Let The Scholars Beware'[2]

Faisal states:

---

[1] Shaykh, Dr Sālih bin Fawzān al-Fawzān, Muhammad bin Fahd al-Husayn (ed.), *al-Ijabāt al-Muhimmah fi'l-Mashākil al-Mumilah* (Riyadh: Matābi' al-Humaydī, 1425 AH/2004 CE, 2nd Edn.), p.156.
[2] http://www.kalamullah.com/faisal.html

"Any time takfeer is made on a man, and his wife still stays with him and co-habits with him that woman is committing *zina*. Anytime takfeer is made on a person and this takfeer is made by a scholar of ahl us-Sunnah wa'l-jamā'ah and the woman was told to make bara'ah from her husband, because he has now become a kāfir. If the woman stay with him {sic} we judge you as a kāfir aswell. So what we do is wage jihād against you, we kill your husband and take you as a right-hand possess. This is the Islamic verdict and when you have right-hand possess you don't have to marry them..."

How does his wife become a kāfirah on the sole basis of her husband's apostasy? Would not intellect dictate also that if a man becomes a Muslim that his wife becomes a Muslim too? When such logic is reversed, it is not hard to see the folly that exuberates from this man's mouth. So the husband apostates and what is Faisal's next course of action? To kill him!? Then he says:

"The second evil scholar is a murji'. A murji' is a person who refuse {sic} to pronounce a kāfir a kāfir, even after the evidence {sic} are made clear...the favourite hadeeth of the murji' is the hadeeth in which the Rasool 鄒 said 'Anyone of you who says to his Muslim brother "O kāfir" one of you become a kāfir'..."

So Faisal defines the *murji'iah* as merely "*a person who refuses to pronounce a kāfir a kāfir*" - he mentions nothing about the *murji'ah* with regards to *imān*,

189

as their main issue is with regards to *īmān*, and he mentions nothing about them not allowing *istithnā'* in *īmān*! So Faisal does not even define the *murji'īah* correctly! This again highlights his excessive-compulsive takfeer disorder (ECTD) with the word 'kāfir' and that everything defined or explained must be in some way connected to it no matter how remote from the matter it may be. He states:

"Now I am here giving you a bayān freely and there are many people who'd like to silence me, Faisal. They'd like to see my life go out but they have failed miserably to silence me and every time I challenge them to a debate they refuse, they only speak behind my back like nine-year old girls."

Faisal then says:

"Now if a person says the Qur'ān is created is he a Muslim or a kāfir? I can't hear you! A kāfir! Ma'mūn believed the Qur'ān was created, so if Ma'mūn believed the Qur'ān was created why Ahmad ibn Hanbal did not {sic} make takfeer on him? The answer to that: because he (i.e. Ma'mūn) implement {sic} [1] the Sharī'ah to the letter, this is why Ahmad ibn Hanbal didn't make takfeer on him."

---

[1] Again, this is direct from Faisal's own words, he did not use the past tense 'implemented' he rather said 'he implement' even though he is talking about something in the past.

"I can't hear you" - sounds like something from a pantomime character or from a Punch and Judy Show! Swiftly moving on, where is the proof for this statement about Ma'mūn? Faisal says this and provides no evidence whatsoever of whom from the people of knowledge stated this.[1] There is no mention of *"implementation of the Sharī'ah"* in *Usūl us-Sunnah*[2] of Imām Ahmad, nor in *Tabaqāt ul-Hanābilah*[3] of Qādī Muhammmad ibn Abī Ya'la[4] nor in *Sharh Usūl I'tiqād Ahlis-Sunnah* of Imām al-Lālikā'ī. There is nothing about *"Ahmad not making takfeer due to the implementation of the Sharī'ah"* and in any case, believing that the Qur'ān is created is not *"implementing the Sharī'ah to the letter"*. Implementing the Shari'iah of Allāh includes correct aqeedah, so what is Faisal on about? Actually, correct belief in Allāh and performing righteous good deeds are two things that bring into effect the following verse of Allāh:

---

[1] Faisal also repeats this issue of the **"implementation of Sharī'ah"** in the lecture *'The Devil's Deception of the Saudi Salafis'* with regards to Hajjāj ibn Yūsuf, about an hour and twenty minutes into the lecture.

[2] Edited by Fawwāz Ahmad Zumarlī in 1411 AH

[3] Abdurrahmān al-'Uthaymeen (ed.), Riyadh: Maktabah al-'Ubaykān, 2005 CE; also Muhammad Hāmid al-Faqīhī (ed.), Cairo: 1952 CE; Beirut: Dār ul-Ma'rifah

[4] He is al-Qādī Abū Ya'la Muhammad bin Husayn bin Muhammad bin Khalaf bin Ahmad al-Baghdādī and he authored some of the major classifications of the Hanbalī madhhab. He was born in 380 AH/ 990 CE and studied under many scholars including 'Īsā Ibn Wazeer. He excelled in *fiqh, tafseer, usūl* and was the Imām of 'Irāq during his time, he died in 458 AH/ 1065 CE. He authored *Ahkām ul-Qur'ān, Masā'il-Īmān, al-Mu'tamid fī Usūl id-Deen* (edited by W.Z. Haddād, Beirut, 1974 CE), *'Uyūn ul-Masā'il, Rad 'alā Karāmiyyah, Rad 'alā Sālimiyyah wa'l-Mujassimah, Rad 'alā Jahmiyyah, al-Kalām fī'l-Istiwā, Fadā'ilu Ahmad, at-Tibb, Tareekh ul-Islām* and other works.

﴿ وَعَدَ ٱللَّهُ ٱلَّذِينَ ءَامَنُوا۟ مِنكُمْ وَعَمِلُوا۟ ٱلصَّٰلِحَٰتِ لَيَسْتَخْلِفَنَّهُمْ فِى ٱلْأَرْضِ كَمَا ٱسْتَخْلَفَ ٱلَّذِينَ مِن قَبْلِهِمْ وَلَيُمَكِّنَنَّ لَهُمْ دِينَهُمُ ٱلَّذِى ٱرْتَضَىٰ لَهُمْ وَلَيُبَدِّلَنَّهُم مِّنۢ بَعْدِ خَوْفِهِمْ أَمْنًا يَعْبُدُونَنِى لَا يُشْرِكُونَ بِى شَيْـًٔا وَمَن كَفَرَ بَعْدَ ذَٰلِكَ فَأُو۟لَٰٓئِكَ هُمُ ٱلْفَٰسِقُونَ ﴾

Allāh has promised those among you who believe, and do righteous good deeds, that He will certainly grant them succession to (the present rulers) in the earth, as He granted it to those before them, and that He will grant them the authority to practise their religion, that which He has chosen for them (i.e. Islam). And He will surely give them in exchange a safe security after their fear (provided) they (believers) worship Me and do not associate anything (in worship) with Me. But whoever disbelieved after this, they are the Fasiqun (rebellious, disobedient to Allāh). *{An-Nūr (24): 55}*

This is one of the common doubts of the people of *takfeer*, they apply this new modern interpretation about *"takfeer not being made due to the implementation of the Sharī'ah"* but the reality is that Imām Ahmad mentions in his *Usūl us-Sunnah* that revolt against a Muslim leader is not to be made. He states under point 53:

And whoever revolts against a leader from among the leaders of the Muslims, after the people had agreed upon him and united themselves behind him, after they had affirmed the khilāfah for him, in whatever way this khilāfah may have been, by their pleasure and acceptance or by (his) force and domination (over them), then this revolter has disobeyed the Muslims, and has contradicted the narrations of the Messenger of Allāh ﷺ. And if the one who revolted against the ruler died he would have died the death of ignorance.

Then point 54:

And the killing of the one in power is not lawful, and nor is it permissible for anyone amongst the people to revolt against him. Whoever does that is an innovator, (and is) upon other than the Sunnah and the (correct) path.[1]

Imām Ahmad ﷺ did not mention anything whatsoever about the *"implementation of the Sharī'ah"* he states that *any* Muslim ruler that assumes power must be obeyed and that revolting against him is not permissible. Imām Abū Ja'far at-Tahāwī, author of *'Aqeedah Tahāwiyyah'*, which was explained by Ibn Abi'l-'Izz al-Hanafī, states:

We do not view (that it is permissible to) revolt against our leaders or those who are responsible for our affairs and even if they transgress we do not make du'ā against them[2] and we do not take back the covenant of

---

[1] For both the Arabic and English texts see *Foundations of the Sunnah by Imām Ahmad ibn Hanbal* (Birmingham: Salafi Publications, 1417 AH/1997 CE), pp.37-38.

[2] Shaykh 'Ali Hasan al-Halabī stated in a lesson at the *Imām Albānī Centre* (in 'Ammān, Jordan) in March 2006 CE: "Some people make du'ā against the Muslim leaders or curse and slander them and this is not from the characteristics of the people of truth."

obedience from them[1] and we view that obedience to them is from obedience to Allāh and obligatory[2] as long as they do not command to disobedience and we make du'ā to Allāh for them to have correctness and good health.[3]

As for the consensus, which clearly indicates this, is that which was stated by Imām an-Nawawī ؓ in his explanation of *Saheeh Muslim* wherein he stated:

وأما الخروج عليهم، وقتالهم، فحرام بإجماع المسلمين، وإن كانوا فسقة ظالمين

"As for revolting against the rulers and leaders and fighting against them then it is harām (impermissible) according to the consensus of the Muslims, <u>even if they are sinful transgressors</u>."[4]

This principle can also be found in another monumental work, the Imām of the Sunnah, the Shaykh of the *Hanābalah*, al-Barbahārī in his work *Sharh us-Sunnah*:

---

[1] Shaykh 'Ali said: "This obviously means by extension removing themselves from the obedience of Allāh as the Prophet ﷺ said '*There is no obedience to the creation in disobedience to the Creator*' and he ﷺ also said '*Obedience is only in that which is good.*' If the issue is in regards to that which opposes the Divine Legislation and the affair of the Allāh and His Messenger, then obedience in this regard is not permissible."

[2] Meaning: responding in obedience to the leader is as if you have responded in obedience to Allāh, it is obligatory. (Shaykh 'Ali Hasan)

[3] Shaykh 'Ali stated: "Instead of making *du'ā* against them we make *du'ā* for them as Imām Ahmad ؓ mentioned."

[4] Meaning: 'even if those Muslim rulers are sinners and transgressors'. This is found in vol.12, p.229 of Imām an-Nawawī's *Sharh* of Saheeh Muslim.

ولا يحل قتال السلطان, والخروج عليهم وإن جاروا وذلك قول رسول الله —صلى

الله عليه وسلم – لأبي ذر (الغفاري): " اصبر وإن كان عبدا حبشيا" و قوله

للأنصار: "اصبروا حتى تلقوني على الحوض".

It is not permissible to fight the ruler or rebel against them, even if they are oppressive. This is due to the statement of Allāh's Messenger ﷺ to Abū Dharr: '*Have patience (with the ruler), even if he is an Abyssian slave.*' Moreover, his ﷺ statement to the Ansār: '*Have patience until you meet me at the Hawd.*'[1]

This contemporary argument about *"takfeer not being made due to the implementation of the Sharī'ah"* is also feebly used by the *takfīrīs* to rebut the following *hadeeth*:

أخرج مسلم في " صحيحه " عن حذيفة بن اليمان – رضي الله عنهما – قال:

قلت : يا رسول الله ! إنا كنا بشر فجاء الله بخير فنحن فيه فهل من وراء هذا الخير

شر ؟ قال "نعم "، قلت : هل وراء ذلك الشر خير ؟ قال " نعم " قلت فهل وراء

الخير شر ؟ قال : " نعم " قلت : كيف ؟ قال " يكون بعدي أئمة لا يهتدون

بهداي، ولا يستنون بسنتي، وسيقوم فيهم رجال قلوبهم قلوب الشياطين في جثمان

---

[1] Sharhus Sunnah, p. 70.

إنس " قال : قلت : كيف أصنع يا رسول الله – أن أدركت ذلك؟ قال : " تسمع

وتطيع للأمير وإن ضرب ظهرك وأخذ مالك فاسمع وأطع".

Reported in *Saheeh Muslim*[1] from Hudhayfah ibn al-Yamān ﷺ wherein he asked the Prophet ﷺ if there was any evil after this good and the Prophet ﷺ responded saying '*Yes.*' Hudhayfah asked 'how can this be?' The Prophet ﷺ said '*There will be after me leaders who will neither be guided by my guidance nor follow my Sunnah and men will emerge from them who will have the hearts of devils in the bodies of men.*' Hudhayfah asked 'What should be done if that happens?' The Prophet ﷺ said '*Listen and obey the leader, even if he beats your back and takes your money, listen and obey!*'

So if a leader "does not follow the guidance of the Prophet ﷺ" is this *"implementing the Sharī'ah"*? If the leader "will not follow the *Sunnah* of the Prophet ﷺ" is this *"implementing the Sharī'ah"*? If the leader "beats your back" (unjustly) is this *"implementing the Sharī'ah"*? If the leader "takes your money" after doing this beating, is this *"implementing the Sharī'ah"*? If a leader has a heart of a devil in human form is this *"implementing the Sharī'ah"*?? Yet the Takfīrīs conjure up, with no precedence from any scholar from the *Salaf*, that this *hadeeth* is only applied to *"those Muslim leaders who are implementing the Sharī'ah"*! So they seek to append to the words of the Prophet ﷺ. Faisal

---

[1] Vol.3, p.1476

196

continues by making *takfeer* of Muslim countries which are part of the UN and this is again false. Faisal states:

"Even if they implemented the Sharī'ah still they'd be kāfirs because they give their allegiance, their bay'ah, their oath of allegiance, to the UN..."

Shaykh 'Abdul'Azeez bin Rayyis ar-Rayyis *(hafidhahullāh)* has dealt with this issue thoroughly in his book *al-Burhan al-Muneer fi Dhad Shubuhāt Ahl it-Takfeer wa't-Tafjeer* [The Clear Proofs for Refuting the Doubts of the People of Takfeer and Bombing] in a chapter dealing with the issue of *takfeer* due to being in the UN. Shaykh 'Abdul'Azeez bin Rayyis ar-Rayyis notes that:

فهي هيئة ذات أنظمة وقرارات وعهود ومواثيق انضمت إليها أكثر دول العالم، ومنها الدولة السعودية — حرسها الله ورعاها —، وقد نشأت إبان الحرب العالمية الثانية، والهدف الرئيس من إنشائها تقريب وجهات النظر بين الأمم، وتضييق الثغرات التي قد تنشأ بين الدول، والتي من شأنها إن استمرت أن تشكل خطراً على السلم والأمن الدوليين إلى جانب تحقيق السلام، ومنع اللجوء إلى استخدام القوة كحل للمشكلات العالمية.

(The UN) is an organisational system of resolutions, agreements and covenants which most of the world's states are affiliated to, including the state of Saudi, may Allāh protect it. It (i.e. the UN) developed …. after

197

the second world war and the main aim of its development was to bring together nations and views and to narrow the variances which can emerge between nation-states which if left to continue would lead to dangerous consequences for peace and security between two states alongside achieving peace. It was also set-up to prevent the use of power as a solution to global problems.

Shaykh 'Abdul'Azeez ar-Rayyis *(hafidhahullāh)* then mentioned King Faisal ﷺ highlighting this about the UN and then the Shaykh stated:

وبما أن الغلبة في هذه الهيئة للكفار فإن بها أنظمة لا توافق الشرع ؛ فلذا عارضت السعودية بعض الأنظمة، ولم توافق على كل ما فيها. وإليك جملة من العهود والمواثيق التي لم تقبلها الدولة السعودية — حرسها الله — :

1– لم توافق المملكة العربية السعودية على الاتفاقية التي تنص على القضاء على جميع أشكال التميز ضد المرأة. قال طلال محمد نور عطا: تحفظت المملكة العربية السعودية على هذه الاتفاقية، ولا تلزم نفسها بما يتعارض مع أحكام الشريعة الإسلامية ا.هـ[1]

[1] حاشية كتابه المملكة العربية السعودية والمنظمات الدولية ص181.

2- لم توافق المملكة العربية السعودية على المادة السادسة عشرة في حقوق الإنسان القائلة " للرجل والمرأة متى بلغا سن الزواج الحق بالتزوج بدون قيد بسبب الدين " فقالت دولة التوحيد في مذكرة أرسلتها إلى الأمم المتحدة : إن زواج المسلم من امرأة وثنية وغير مؤمنة بوجود الله أمر حرمه الإسلام، وأيضاً زواج المسلم من كتابية يهودية أم مسيحية أباحه الإسلام، أما زواج غير المسلم بمسلمة فغير مباح.[1]

3- لم توافق دولة التوحيد على المادة العاشرة من الإعلان العالمي لحقوق الإنسان التي أعطت كل شخص حرية تغيير دينه.[2]

4- أن المملكة العربية السعودية لم تنظم إلى المعاهدتين الدوليتين: الأولى الخاصة بالحقوق الاقتصادية والاجتماعية والثقافية. والثانية المتعلقة بالحقوق السياسية والمدنية، بسبب احتواء كل من هاتين المعاهدتين على مواد لا تساير تعاليم الشريعة الإسلامية السمحة.[3]

فإذا كانت هذه حال الدولة السعودية مع هيئة الأمم المتحدة، من أنها لا تقبل الأنظمة التي تخالف الشريعة الإسلامية باعتراف قادات هذه الدولة — وفقهم الله لما

---

[1] مذكرة الحكومة السعودية إلى منظمة الأمم المتحدة حول تطبيق حقوق الإنسان في المملكة عملاً بالشريعة الإسلامية. نشر في العدد الأول من المجلة العربية ص182، وانظر كتاب موقف المملكة العربية السعودية من القضايا العالمية في هيئة الأمم المتحدة ص98.
[2] المرجع السابق.
[3] موقف المملكة العربية السعودية من القضايا العالمية في هيئة الأمم المتحدة ص98.

فيه هداه —، وبتطبيقهم لها عملياً، وذلك بأن يتحفظوا على الأنظمة والقرارات المخالفة للشريعة الإسلامية، إذا كان هكذا حال الدولة مع هيئة الأمم المتحدة فلماذا — يا منصفون — يُشنع عليها وتُكفر ؟! أليس من حقها أن تشكر بدل أن تكفر، من أجل امتناعها عن القرارات المخالفة للشريعة ؟ أليس من حقها أن تؤازر وتساند على اعتزازها وحدها من بين جميع الدول الإسلامية بشريعة الإسلام وتحفظها على كل ما يخالفه؟

ب/ أن المصلحة تقتضي انضمام الدولة السعودية لهذه الهيئة حماية لنفسها من أعدائها الكفار، بل وبعض الدول الإسلامية المخالفة للمعتقد السلفي، فإنهم يتربصون بدولة التوحيد الدوائر لدوافع متعددة معلومة، ومن أوضح البراهين حرب الخليج الأولى، فدولة تهجم وأخرى عن أنيابها تكشر .

ومن المتقرر شرعاً أن للضعف أحكاماً مغايرة لحالة القوة، وبنود صلح الحديبية خير شاهد ودليل على هذا. وقد ذكر الشيخ المؤرخ إبراهيم بن عبيد آل عبدالمحسن في كتابه التاريخي" تذكرة أولي النهى والعرفان بأيام الله الواحد الديان " كتب معاهدات مع بريطانيا ظاهرها الرضا بالضيم فقال: سادساً : يتعهد ابن سعود كما تعهد آباؤه من قبل أن يتحاشى الاعتداء على أقطار الكويت والبحرين ومشائخ

200

قطر وسواحل عمان التي هي تحت حماية الحكومة البريطانية، ولها صلات عهدية مع الحكومة المذكورة، وأن لا يتدخل في شؤوفا وتخوم الأقطار الخاصة بهؤلاء ستعين فيما بعد. وجرى توقيعها في 18 صفر من هذه السنة الموافق 26 ديسمبر 1915، ولا ريب أن هذه الاتفاقية جائرة... وقد انتقدها الكتاب فقال عنها الضليع فؤاد حمزة لما أشرف عليها إنّها معاهدة جائرة. وقال عنها الماهر الذكي حافظ وهبة المشهور بحرية الفكر ورجاحة العقل واستقلال الرأي ما نصه: تجلى قصر نظر مستشاري ابن سعود بما يجري في العالم والاستفادة من الفرص ولكن يقال عنها إنّ الظروف والأحوال ذلك الوقت دعت إلى توقيعها. ولما خلى ابن سعود وصحبه الذين فيهم الشرف والدين والقوة غير أفم لا يعرفون لغة السياسة وأساليب الاستعمار ولا يصدقون بالظفر لغير الصارم البتار واستشارهم كعادته أجابوه بأننا في حال ضعف وخصمنا قوي جبار، فنراها تنفعنا بإذن الله في الحال ولا تضرنا إذا كنا في حالة منعة وقوة، ويمكن تعديلها فيما بعد، فالعبرة بالقوة في كل وقت وحال، فقم وتوكل على الله ووقعها، كما أنه أدرك بأنه لا يبيع ولا يتخلى ولا يرهن من نيته حسن الجوار، وتسهيل طرق الحجاج. فما أحسن نتائج هذه الآراء والأفكار، ولنا أسوة في صلح الحديبية، أضف إلى ذلك أنها ألغيت بعد سبع سنوات وعدلت

فيما بعد ذلك لما فتح الله له الحجاز واعترفت له بريطانيا بالاستقلال التام يفعل ما

يشاء ويحكم ما يريد. ا.هـ [1]

ج/ أنه لو قدر جدلاً أن الانضمام إلى هيئة الأمم المتحدة من الحكم بغير ما أنزل الله

لما كفرت الدولة السعودية بفعلها ؛ لأنه تقدم بيان أن الحكم بغير ما أنزل الله على

شناعته وكونه سبباً للضعف وتسلط الأعداء، إلا أنه لا يخرج من الملة، وبهذا كان

يفتي شيخنا عبدالعزيز بن باز والشيخ الألباني – رحمهما الله – كما تقدم.

تنبيه/ لو كان الانضمام إلى هيئة الأمم المتحدة من الحكم بغير ما أنزل الله لرأيت

علماءنا كالشيخ محمد بن إبراهيم والشيخ سعد ابن عتيق والشيخ عبدالعزيز ابن باز

والشيخ محمد العثيمين – رحمهم الله – أنكروه وبينوا حرمته، بل نص على جوازه

بعضهم فقد سئل الشيخ محمد بن صالح بن عثيمين: بعض الناس يقول إن الانضمام

إلى الأمم المتحدة تحاكم أيضاً إلى غير الله سبحانه وتعالى، فهل هذا صحيح ؟

فأجاب: هذا ليس بصحيح، فكل يحكم في بلده بما يقتضيه النظام عنده، فأهل

الإسلام يحتكمون إلى الكتاب والسنة، وغيرهم إلى قوانينهم، ولا تجبر الأمم المتحدة

أحداً أن يحكم بغير ما يحكم به في بلاده، وليس الانضمام إليها إلا من باب

---

[1]. (198/2).

202

المعاهدات التي تقع بين المسلمين والكفار ا.هـ[1]، بل واستمر هؤلاء العلماء الأجلاء

يرددون أن الدولة السعودية – حرسها الله – تحكم بما أنزل الله، وزكوها بهذا .

And as the majority of the member states are kuffār there are aspects which do not agree with the Divine Legislation and for that reason Saudi rejected some of the system and did not agree with all that is in it. Here, unto you are some of the agreements and treatises that the Saudi state, may Allāh protect it, did not accept:

1.   The Kingdom of Saudi Arabia did not agree with the agreement judging all forms of discrimination against women. Talāl Muhammad Nūh 'Atā stated: 'The Kingdom of Saudi Arabia preserved this agreement but did not adhere itself to what opposed the Divine Legislation of Islām.'

2.   The Kingdom of Saudi Arabia did not agree with article 16, which says that a man and a woman, when they reach the age of marriage, they have the right to marry without any religious conditions. Saudi Arabia stated in a memo sent to the United Nations 'The marriage of a Muslim male to a polytheist woman or to a woman who does not believe in the existence of Allāh is a matter that Islām has prohibited. Also, the marriage of a Muslim male to a woman of the book, being a Christian woman or a Jewish woman is a matter that Islām has allowed. As for the

---

[1] مجلة الدعوة – العدد 1608 – 10 جمادى الأولى 1418هـ - 11 سبتمبر 1997م.

marriage of a non-Muslim male to a Muslim female then this is impermissible.'[1]

3. 'The state of Tawheed' did not agree with article 10 of the Universal Declaration of Human Rights, which gives anyone the right to change their religion.[2]

4. The Kingdom of Saudi Arabia did not implement two state covenants, the first being particular to economic, social and cultural rights and the second being related to political and civic rights due to the contents of these covenants which do not conform with the Divine Legislation of Islām.[3]

So if this was the situation of the Saudi state with the UN, in that it does not accept those aspects of the system which contradict the Divine Legislation of Islām, by the admission of the leaders of this state (i.e. Saudi), may Allāh grant them success with His guidance of what is in it, and their application of the Divine Legislation practically and preserving

---

[1] *Mudhakirat ul-Hukūmah Saudiyyah ilā Munnadhmat il-Ummamil-Muhtahidah Hawla Tatbeeq Huqūq ul-Insān fi'l-Mamlakah 'Amalan bi'sh-Sharī'ah Islāmiyyah* [Memo of the Saudi Government to the United Nations Organisation About the Application of Human Rights in the Kingdom According to the Divine Legislation of Islām], *Majallah 'Arabiyyah*, no.1, p.182. Also see *Kitāb Mawqif Mamlakat il-'Arabiyyat is-Saudiyyah min al-Qadāyah al-'Ālamiyyah fī Hay'at il-Ummamil-Muhtahidah* [The Position of the Kingdom of Saudi Arabia in Regards to World Affairs in the United Nations Organisation], p.98.

[2] Ibid.

[3] *Kitāb Mawqif Mamlakat il-'Arabiyyat is-Saudiyyah min al-Qadāyah al-'Ālamiyyah fī Hay'at il-Ummamil-Muhtahidah* [The Position of the Kingdom of Saudi Arabia in Regards to World Affairs in the United Nations Organisation], p.98.

the Divine Legislation in face of the system and contradictory resolutions. If this is the condition of the Saudi state in its dealings with the UN, why then, O people of justice, is it abused and made takfeer of? Is it not from its right that it is thanked rather than made takfeer of due to its avoidance of resolutions, which oppose the Divine Legislation of Islām? Is it not from its right that it is supported and trusted due to its unique pride in, amongst all of the Islamic countries, the Divine Legislation of Islām and preserving it against whatever contradicts it?

[B] The benefit Depends on the entry of the Saudi State to this organisation
To protect itself from its kuffār enemies, or even rather, some Islamic countries which oppose the creed of the Salaf, to meet with disaster lay in wait for the state of Tawheed for many well-known reasons. From the clearest proofs of this is the first Gulf war wherein one state attacked another. What is oft repeated in the Divine Legislation is that circumstances of weakness are different from a state of strength. The treaty of Hudaybiyah is the best witness and proof for this. The historian, Shaykh Ibrāheem Bin 'Ubayd Āl 'AbdulMuhsin stated in his historical book *Tadhkiratu Awlī wa'n-Nahy wa'l-'Irfān bi-Ayām Allāh al-Wāhid ad-Dayān*:

'Sixthly: Ibn Saud made agreements just as his fathers did in order to keep away the enemies from the regions of Kuwait, Bahrayn, the Sheikhs of Qatar,[1] the coastal areas of 'Uman (Oman) which were under the rule of the British and had treaty relations with the aforementioned government. Also, the agreements were to neither interfere in the affairs of these countries nor to settle in those areas, the treaty was signed on (circa) 18 Safar 1334 AH corresponding to 16 December 1915 CE. There is no doubt that this type of agreement is allowed... and the well-versed historian Fu'ad Hamza[2] stated about it that the treaty was permitted. The adept intelligent memoriser who was gifted with fame for free thinking, composure of intellect and independent opinion stated: "The short-sightedness of the advisor of Ibn Sa'ud of what was taking place in the world was clear and he was merely taking advantage of the opportunities." However, it was said about the opportunity that the circumstances of the time necessitated a treaty to be signed...'[3]

[C] To assume, for arguements sake, that joining the UN was ruling by other than what Allāh has revealed.

The Saudi state still could not be made takfeer of by being in it, because, as has been explained, not ruling by what Allāh has revealed is due to

---

[1] The Ottoman Turks were driven out of these three regions in 1913 CE after Ibn Sa'ud finally defeated them at al-Ahsa. [TN]

[2] He is the author of *Qalb Jazeerat ul-'Arab* (Riyadh: Maktabat an-Nasr al-Hadeethah, 1968 CE). [TN]

[3] Vol.2, p.198

weakness and the reign of the enemy, so it does not expel from the religion, this is what our Shaykh 'Abdul'Azeez Bin Bāz and Shaykh al-Albānī ؄ judged as has preceded.[1]

ATTENTION: If joining the UN was ruling by other than what Allāh has revealed you would have seen our scholars such as Shaykh Muhammad ibn Ibrāheem, Shaykh Sa'd bin 'Ateeq, Shaykh 'Abdul'Azeez bin Bāz and Shaykh Muhammad ibn Sālih al-'Uthaymeen G reject it and clarify its prohibition. Rather, it is transmitted from some of them its permissibility (being part of the UN), Shaykh 'Uthaymeen was asked: 'Some people say that joining the UN is rule by other than Allāh, is this correct?'

He answered: 'This is not correct, as each one in his country rules by what is required of him. So the people of Islām rule by the Book (Qur'ān) and Sunnah and others rule by their laws. The UN does not force anyone to rule by other than what they rule by within their countries. Being in the UN is nothing other than from the aspect of treaties which take place between the Muslims and the kuffār.'[2]

---

[1] For these statements from Imāms al-Albānī and Bin Bāz refer to the complete translation of Shaykh Rayyis' book here: http://www.salafimanhaj.com/pdf/SalafiManhaj_TakfeerAndBombing.pdf
[2] *Majallat ud-Da'wah*, no.1608, dated: 10 Jumadā al-Ulā 1418 AH/September 11 1997 CE.

So rather, such scholars (which have just been mentioned above) constantly repeat that the Saudi state rules by what Allāh has revealed.

Faisal states:

"These scholars who have given their allegiance to the leaders it is harām for you to respect these scholars…"

Even though the scholars from the *Salaf* have all agreed upon obedience to the Muslim rulers! We will deal more with this in the last chapter, inshā'Allāh. Faisal states, in his pure ignorance and hatred of the people of Sunnah, an hour into the lecture:

"I suggest you don't embarrass yourself and promote the 'aqeedah of kufr dūna kufr…because when you promote this dodgy 'aqeedah and this is the 'aqeedah of the Salafis, may the curse of Allāh be upon them in this life and the hereafter, and anyone who promote {sic} the 'aqeedah of kufr dūna kufr this person is an enemy of Allāh, His Rasūl and al-Islām."

The issue of '*kufr dūna kufr*' has been dealt with by us earlier[1] and yet again we observe here that Faisal saves his most harsh criticisms for the *Salafis* saying "may the curse of Allāh be upon them in this life and the hereafter". Yet the

---

[1] For a detailed critique of Faisal and other new age *takfiri* activists in regards to their criticisms of the *tafseer* of 'Abdullāh ibn Abbās "kufr dūna kufr" refer to: http://www.salafimanhaj.com/pdf/SalafiManhaj_KufrDoonaKufr.pdf

people of Sunnah are not harmed by those who oppose them and thus his oppression will not yield any results, inshā'Allāh! He continues:

"The Jews love Judaism more than the Muslims love al-Islām, this is why they have a Jewish state and we don't have an Islamic state. The Jewish Rabbis are more sincere to their false religion more than our Islamic scholars who are not sincere to our religion...Islām is a religion without scholars..."

What more is there than this to indicate Faisal's *Khārijiyyah*? He praises the Jews and Christians for having scholars and then attacks the Muslims by claiming that the Muslims have no scholars whatsoever on the face of the earth! Twenty minutes before the end of the lecture, Faisal says:

"The fitna of our time is the Sharī'ah there is no Sharī'ah anyway and only the Tālibān is trying..."[1]

This is where we find one of Faisal's huge blunders, he said earlier:

"Even if they implemented the Sharī'ah still they'd be kāfirs because they give their allegiance, their bay'ah, their oath of allegiance, to the UN..."

---

[1] Over 56 minutes into another lecture entitled *'Islam Under Siege'* Faisal again praises the Tālibān for having "*implemented Sharī'ah*" and being a "*Sharī'ah state.*"

Yet even the Tālibān sent its envoy to the USA in December 1997 CE to meet *UNOCAL* there to discuss the proposed gas pipeline from Turkmenistan and Khazakhistan via Afghanistan! The Tālibān delegation included *Acting Minister for Mines and Industry* Ahmed Jan, *Acting Minister for Culture and Information* Amir Muttaqi, *Acting Minister for Planning* Din Muhammad, and appointed *'Taliban Permanent Delegate to the United Nations'*, Mujahid![1] The article states:

> Dec. 15, 1997 A Taliban delegation has visited Washington and was received by some State Department officials. The Talib *{sic}* delegation's meeting with U.S. Undersecretary of State for South Asia Karl Inderforth was arranged by the UNOCAL, which is eager to build a pipeline to pump gas from Turkmenistan to Pakistan via Afghan territory.

'We made our position clear, namely that the pipeline could be useful for Afghanistan's rehabilitation, but only if the situation was settled there by political means', a State Department official said on condition of anonymity. He stated that the Taliban representatives were told that they should form 'a broadly-based government together with their rivals before the ambitious project to build an oil and gas pipeline is launched'.

According to Taliban assessments, only one pipeline could yield almost $300 mm for rehabilitating the war-ravaged Afghanistan. **The Taliban delegation included Acting Minister for Mines and Industry Ahmed**

---

[1] http://www.gasandoil.com/goc/news/ntn80956.htm (Accessed Online on Wednesday 10 November 2010).

210

Jan, Acting Minister for Culture and Information Amir Muttaqi, Acting Minister for Planning Din Muhammad, and recently appointed Taliban Permanent Delegate on the United Nations Mujahid. A State Department official described the talks as "open and useful". He said that they also touched on the production of opium and open poppy on the Taliban-controlled territory, human rights, treatment of women, and on America's attitude to the projected pipeline. Asked whether there could be problems for the U.S. government if it backed the commercial investments into a country, which is ruled by Islamic fundamentalists, who, according to western standards, are oppressing women, the State Department official said that any real "political settlement" would resolve this problem.

In the meantime, Secretary of State, Madeleine Albright described the Talib government only a month ago as something quite disgusting due to its policy of oppressing women.

So did the Tāliban have allegiance to the UN which thus makes them kuffār too, according to Faisal? Indeed, this extremism and simplistic reasoning did even lead to some of the Khawārij of the era to make *takfeer* of the Tāliban and view their country as being *'Dār ul-Kufr'!* This was stated by the *mudallis* Omar Bakri Muhammad.[1] This is in fact the logical deduction of the ideas and thinking of the likes of ("el") Faisal. In March 2000 CE the Tāliban sent its

---

[1] *As-Sharq al-Awsat* newspaper, no.2, August 2001 CE.

roving representative (Syed Rahmatullah Hashemi) to meet with US officials to discuss issues related to oil and gas. Not to mention, what has been stated, regarding their taking training, weapons and other munitions from the CIA; but the *Salafis* do not rush to make *takfeer* of the Tālibān, and Faisal didn't due to his contradictory stances, but actually in keeping with his *khawārij manhaj* he should have also made *takfeer* of Afghānistān and the Tālibān for the same reasons that Omar Bakri Muhammad did.

Sample Lecture Number Ten: 'Rejecting The Taghut'

With this lecture Faisal attributes *kufr* even to his own audience (!) some 30 minutes into the lecture saying:

"Many of you your Shāhadah has gone even without you realising it"!!

Continuing with his mass *takfeer* of Muslims Faisal states around forty minutes into the lecture, in yet another statement that reveals his *khārijiyyah*:

"So today the Muslims are like the kāfirs of Quraysh…"

Sample Lecture Number Eleven: 'Treachery From Within'[1]

He states:

"The Saudi Salafis, they are your enemies, in fact they are your greatest enemies because they guise themselves, they hide themselves, in clothing of righteousness and piety with a beard and a white thowb, some of them speak Arabic, yet they use their knowledge of Arabic to cement the throne of the apostate leaders...these are the nine enemies who you have to fight in this world today."

Reflect on this enmity. Indeed some of the brothers of north-west London, who used to be with Faisal for about three years, then left him narrate to us that El-Faisal used to tell them to *"prepare themselves against the Salafis, as I have heard that they are coming"*. To which the blind followers of Faisal would arm themselves with Uzis, machetes and other weapons to use against Salafis! This is the so-called jihād of Faisal! Towards the end of the lecture, a couple of minutes passed the hour, Faisal states:

"To say 'the Rabbi Bin Bāz', that's more befitting."!!!

Indeed, this is the real treachery from within the ranks of the Muslims, from the *khawārij*!

---

[1] http://www.kalamullah.com/faisal.html

Sample Lecture Number Twelve: '40 Signs Of The Wicked Scholar'

This lecture is 1 hour and 35 minutes of attempting to discredit the senior scholars of the Sunnah, Imām Bin Bāz G in particular. The ruined ("el") Faisal Jamaykī states:

> **"Evil scholars do not take direct questions from the floor because they cannot afford to be exposed."**

Here then Faisal is again trying to hoodwink the audience against the scholars by making this foolish claim; and in any case it does not apply to the major scholars as they are all well-known for taking direct questions from the floor, so this is just another example of Faisal's scare-mongering. In continuing with his propaganda, Faisal says:

> **"They even have talks, speakers and conferences and then they plant a man in the crowd to ask them questions (such as) 'what do you think about so and so?' 'what do you think about this Shaykh and that Shaykh?' to use that opportunity to kill the character of that particular Shaykh, so they plant people in the crowd to ask them questions about certain personalities..."**

How does Faisal know this? Where are the examples of this? Faisal mentions this yet provides no evidence of this taking place whatsoever, its based on conjecture and evil suspicion. He continues with his nonsense after one hour and twenty minutes:

"There is absolutely no Salafi scholar who will teach you shirk al-Hākimiyyah and mention shirk al-Hākimiyyah, the shirk of a leader throwing the Qur'ān behind his back and govern the people with his evil and corrupted desires."

Again, we are forced to correct and expose the subtle deceptions of this man. If only he had been truthful and added the words in his sentence: "There is absolutely no Salafi scholar who will teach you shirk al-Hākimiyyah [as a fourth category]." In addition, to *"govern the people with evil and corrupted desires"* does not necessitate revolting, fighting or attempting to remove a leader. The Prophet ﷺ stated in a hadeeth, that Faisal never quotes in any of his lectures, in *Saheeh Muslim*[1] from Hudhayfah ibn al-Yamān ؓ wherein "he asked the Prophet ﷺ if there was any evil after this good and the Prophet responded saying *'Yes.'* Hudhayfah asked 'how can this be?' The Prophet ﷺ said *'There will be after me leaders who will neither be guided by my guidance nor follow my Sunnah and men will emerge from them who will have the hearts of devils in the bodies of men'.* Hudhayfah asked, 'What should be done if that happens?' The Prophet ﷺ said, *'Listen and obey the leader, even if he beats your back and takes your money, listen and obey!'"*

---

[1] Vol.3, p.1476.

Faisal continues just before the end of the lecture by saying:

"Anyone who says that Algeria is fitna because it is Muslims killing Muslims then he is passing fatwa to suit the UN, USA, France and is in the pocket of evil and kāfir governments…"

Firstly, irrespective of the reason, how can 'Muslims killing Muslims' not be a fitnah? Anyone who does not agree with his own *khawārij* views must therefore "be in the pocket of *kuffār* governments", and of course, this is false.

Sample Lecture Number Thirteen: 'Knowledge'

Faisal states seven minutes into this lecture:

"Your scholars have failed you miserably, they don't guide you to the straight path. Many of you did not even know that there is something called *Tawheed al-Hākimiyyah*…many of you don't know that there is something called *Shirk al-Hākimiyyah*."[1]

Here we see the pattern of Faisal yet again droning on about his infatuation with *al-Hākimiyyah*. In doing so, Faisal hopes to place himself in their stead so that people turn to him for guidance. 50 minutes into the lecture Faisal

---

[1] We have commented on Faisal's infatuation with this previously.

216

continues in his random *takfeer* of general Muslims and claiming to know what is in the hearts by stating:

"So the Muslims in this country (i.e. the UK), the majority of them, they have no īmān and no taqwā, the average Muslim you meet on the street he has no īmān and no taqwā..."

Faisal mentions, an hour and twelve minutes into this wretched lecture:

"Another quality of the student of knowledge is to abstain from arguing, do not argue with anyone, al-jidāl, do not dispute or argue with anyone, do not get yourself involved in too many debates...as for inviting someone to debate with you and then you show off this is not allowed as a student of knowledge."

Herein Faisal blatantly contradicts himself, as in the lecture *Let the Scholars Beware* he states:

"...and every time I challenge them to a debate they refuse..."

So Faisal himself is guilty of entering into "**too many debates**" based upon *bātil*, in *Jewish Traits in the Ummah* Faisal stated:

"...if I challenge you to a debate I become a kāfir. Likewise, if I challenge you, and the Salafis we have given them this challenge then they runaway and hide. If a Salafi should open his mouth and challenge saying "I'm going to have a debate, a public debate, in regards to

Tawheed al-Hākimiyyah" if he (i.e. the Salafi) throws that challenge out to you, that person becomes a kāfir! Are you convinced or you're not convinced?"

Faisal in fact is the most notable for his ridiculous debates, even debating with the likes of Abū Hamza and Abū Qatādah, with even both of them calling Faisal a Khārijī! As took place in Abū Hamza's refutation of Faisal[1] and with Abū Qatādah in the debate *Are the Salafis Muslims?* An hour and fifty minutes into the lecture Faisal states:

"Abū Qatādah is your Sheikh because I get my knowledge, some of it, from Abū Qatādah and I pass it on to you."

Enough said! Refer to Shaykh 'AbdulMālik ar-Ramadānī al-Jazā'irī's refutation.[2] Ten minutes before saying this Faisal stated:

"The reason why he (i.e. Abū Qatādah) did not make takfeer of the Salafis is because, I think, his knowledge of the Salafis is not very vast because when I played the tape when the Salafi said those who believe in jihād and do jihād are the brothers of the Shaytān he was taken aback. He didn't know that Salafis believe that those people who do jihād are the brothers of the Shaytān."

---

[1] See: http://www.scribd.com/doc/2402521/Beware-of-Takfir-Abu-Hamza-AlMisri
[2] http://www.salafimanhaj.com/pdf/SalafiManhajQatādah.pdf

Here Faisal makes another farcical allegation, the statement about those being *"brothers of the devils"* is related to those people who bomb innocent people *in the name of jihād*, not people who wage jihād (whether defensive or offensive) generally. So here Faisal tricks his audience with a archetypal Straw Man argument into thinking that the Salafis hold the sincere and real *mujāhideen* as being *"brothers of the Shaytān"* and dupes the audience into following this, when the reality is that the *fatwa* was regarding terrorists, unless Faisal supports the likes of the actions about which the *fatwa* was referring?

Sample Lecture Number Fourteen: 'Sacrifice'

He states 25 minutes into the lecture:

"In the Muslim world today most of our scholars are not prepared to sacrifice, they are not prepared to speak the truth and this is why we are in a pathetic state...Where are the sacrifices that are being made by the scholars of Islām? Where they {sic} are afraid of men instead of being afraid of Allāh."

Sample Lecture Number Fifteen: 'The Role Of The Masjid'

This lecture is merely another display of false accusations against the Salafis, he states after eighteen minutes into the lecture:

> "...and today noses are being broken in the mosque, on many occasions noses were broken in Brixton Mosque; if you go there and speak about King Fahd they give you a black eye."

We will see that Faisal repeats this allegation in some later lectures in order to create propaganda against the Salafis of Brixton Mosque.[1]

Sample Lecture Number Sixteen: 'What's your Aim, What's your Objective'[2]

In this lecture of agitation, Faisal states just two minutes before the end:

> "...Today Muslims are starving and we have Muslim governments who turn a blind eye to their starving brothers and sisters and send money to feed the monkeys in the London Zoo!"[3]

---

[1] Indeed, even according to the likes of Abū Hamza al-Misrī, Faisal only stated this as he himself got his nose broken! Refer to Abū Hamza's own words on page 68 here at this link: http://www.scribd.com/doc/2402521/Beware-of-Takfir-Abu-Hamza-AlMisri - however this is not trustworthy but it shows that even Faisal's own *takfiri* thinkers question this oft-repeated allegation of Faisal.

[2] www.clickislam.org

[3] Faisal then states in a quote, which owes more to communism and socialism: "**Wealthy Muslims who Allāh has blessed and this wealth is for all, for the ummah.**"

This is another unjust and transgressing statement, as the Saudi government for example is at the forefront of assisting needy Muslims around the world and this has to be acknowledged and admitted with no blame, shame or *kibr*.

We will now present clear examples of Muslim governments contributing to end hunger, starvation and famine in Muslim countries. So the questions to Faisal, his cult followers and other similar arm-chair activists are: When the Saudi Arabian people donated 200 million Saudi Riyals to the Muslims of Gaza in 2009,[1] and one Saudi businessman gave $6.7 million, was this *"turning a*

---

[1] According to Mohammed Al-Kinani reporting for the *Arab News* and *Saudi Gazette* on January 4 2009:

SR100 million and counting!

JEDDAH - King Abdullah, Custodian of the Two Holy Mosques, donated SR30 million to give the countrywide fund-raising campaign in aid of the Gaza Palestinians a strong boost at its launch on Saturday across Saudi Arabia. The 11-hour telethon that started on Saudi TV at 4 P.M. as part of the Custodian of the Two Holy Mosques' Campaign for the Relief of the Palestinian People in Gaza, raised SR94, 459,313 by midnight. The telethon opened with two pediatric societies contributing medical equipment worth SR250,000, and that set the pace with donations pouring in from callers immediately afterwards.

Some 150 participants talked to Saudi TV from the Grand Mosque in Makkah, the Prophet's Mosque in Madina, and Imam Turki Bin Abdullah Mosque in Riyadh, explaining the plight of the Gazans and condemning the poor international response to Israel's continuing bombardment of the territory. Jamal Al-Shoubaky, the Palestinian Ambassador to the Kingdom, said in his appeal: 'The whole world should immediately do something to stop this catastrophe - every single minute means more innocent bloods.' 'We need medical treatment and basic food supplies,' he said. The ambassador expressed gratitude for the donation campaign, called for by King Abdullah, Custodan of the Two Holy Mosques, noting that the King was moving politically to discuss with world leaders ways to stop the Israeli assault. King Abdullah has also issued urgent directives to airlift wounded Palestinians to Saudi

blind eye to their starving brothers and sisters"? When the Saudi government donated $2.6 million to Palestinians in Ramadān 2006 CE was this *"turning a blind eye to their starving brothers and sisters"?* When Saudi Arabia gave $500 million to help in the situation in Lebanon in 2006 CE, the Saudi government gave Lebanon $1 billion and the Saudi people via a telethon donated around $50 million to Lebanon. Was all of this *"turning a blind eye to their starving brothers and sisters"?* When the Saudi government gave $10 million dollars to poor countries in the Horn of Africa and East Africa, was this *"turning a blind eye to their starving brothers and sisters"?* When Saudi gave $2 million to help the poor within its own country was this *"turning a blind eye to their poor starving brothers and sisters"?*[1] When the Saudi government donated 45

---

hospitals. Al-Shoubaky said that what the Palestinians really need is an end to the Israeli attacks on innocent people in Gaza. Dr. Saleh Al-Wohaibi, general secretary for the World Assembly of Muslim Youth (WAMY), described the fund-raising campaign as humane. 'Even if those attacked were non-Muslims, we have to lend them a hand. It is truly a calamity against humanity,' said Al-Wohaibi. One businessman from the Eastern Province donated 30 ambulances of the year 2009 model.

Thousands of Saudi citizens and expatriates, men, women and children, gatherd at donation centers Kingdom-wide. All sports stadiums and Saudi TV centers in the country's 13 governorates would remain open round the clock to receive donations. Many international satellite TV channels have also contributed to the Custodian of the Two Holy Mosques' campaign to support the Gazans. 'All WAMY centers are open day and night to receive donations,' said WAMY assistant secretary general, Dr. Mohammed Badahdah. The collection process is closely monitored by committees of local authorities. Separate halls have been allocated for female donors. Many women gave, in addition to cash, their jewellery to help the Palestinians. In Dammam, the Sharqiya Chamber of Commerce and Industry held a separate internal fund-raiser for Gaza.

[1] According to P.K. Abdul Ghafour reporting for the *Arab News* on Sunday 8 January 2006 CE corresponding to 9 Dhu'l-Hijjah 1426 AH:

million Saudi Riyals[1] to help the Muslims in Chechnya and the Qatari people gave 8 million in a telethon in 1999 CE, was all this *"turning a blind eye to their starving brothers and sisters"*? When Saudi donated SR18 billion to the poor Muslims in Bosnia was this *"turning a blind eye to their starving brothers and sisters"*? According to the *Bosnian Muslims* themselves, and even non-Muslims, Saudi funded and financed schools, medical services, clinics, restored water supplies, financed the care of 7000 orphans, rebuilt *masājid* and houses etc. When Pakistan was hit by the earthquake, the Saudi people through a

---

King Donates SR2bn for Housing Poor

JEDDAH, 8 January 2006 — Custodian of the Two Holy Mosques, King Abdullah has donated SR2 billion for housing projects to provide decent housing for the Kingdom's poor and needy. According to a report in Asharq Al-Awsat, this was the largest single donation to a charity in the Kingdom's history. Yousuf Al-Othaimeen, secretary-general of the King Abdullah Charitable Housing Foundation, said the king had given land in Madinah worth SR2 billion to the foundation. He estimated the total area of the land at five million square meters. It is located between the Prophet's Mosque and the Madinah airport. 'This land will be administered as a source of income for the foundation's charitable projects,'Al-Othaimeen told the Arabic daily. 'Part of the land will be sold while the rest will be used for development projects,' he said. Al-Othaimeen said King Abdullah earlier gave 10,000 square meters of land in Riyadh for the foundation's permanent headquarters. 'King Abdullah bought the land for SR15 million specifically for that purpose,' he said. The foundation, which was established three years ago, has already constructed a large number of low-cost housing projects for the poor in various parts of the country. The housing units are provided along with other facilities including heath care and education. Al-Othaimeen said the foundation intended to establish 7,000 housing units in different parts of the Kingdom, which would benefit some 50,000 citizens. King Abdullah ordered a national strategy to fight poverty in the country after visiting a Riyadh slum three years ago when he was crown prince. He set aside SR2 billion from the budget surplus for a low-cost housing scheme.

[1] This is the equivalent to about £6 million, $12 million or 10 million Euros.

concerted telethon donated 450 million Saudi Riyals, was this *"turning a blind eye to their starving brothers and sisters"*?

Saudis donated 308 million Saudi Riyals to Tsunami hit areas, and in the same year they gathered 746 million Saudi Riyals for Palestinian families, is this *"turning a blind eye to their starving brothers and sisters"*? When the Saudi government donated $185 million in 1984 CE to help pay the cost of transporting food, drilling wells and installing water pumps in poor countries in Africa, was this *"turning a blind eye to their starving brothers and sisters"*? When Saudi also put up $30 million and $45 million in 1985 CE for food aid in Eritrea, Chad, Sudan and Somalia is this *"turning a blind eye to their starving brothers and sisters"*? When Saudi donated $135 from 1982-84 to the *International Fund for Agricultural Development (IFAD)*, and was the second largest donor after the USA, was this *"turning a blind eye to their starving brothers and sisters"*? As a result of all of this, 'Abdul'Azeez ar-Rukbān, the *World Food Programme's* former special ambassador stated:

> "The Kingdom of Saudi Arabia has donated billions of dollars bilaterally or multilaterally to relief and development projects over the last thirty years and the recent donations to the WFP are examples of its ongoing commitment to help humanity."

Abdul Wahab Bashir stated, reporting for the *Arab News* (dated: Friday 12 April 2002 CE/30 Muharram 1423 AH):

Saudi telethon raises SR210 million for Palestinians

JEDDAH, 12 April — Viewers from inside Saudi Arabia and abroad strongly responded to last night's national telethon for the Palestinian people giving millions of dollars in donations. The donations include gold, cars and even slingshots sent by Saudi children to help their Palestinian brethren fight Israeli occupation. By the time this paper went to press, an hour before the early morning deadline for the end of the telethon, the amount had reached SR210 million ($56 million). Throughout the telethon, the second since the start of the current Palestinian intifada 18 months ago, the 'Ulema on screen urged Saudis and expatriate workers to give generously to relieve the suffering of the Palestinian people. The viewers' response turned the courtyard of the television studios in Riyadh and Jeddah into a giant warehouse. Roads leading to the two TV stations were clogged with vehicles and entire families were seen heading toward the site to give their contributions. Four Indonesian Muslim maids on their way home to spend vacation with their families paid SR100 each to the authorities at King Khaled International Airport in Riyadh saying they wanted to join in the campaign to help the Palestinians. Westerners, too, joined in the campaign. A Briton from Dammam in eastern Saudi Arabia contributed cash and blamed the United States for what is happening in the occupied land and the suffering of the Palestinians. A Saudi businessman based in Jeddah said giving money is the least Saudis could do to help the

Palestinian. At the television stations the yards overflowed with goods of every kind from giant tin trunks bursting with heavy gold bangles and pearl necklaces to cars including ambulances, electrical appliances and dresses. One Saudi man offered to donate one kidney and to give blood 13 times to Palestinians in need of medical treatment. Another came up with a rare copy of the Holy Qur'ān, which he put for auction, and it fetched SR150 million soon after the start of the bidding. Custodian of the Two Holy Mosques, King Fahd, who donated SR10 million, had ordered the 11 hour telethon. Generous donations also came from Crown Prince Abdullāh, deputy premier and commander of the National Guard, and Prince Sultan, second deputy premier and minister of defence and aviation, and other members of the royal family. A unified bank account was set up for the event by the Saudi Committee for the Support of the Intifada headed by Interior Minister Prince Naif. The committee coordinates assistance to the Palestinians. The last telethon for Palestinians saw support pouring in from all over the world and by the end of the day SR40 million had been raised. The committee has urged Saudi citizens and expatriates to support the intifada and help provide food, medicines and clothes for the Palestinians and contribute to rebuilding homes and other infrastructure destroyed by the Israeli Army. It said it would continue to provide direct assistance to the families of Palestinian martyrs, the wounded and families suffering under the occupation. A spokesman for the committee called the station to say the committee will start sending 100 vehicles loaded with food, medicines and other relief material in addition to ambulances to the Palestinians through Jordan. 'The telethon reflects the solidarity the Saudis and expatriates in the Kingdom feel toward the Palestinian people. What is happening in Palestine stirs mixed feelings of pain and hope in Muslims. They feel pain and anger seeing the killings and destruction that the Palestinians continue to suffer and the conspiracies being directed against the Muslim identity and sanctuaries. But at the same time there is hope because this event is being launched from the land of the two holy mosques (in Makkah and Madinah) which is closely linked to the land of Al-Aqsa Mosque,' said Sheikh Abdul Rahman Al-Sudais, imam of the Grand Mosque in Makkah. He was referring to the ascension of Prophet Muhammad (PBUH) who was transported from the Sacred Mosque in Makkah to the Farthest (Al-Aqsa) Mosque of Jerusalem in one night and shown the Signs of Allāh."[1]

Mashā'Allāh! This was in 2002 CE! Is this *"turning a blind eye to their starving brothers and sisters"* as Faisal claims?? We should like to know what the likes of him are doing practically for the people, after his pompous accusations against the Salafis and their scholars?! In 2000 CE:

---

[1]

http://www.arabnews.com/?page=1&section=0&article=14239&d=12&m=4&y=2002

"The International Islamic Relief Organization has provided SR 2 million [U.S. $ 0.5 million] as a first installment to help the Palestinian people in their present ordeal. The organization's Secretary-General Dr. Adnan bin Khalil Basha called for the provision of all possible assistance, specifically $1,000 for the family of each martyr, $500 for the family of each injured person, $25,000 dollars to support each hospital in Al-Quds and the West Bank, $35,000 for the purchase of an ambulance for the Holy Mosque in Al-Quds, $100,000 to equip an emergency room in the mosque's clinic, and $70,000 to establish a fire-fighting center in the mosque. For those wishing to participate in this charitable work, an account has been set up in the Alrajhi Bank."[1]

Is this *"turning a blind eye to their starving brothers and sisters"* as Faisal claims?? Also during the bombing of Lebanon in 2006 by the Zionist state:

LEBANON: Arab nations more generous than Western counterparts:

So far Saudi Arabia is the Arab world's major donor to Lebanon. On Wednesday, Saudi Arabia's King Abdullāh ordered the transfer of US $1 billion to Lebanon's central bank, in an effort to consolidate the stability of the Lebanese pound. Although the Lebanese central bank had some US $14 billion of foreign reserves, pressure was mounting on the pound and there was increased demand for the US dollar. According to

---

[1] http://www.saudiembassy.net/2000News/News/ForDetail.asp?cIndex=2558

economists, the Saudis have been supporting the Lebanese currency since 1990.

The article continues:

A further donation of US $32 million was raised through a Saudi television appeal on Thursday. A similar telethon conducted on Friday in the United Arab Emirates (UAE) raised Dh49 million (US $13.5 million). The telethon was organised by Dubai Media Incorporated, the Sheikh Mohammed Bin Rashid Humanitarian and Charitable Foundation and the UAE Red Crescent Authority. UAE President Sheikh Khalifa bin Zayed al-Nahayan has ordered a US $20 million donation to provide medical and other aid supplies to the Lebanese people. A similar sum – US $20 million – has been promised by Kuwait's Emir Sheikh Sabah al Ahmed al Sabah to help secure the transportation of emergency aid to the Lebanese. Kuwait was among the first countries to help Lebanon since its current crisis with Israel started. In addition to official donations by Arab governments and NGOs, individuals throughout the Arab world have been contributing generously to assist the Lebanese people, according to local media reports.

The Qatari authorities, for example, have collected about US $ 3.9 million in donations towards that goal. Some US $250,000 has been wired to the Lebanese Red Cross by the Kuwait Red Crescent Society from private donations, according to its head, Berjas al-Berjas. Al-Berjas said a Kuwait plane carrying tonnes of first aid medicine will arrive in Damascus on Sunday en route to Beirut and that 290 electric power generators were sent to Lebanon from Kuwait on Wednesday. On the same day, a Jordanian military plane arrived in Beirut carrying humanitarian relief aid supplies, including tonnes of food and medical supplies. The figure of total donations by individuals in the Arab world is higher probably than that officially released as Muslims are discouraged from pupblicising acts of goodwill, including charitable donations. 'It is important to note that the figure that we see coming out of the Arab states may not necessarily reflect the totality of assistance since there is also a lot of discreet assistance which is provided by individuals or groups of individuals who are not concerned to have their generosity advertised as per the principle of giving in Islam,' said Freijsen."[1]

And according to Adel al-Malki reporting for the *Saudi Gazette* on Friday 28 July 2006 CE it is reported:

AID Lebanon Telethon Closes with SR108 Plus:

JEDDAH - Mohammed Zāl Al-Otaibi wanted to donate 100 she-camels to the people of Lebanon. Donation officials were happy with Otaibi's donation, but politely asked him to sell them off and then come back with the cash. Each she-camel can fetch anywhere from SR5000 to SR2

---

[1]Source:
http://www.irinnews.org/report.asp?ReportID=54880&SelectRegion=Middle_East&SelectCountry=LEBANON

million, depending on the breed of the she-camel. Likewise, some teenagers and men in their twenties went down to donation centers and handed over their car keys to donation officials, telling them they had no money, but they were sure the cars would fetch a pretty price. Officials again asked them for help and said "please sell them and come back with the money." Towards the early hours of Thursday morning, Saudi Television reported that the Kingdom had gathered more than SR108 million in donations from the public. The one day telethon to promote donations for Lebanon was kick-started by an extremely generous endowment announced by King Abdullāh Bin Abdul Aziz, Custodian of the Two Holy Mosques Tuesday, when the King pledged a $500 million grant for the reconstruction of Lebanon and $250 million for the reconstruction of Palestine.

King Abdullāh further promised a deposit of $1 billion to the Central Bank of Lebanon to aid the Arab tourism destination's ailing economy. The King, who came to Jeddah on Wednesday after visiting Baha earlier this week, donated another SR10 million upon his arrival on Wednesday. Crown Prince Sultan put forth another SR5 million and Minister of Interior Prince Naif Bin Abdul Aziz, chairman of the donation effort, presented another two million riyals. Other Saudi royals gave generously, but mostly said they preferred their names be withheld. Also on Wednesday, the King ordered the dispatch of a mobile hospital to Lebanon that will travel by road through Jordan and Syria to

Lebanon. Earlier on Wednesday, a Jordanian plane equipped with a mobile hospital managed to land at Beirut International Airport, after receiving clearance from the Israelis earlier in the morning to fly in. Women thronged centers with gold and silver jewelry. Children brought their toys, with one girl breaking open her piggy bank at a donation box to pour out all of her savings. One 13-year-old sold his moped to a friend on the spot and walked into a donation center and handed over the money. The donation campaign will last for the coming 15 days, with cash donations being accepted by Ahli Bank and 'giveaways' being processed by the Saudi Red Crescent at Jeddah Islamic Port. 'Giveaways' are sorted by the Saudi Red Crescent at its port warehouses, with jewelry being sold in public auctions, and medical supplies and the like being packaged ready for shipping to the war-torn country. Likewise for food supplies, and clothes and toys.

The telethon started Wednesday at 1 P.M. local time and ended with SR9.245 million in donations from the Saudi public and foreign residents living in the Kingdom in the first two hours. Saudi Fransi Chairman, Ibrahim Al-Touqi, gave the first donation in the amount of SR1 million. "This is the last 50 riyals in my pocket," one man, who identified himself with his initials told the television presenter, as he pledged the money for donation on Wednesday. "I do not even have a car, but I do not believe that I cannot give this money to the Lebanese people," he added. Shar Al-Shihri said he had donated his IPO money instead of subscribing with it on Wednesday. "I came over to the ATM machine and saw the announcement for donations. Instead of subscribing to the King Abdullāh Economic City IPO, I donated the money," Shihri told The Saudi Gazette, as he left a bank branch in Al-Nuzha district. "The pictures of all those Lebanese children say it all," he added. This is the 10th telethon to generate donations from the public for a grief stricken country.

When Pakistan was hit by an earth shattering earthquake earlier this year, the public in Saudi Arabia donated over SR450 million in cash and assets. Saudis donated SR308 million to Tsunami-hit Indonesians at the end of 2004, while they gathered SR746 million in other donations for Palestinian families that same year. The Kingdom's chief Islamic cleric, Grand Mufti Sheikh Abdul Aziz Bin Abdul Rahman Āl Al-Sheikh gave a passionate plea for donations, urging the public to look deep in their hearts and give. Abdul Rauf Rajab, a spokesman for the Organization of the Islamic Conference, said the Lebanese government had given the OIC a list of items much needed by the country's war-stricken population that mostly included medical supplies and provisions needed to care for children. 'The UN will be getting in supplies through Al-Reeda corridor,'he said. The World Health Organization is asking for $32.4 million, on behalf of the partners working on health issues like UNICEF, UNFPA and UNRWA to serve the medical needs of 800,000 people over the next three months. According to the UN this appeal is part of the total United Nations' Flash Appeal for Lebanon, which seeks a total of $150 million. Some 1,200 people have been injured and 346 killed. Several hundred thousand Lebanese have fled their homes, some to neighboring Syria."

Is all this, *"turning a blind eye to their starving brothers and sisters"* as Faisal claims?? Then let's turn to:

Saudi Arabia to finance new Palestinian homes in Hebron:

The Saudi Committee for the Relief of the Palestinian People has said it will finance the construction of 100 housing units in the West Bank city of Hebron at cost of US$ 6.3 million. The project, to be undertaken in cooperation with UN-HABITAT, was approved on the instructions of His Majesty King Abdullāh Bin Abdul Aziz Al Saud, and Prince Naif Bin Abdul Aziz Al Saud, Minister of Interior and General Supervisor of the Saudi Committee for the Relief of the Palestinian People. Officials said the new homes would be allocated to underprivileged or widowed women. The Chairman of the Saudi Committee for the Relief of the Palestinian People, Mr. Said Al Orabi Al-Harthi, who also serves as Advisor to the Minister of Interior, said the idea was to improve the living conditions of widowed women and their families. The project would be implemented, during a period of 24 months, through the Special Human Settlements Programme of UN-HABITAT and in cooperation with the Ministry of Labour and Social Affairs, and the Ministry of Public Works and Housing of the Palestinian National

Authority and local NGOs. He cited the Kingdom of Saudi Arabia's deep commitment to mitigate the suffering of the Palestinian people and help meet their essential needs. To date, he added, it had financed more than 36 relief and humanitarian programmes in the Palestinian territories in cooperation with a number of international organizations. UN-HABITAT and the Saudi Committee for the Relief of the Palestinian People will soon sign a Memorandum of Understanding to commence the implementation of the project."[1]

Is this *"turning a blind eye to their starving brothers and sisters"* as Faisal asserts? How about:

Saudi Committee for the Relief of Palestinian People donates $3 million to Palestinian children:

JERUSALEM / RIYADH, SEPT 6, 2005 - The Saudi Committee for the Relief of Palestinian People is giving US$3.6 million to the United Nations Children's Fund (UNICEF) towards critical projects supporting children in the Occupied Palestinian Territory (OPT). The contribution is part of a new strategic framework with UNICEF for assistance to children in OPT. It emerged from meetings this spring between representatives from UNICEF's Gulf Area Office and OPT and senior officials from the Saudi Ministry of the Interior. The fresh funding will focus on assistance in education and health for the new generation of

---

[1] http://www.unhabitat.org/content.asp?cid=3739&catid=7&typeid=6&subMenuId=0

Palestinian adolescents. 'UNICEF and the Saudi Committee for the Relief of Palestinian People come together at this critical time when assistance in the West Bank and the Gaza Strip are more important than ever following disengagement,' said Dan Rohrmann, the UNICEF Special Representative in OPT. 'There are immense challenges but also immense opportunities in terms of improving the lives of children. It is heartening to see the Saudi Committee providing such a major boost.' June Kunugi, UNICEF Representative for the Gulf countries, said: 'This generous contribution is a landmark agreement and we thank the Custodian of the Two Holy Mosques King Abdullāh bin Abdul Aziz, the Kingdom of Saudi Arabia, and its people for partnering with UNICEF to safeguard the well-being and rights of children, in this instance in the occupied Palestinian territories.' The Saudi Committee for the Relief of Palestinian People was established in 2000, and has since donated some US$200 million to projects in OPT. The Committee has provided cash and in-kind assistance in addition to funding educational and medical activities as well as reconstruction schemes."[1]

Is this *"turning a blind eye to their starving brothers and sisters"* as Faisal, the arm-chair activist, claims? In 1996 CE:

Saudi Arabia launches fund-raising week for Bosnia:

---

[1] http://www.reliefweb.int/rw/rwb.nsf/db900SID/HMYT-6FYL76?OpenDocument

The Kingdom of Saudi Arabia today launched a week-long fund-raising campaign to help rebuild the war-ravaged Republic of Bosnia-Herzegovina. This is the third such 'Bosnia Week', and is in line with the directives of HRH Prince Salman Bin Abdul Aziz, Governor of Riyadh Province and head of the Supreme Commission for Collection of Donations for Bosnian Muslims. Two-thirds of all that is collected by the Commission is remitted directly to the Bosnian government either in a dedicated bank account, or through the Bosnian Embassy in Riyadh, or to President Izetbegovic by a delegation visiting Bosnia. One-third of the donations are used to purchase relief aid or extend monetary assistance to individuals in need, as well as to secure health care, restore gas supplies, and repatriate displaced persons.

Seventeen shiploads of food, clothes, vehicles and other supplies have been sent to the Commission's office in Bosnia, which distributes aid to Muslims in Bosnian towns through eight affiliated centers. In addition, the Commission distributes religious books and organizes seminars and training courses, including Qur'ān memorization. The media is asked to highlight the need in Bosnia for rebuilding mosques as well as factories and agricultural centers. In appealing to all Muslims to contribute to the fund-raising, the Commission praises the generosity of the Saudi people and of Custodian of the Two Holy Mosques King Fahd Bin Abdul Aziz."[1]

---

[1] http://www.saudiembassy.net/1996News/News/ForDetail.asp?cIndex=4213

Saudi even donated money (some accounts say $250 million) to help poor non-Muslims, mostly African-Americans, who had been left out in the cold and left to drown by their own government, during Hurricane Katrina! Anyone would have thought that it was a poor African country, the way the people were struggling there, and there is no doubt that racism on the part of the government of the day played a role in their treatment. So what have Faisal and his blind followers given to the *ummah*, except for *fitna*, falsehood, controversy and those who justify killing and attacking innocent people and civilians in the name of jihād? In August/September 2010, out of the top ten donors to the flood victims of Pakistan, there existed only one Muslim country in this list and their donations are purely uncommitted pledges – Saudi Arabia:

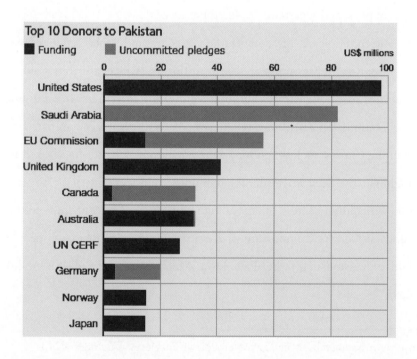

The *Arab News* newspaper reported on August 20 2010:

"JEDDAH: Second Deputy Premier and Interior Minister Prince Naif, who is also the supervisor general of the King Abdullāh Campaign for Pakistan, expressed his pleasure at the king's donation of SR300 million on behalf of the people of Saudi Arabia.

"In truth the policy of King Abdullāh to offer instant relief to the victims of calamities anywhere in the world has put the Kingdom in the forefront of nations that offer assistance and relief to victims of afflictions. It has also made the Kingdom eligible for the title 'the Humanitarian Kingdom," Prince Naif said.

Prince Naif also called on all people in the Kingdom to make the campaign a huge success, in a statement quoted by the Saudi Press Agency on Friday. The Kingdom launched a nationwide fundraising campaign on Monday for Pakistan's flood victims, on the instructions of the king. The king inaugurated the campaign by giving SR20 million while Crown Prince Sultan, deputy premier and minister of defence and aviation, donated SR10 million and Prince Naif SR5 million to the fund.[1]

---

[1] http://arabnews.com/saudiarabia/article108061.ece - accesse 29 August 2010

The *Arab News* newspaper also reported on 28 August 2010, in an article entitled *"SR810,000 raised for pak flood aid"*:

RIYADH: Pakistani expatriates in Riyadh donated SR810,000 to flood victims at a fund-raising campaign organized by the country's mission in Riyadh on Thursday.

The Pakistan Embassy organized the event in cooperation with a group of volunteers, who were instrumental in making a large gathering of more than 500 philanthropists. One expatriate donated SR50,000 toward the fund. Thanking all Pakistanis who were present on the occasion, Pakistan Ambassador Umar Khan Alisherzai told his countrymen that their motherland was faced with the calamity of unprecedented scale and nature and it was the paramount duty of all Pakistanis to do their part in sharing the burden of the people and the government of Pakistan. He said he was very happy to see people rising above their political and other affiliations for a noble cause of extending help to their fellow citizens who were desperately looking forward to their assistance.

The ambassador also thanked all the countries that had extended help. He made a special mention of Saudi Arabia, which proved that it was a true friend of Pakistan and its people. He thanked the Custodian of the Two Holy Mosques, King Abdullāh, for ordering to form an air bridge of relief supplies between Riyadh and Islamabad. He also thanked the government and the people of the United States, the European Union,

UK, France, Germany, Japan, China, Turkey, Kuwait, Qatar, UAE and all those who had contributed in several ways to help the distressed people. Zahoor Hasan Gilani, community welfare attaché, made a presentation on the flood situation in Arabic for the benefit of the Saudi guests. The Deputy Head of the mission, Ayaz Mohammad Khan, made a multimedia presentation on the current status of the disaster and the international help that Pakistan has received so far.[1]

The *Arab News* newspaper reported on 28 August 2010:

JEDDAH: Saudi Arabia will distribute 1,000 truckloads of relief supplies to Pakistan flood victims beginning Monday, an official statement said.

The relief is being arranged on the directives of Custodian of the Two Holy Mosques, King Abdullāh, it said, adding that Second Deputy Premier and Minister of Interior, Prince Naif, would supervise the program. During the two month long relief program, trucks will carry foodstuffs such as rice, flour, cooking oil and milk, beans and lentils, the statement added. In the first phase, 80 trucks will go to the flood-affected areas of Punjab and Kashmir. About 8,000 families in Punjab will receive 160 tons of flour, 40 tons of rice, 40 tons of lentils, 16 tons of milk and 40,000 litres of cooking oil.

---

[1] http://arabnews.com/saudiarabia/article116286.ece - accessed 29 August 2010

241

Around 12,000 families in Kashmir will get 240 tons of flour, 60 tons of rice, 24 tons of lentils, 24 tons of beans, 25 tons of milk and 60,000 litres of cooking oil. King Abdullāh had earlier ordered a nationwide fundraising campaign to support Pakistan's flood victims, which raised more than SR400 million. On Saturday, eight Saudi planes arrived in Islamabad carrying medical equipment for a field hospital.

The floods are Pakistan's worst-ever natural disaster in terms of the amount of damage and the number of people affected, with more than six million people forced from their homes, about a million of them in the last few days as the water flows south. The disaster has killed about 1,600 people, inflicted billions of dollars in damage to homes, infrastructure and the vital agriculture sector.[1]

Sa'eed Shah stated, reporting for *The Guardian*, on Wednesday 18 August 2010:

Saudi Arabia has overtaken the US as the largest donor to Pakistan's flood relief effort, following criticism that Muslim countries were not giving enough for victims of the disaster. The oil-rich country is to give $105m (£67m) in aid, according to Pakistan's National Disaster Management Authority, though just $5m of this is in cash, with the rest in the form of relief goods. The Saudi public has separately raised $19m.

---

[1] http://arabnews.com/saudiarabia/article117623.ece - accessed 29 August 2010

The pledge was made as a spurt of other money came in for the still sluggish fundraising drive. The European Union increased its contribution, by €30m (£24m) to €70m, and the UN said that its appeal was now half funded. The flooding is still inundating new areas, with two or more weeks of the monsoon season yet to run, whilst the threat of disease means the crisis could grow much worse. A second wave of flooding has hit new areas of the southern provinces of Sindh and Balochistan.

In Britain, the Disasters Emergency Committee expressed "grave concern" today that cholera cases had been confirmed. Until now, the US had been the leading contributor towards relief efforts, and its generosity was seen as a way for Washington to improve its image in Pakistan. Muslim countries, meanwhile, had been slow to give and may have been 'stung' into donating by criticism in the Pakistani media. Saudi Arabia has strong links with Pakistan, with many Saudi charities promoting its brand of conservative Islam in the country for decades, including the funding of religious seminaries often accused of promoting Islamist extremism. The US is giving $76m in cash but says its contribution is worth $87m, including aid-in-kind. In addition, the US has 19 helicopters operating in northern Pakistan, ferrying supplies and people.

Last week, Richard Holbrooke, the US special representative for Afghanistan and Pakistan, said: 'The people of Pakistan will see that when the crisis hits, it's not the Chinese. It's not the Iranians. It's not other countries. It's not the EU. It's the US that always leads.' In total $466m has been pledged in aid so far, including contributions to the UN and non-governmental organisations. An appeal by the Pakistani prime minister, Yousaf Raza Gillani, attracted less than £1m at the start of this week. Today, the cricketer turned politician, Imran Khan, launched a challenge to the government by starting his own flood appeal, saying the Pakistani public did not trust giving to the state.

Britain is giving £31m, said the international development secretary, Andrew Mitchell, who was today visiting flood-hit areas in Pakistan. 'The people of Pakistan need help and they need it now,' said Mitchell. 'It is difficult to comprehend the extent of this tragedy. Nothing could have prepared me for the horrific scenes of destruction and devastation I have seen today. But the worst could still be to come.' According to Oxfam, within the first 10 days after the Haitian earthquake, donors had committed $742m and pledged a further $920m. For Pakistan, the figures over the same period were $45m and $91m. The money already donated is for the immediate relief of the 20 million people affected by flooding. A vast area slicing through the middle of Pakistan, running from the mountains of the north to the desert areas of Sindh province in the south, has been affected. It is estimated that billions of dollars will be needed to rehabilitate the ravaged areas, rebuilding infrastructure and the economy. The UN appealed last week for $460m to cover the first 90 days of the emergency. It said today that half the target had been reached, but warned that it was able to reach less than a quarter of the 6 million people in urgent need for food and clean drinking water. The cost of providing clean water alone is about $2m a day.[1]

The Arab News also reported on 16 August 2010:

JEDDAH: Saudi Arabia launched a nationwide fundraising campaign on Monday for Pakistan's flood victims, on the instructions of Custodian of the Two Holy Mosques King Abdullāh, Second Deputy Premier and Minister of Interior Prince Naif said.
King Abdullāh inaugurated the campaign by giving SR20 million while Crown Prince Sultan, deputy premier and Minister of Defence and aviation, donated SR10 million and Second Deputy Premier and Minister of Interior, Prince Naif, SR5 million to the fund. 'We have instructed all regional governors to set up subsidiary committees to collect donations and encourage businessmen and other citizens to participate actively in the campaign, which is named after King Abdullāh,' Prince Naif told the Saudi Press Agency.

---

[1] http://www.guardian.co.uk/world/2010/aug/18/pakistan-floods-saudi-arabia-pledges - accessed 29 August 2010

He said potential donors could deposit their money in account No. SA8710000020162400000107 at National Commercial Bank or transfer their money using NCB's telebanking service or ATMs or Al-Ahli online service. In response to the king's call, Tabuk Gov. Prince Fahd bin Sultan identified locations in the region to collect donations. They include the headquarters of the King Abdul Aziz Charitable Society and Prince Fahd bin Sultan Social Program. The governor also set up a committee to organize the fundraising.

Saudi Arabia has already sent 16 planeloads of relief supplies to Pakistan after the country was hit by the worst floods in its history. On Sunday, the 15th and 16th cargo flights arrived in Pakistani airports with Saudi supplies. Saudi Finance Ministry officials Abdullāh Al-Muhaisen, Abdul Aziz Al-Fayad and Abdullāh Al-Dossary handed over the relief supplies to Pakistani authorities. The Saudi Embassy in Islamabad is supervising the distribution of Saudi aid among the victims. The Kingdom has pledged $100 million relief for Pakistan. 'We are coordinating with UN agencies to distribute the humanitarian and emergency relief supplies,' an official statement said.

UN Secretary-General Ban Ki-moon, who surveyed the devastation caused by the torrential floods on Sunday, said he had never seen anything like it in his life. He urged foreign donors to speed up assistance to the 20 million people affected. The floods that began more than two weeks ago in Pakistan's mountainous northwest have now affected about a quarter of the country, especially its agricultural heartland. While the death toll of 1,500 is relatively small, the scale of the flooding and number of people whose lives have been disrupted is staggering.

The United Nations has appealed for an initial $460 million to provide relief, but only 20 percent has been given. Once the floods recede, billions more will be needed for reconstruction and getting people back to work.[1]

It seems that Faisal and facts are not very compatible! Which suitably leads us onto the next horrifying lecture:

Sample Lecture Number Seventeen: 'The Devil's Deception Of The 20th Century House Niggers'

The title itself is sufficient to cause hazard signs. This appalling lecture establishes ("El") Faisal's wrath, enmity and kindling of tribulation amongst Muslims; naming this lecture with a term of expression which in no way applies to those whom he aims to condemn at all. Furthermore, Faisal states that he only named this lecture as such based on what "some people told him" demonstrating that Faisal was more concerned in following the desires of his ignorant followers and pandering to them for credibility, even if it is devoid of

---

[1] http://arabnews.com/saudiarabia/article104110.ece - accessed 29 August 2010

247

Islamic *adab* and *akhlāq*. This lecture also shows Faisal's frustration with the Salafī da'wah, which - as he cannot rebut with concise proofs presented academically - leads him to resort to a simplistic attack that is immediately noticeable when one listens. What is immediately noticeable in this lecture is that Faisal totally mimmicks Abū Usāmah's format of refuting 'Umar 'AbdurRahmān! Faisal plays the lecture and stops it in the exact same way as Abū Usāmah does. Nine minutes into the lecture he states:

"These house niggers they break noses of people in different mosques, especially in Brixton Mosque, to protect the so-called honour of King Fahd and the other apostate leaders."

We will not assess this allegation here, which he previously stated in the lecture *The Role of the Masjid*, and regurgitates it twice in this lecture, we will assess it later *inshā'Allāh*. Just twenty minutes into the lecture Faisal states, in another clear indication of his attempting to generate the ideology of *takfeer* and revolt amongst the common Muslims:

"When Ibn Katheer was explaining in his tafseer in Mā'idah 50, he said "it is the ijmā' of all the Muslims" he didn't say the ijmā' of the scholars, he said "Muslims" even the layman on the street knows that this person is a kāfir, that if you don't judge by what Allāh revealed you're a kāfir."

248

Again look at the falsehood of Faisal, when the scholars mention *ijmā'* of course they are referring to the scholars and not the lay people such as the barber, the road-sweeper, the housewife or the dress-maker!! Faisal is merely trying to make *takfeer* to be an easy matter to carry out. For the 'Ulama of Usūl note that the majority view is that *ijmā'* refers to the concensus of the Mujtahid scholars not the "ijmā'", if it can even be called that, of the "layman on the street". Al-'Allāmah Muhammad Ameen ash-Shinqītī stated in *Mudhakkirat Usūl ul-Fiqh 'ala Rawdat un-Nādhir*:

ولا خلاف في اعتبار علماء العصر من أهل الاجتهاد في الإجماع، وأنه لا يعتد فيه بقول الصبيان والمجانين، وأما العوام فلا يعتبر قولهم عند الأكثرين، وقال قوم: يعتبر قولهم لدخولهم في اسم المؤمنين ولفظ الأمة، وهذا القول يقتضي إبطال الإجماع، إذ يستحيل معرفة أقوال الأمة جميعها في مسألة واحدة، والحق أن العوام لا عبرة بهم لجهلهم.

There is no difference of opinion over consideration being given to the Mujtahid scholars of the time in regards to ijmā'. Ijmā does not include the view of the child or insane person, as for the lay people then according to most of the scholars their views are not considered. Some people have said: 'the views of the common people are taken into consideration as they are included under the general title of 'believers' and under the wording of 'Ummah''. This view necessitates annulment of the ijmā' (of the Mujtahid scholars mentioned prior). Yet it is impossible to know the views of the entire Ummah in regards to one matter, and the truth of the matter is that the common lay people are not taken into consideration in regards to the ijmā' due to their ignorance.[1]

Shaykh, Dr 'AbdulKareem bin 'Ali bin Muhammad an-Namlah (Professor in the Usūl ul-Fiqh Department, Sharī'ah College, Imām Muhammad bin Saud Islamic University) states in *Ithāf Dhawī al-Basā'ir bi Sharh Rawdat un-Nādhir fī Usūl il-Fiqh 'alā Madhhab al-Imām Ahmad bin Hanbal*, which is another explanation of Ibn Qudāmah's *Rawdah*:

The first proof, of the proofs for not taking common people into consideration when reaching a consensus, is the analaogy of a common person with a child. The 'Ulama have agreed that the child's view is not believed in regards to reaching a consensus and likewise is the case for a common person, there is no difference between the two. The link between the two is: because a consensus is based on ijtihaad and firm support on inference and neither the child nor common person possess the necessary tools to fulfil that: nadhr (investigation) and istidlāl (inference). A common person is deficient in terms of his legal suitability and capacity to finding the truth so how can he be equal to one who has

---

[1] Al-'Allāmah Shaykh Muhammad al-Ameen ash-Shinqītī, *Mudhakkirat Usūl ul-Fiqh 'ala Rawdat un-Nādhir li-Imām Ibn Qudāmah al-Hanbali* (al-Mansūrah, Egypt: Dār ul-Yaqeen, 1419 AH/1999 CE, ed. Abū Hafs bin al-'Arabī), pp.271-272.

the required legal suitability in this field, the Mujtahids?! This cannot be the case.[1]

This is oft-repeated in Usūl and is well known among the scholars so what exactly did Faisal study when he was at Imam Muhammad bin Saud Islamic University? Moreover, this is taken from an explanation of a Hanbalī work on Usūl authored by Imām Ibn Qudāmah al-Maqdisi

, and Faisal claims to follow the Hanbali madhhab! Imām Ibn 'Āsim al-Ghranātī al-Mālikī stated in *Murtaqā al-Wusūl ilā 'Ilm il-Usūl*:

> *"The non-judge is not taken into consideration, in any consensus of the*
> *common people,*
> *Every scholar who is able to investiage, then the consensus of these people is*
> *considered."*

The explainer of the book, Dr Fakhruddeen bin Zubayr bin 'Ali al-Mahsī, says in regards to the above lines of poetry:

Is it a condition to take common people into consideration for Ijmā'? The composer of the poem mentioned that most of the 'Ulama do not make this condition because Ijmā' is only via the agreement of the Mujtahid scholars of the Ummah.

---

[1] Dr 'AbdulKareem bin 'Ali bin Muhammad an-Namlah (Professor, Sharī'ah College, Department of Usūl ul-Fiqh, Imām Muhammad bin Saud Islamic University, Riyadh), *It-hāf Dhawi'l-Basā'ir bi'sh-Sharh Rawdat an-Nādhir fī Usūl il-Fiqh 'ala Madhhab al-Imām Ahmad bin Hanbal* (Riyadh, KSA: Maktabat ar-Rushd, 1428AH/2007 CE), vol.2, pp.1179-1180.

Then Dr Fakhruddeen bin Zubayr bin 'Ali al-Mahsī states:

The correct view in this issue is the view of the majority in that the views of the Mujtahids is a proof on account of them firmly supporting this on evidence and the common people are not equipped to perform these inferences, hence the view of the common people is not taken into consideration. As for common and apparent issues then they follow Mujtahids.[1]

Faisal then states:

> **"...he is seeking to please his kāfir paymaster..."**

So the question has to be asked: what about Faisal himself who in the 'question and answer session' of the lecture *Challenges Facing the Youth* stated that it is permissible to take welfare state benefits and government hand-outs?! Is this not also receiving "pay from kuffār paymasters"? Indeed it is, in its most debased, dishonourable and subjugated form!

As for Faisal claiming that the refutation on 'Umar 'AbdurRahmān was to *"draw the attention of kuffār intelligence services to him"* then this is another simplistic analogy and *reductio ad absurdum* from Faisal. Just because one

---

[1] Dr Fakhruddeen bin Zubayr bin 'Ali al-Mahsī, *Sharh Nudhm Murtaqā al-Wusūl ilā 'Ilm il-Usūl li-Imām Ibn 'Āsim al-Ghranātī al-Mālikī (d. 829 AH).* 'Ammān, Jordan: Dār ul-Athariyyah, 1428 AH/2007 CE, pp.639-640. Introduction by Shaykh Mashhūr bin Hasan Āl Salmān.

doesn't agree with the extremist, erroneous, incorrect, false and nonsensical beliefs of 'Umar 'AbdurRahmān and those other Takfīrīs this is no way implies that *"this means they are working for kuffār intelligence services"!* This is another one of Faisal's ways of not allowing any criticism of extremists. With regards to Faisal's praise of 'Umar 'AbdurRahmān, it has to be said that Faisal has never even met 'Umar 'AbdurRahmān! Yet he refers to him as being "his Sheikh". Then Faisal states just thirty minutes into the lecture that soldiers in the Egyptian army are *kuffār* and says regarding what Abū Usāmah said:

"...err...what you have just heard is a statement of kufr and some of you detected it and some of you did not detect it, unfortunately...this statement is kufr and if you believe it,[1] it takes you out of the fold of al-Islām."!!

Faisal's initial proof is that he uses what takes place in the UK, in the form of pledging allegiance, and then tries to make an analogy between that and what takes place in a Muslim country. So Faisal compares what non-Muslims do within their procedures to Muslims! This is the typical Khawārij methodology. Then Faisal states:

"The ayah is self-explanatory you don't even need a tafseer for the ayah, but for your convenience I will elaborate..."

---

[1] i.e. that soldiers in the armies of Muslims countries are merely working to feed their families and support themselves!

Observe this: placing himself forward as one who is completely capable of giving *tafseer*, whereas classical *tafāseer* don't even get a mention! Then he says:

"So these tyrannical leaders which we have in our midsts today who have given their allegiance to the UN or the USA or the UK or all the other Dajjāl forces on the face of the earth they are kāfirs and I will explain it later why they are kāfirs. So the soldiers of these leaders are also kāfirs..."

Ibn Taymiyyah stated:

The khawārij are the most apparent of the people of innovation and fighting against the rulers.[1]

See how Faisal makes unequivocal and unrestricted *takfeer* of all of the Muslim countries, Abu'l-Hasan al-'Ash'arī mentioned in *Maqalāt al-Islāmiyyeen* the view of the Khawārij, from the *al-Azāriqah* and *Safariyyah*, that:

They claim the abode, the abode contrary to theirs, is an abode of Tawheed <u>except for the soldiers of the Sultan for indeed it is a state of disbelief</u>.[2]

---

[1] *Majmū' al-Fatāwā*, vol.7, p.217
[2] *Maqālāt al-Islamiyyeen*, p.104

As for his support of the Tālibān regime, then we have discussed this earlier when assessing his lecture *'Let the Scholars Beware'* (no.9 in this study). Faisal then proceeded to note that Egyptians soldiers participate in crimes and transgressions, but again this does not necessitate *takfeer* of them, which Faisal insinuates. Faisal says:

"They kill the men because they are fighting for Sharī'ah, so if a solider kill you {sic} because you're fighting for Sharī'ah how can you pronounce him…err err…{sic} a Muslim?"

Here Faisal stutters as if he is not sure as to what he is saying and how does Faisal know that individuals are *"fighting for the Sharī'ah"* when Faisal doesn't even know them! Then Faisal makes a huge blunder that we observed, he says:

"Those who hate what Allāh has revealed they are kāfirs, Soorah Muhammad verse twenty-five."

And Faisal says it quickly so that the listener almost does not hear it fully. In fact it is in ayah 26 not 25. Even then, the ayah does not say "those who hate what Allāh has revealed they are kāfirs" it actually says:

﴿ إِنَّ ٱلَّذِينَ ٱرْتَدُّواْ عَلَىٰ أَدْبَٰرِهِم مِّنۢ بَعْدِ مَا تَبَيَّنَ لَهُمُ ٱلْهُدَى ٱلشَّيْطَٰنُ سَوَّلَ لَهُمْ وَأَمْلَىٰ لَهُمْ ۚ ذَٰلِكَ بِأَنَّهُمْ قَالُواْ لِلَّذِينَ كَرِهُواْ مَا نَزَّلَ ٱللَّهُ سَنُطِيعُكُمْ فِى بَعْضِ ٱلْأَمْرِ ۖ وَٱللَّهُ يَعْلَمُ إِسْرَارَهُمْ ﴾

255

"Indeed, those who reverted back (to disbelief) after guidance had become clear to them – Satan enticed them and prolonged hope for them. That is because they said to those who disliked what Allāh sent down,[1] 'We will obey you in part of the matter.' And Allāh knows what they conceal." *{Muhammad (47) 25-26}*

Ibn Katheer says in his *Tafseer* about the ayah that it:

Means: they plotted secretly with them and gave them evil advice - as is the common practice of the hypocrites who declare the opposite of what they conceal…whatever they hide and conceal, Allāh is well-acquainted with it and He knows it.

So observe ("El") Faisal's trickery with the Book of Allāh and his simplistic reasoning in order to hoodwink the audience, we will see later how Faisal has problems with this verse and so Faisal should focus on memorising it properly as opposed to making *takfeer*! Indeed, in one narration 'Ali ibn Abī Tālib ﷺ said about the Khawārij that: *"they will hold it (the recitation of the Qur'ān) for them, when it is against them."*[2] The *ayah* was revealed regarding the *yahūd* of Madeenah and Faisal tries to apply it to the Muslims! Forty-seven minutes into the lecture Faisal says:

---

[1] i.e. the Jews of Madeenah
[2] Ibn Abī 'Āsim, *as-Sunnah*, no.916

> "And even if you live in Dār ul-Harb, UK, USA your deen is not protected, every time you give shahādah to someone ten people leave the deen..."

Hereby making out that the UK and the USA are 'abodes of war' yet provides no daleel whatsoever as to why and which scholars have declared these countries to be 'abodes of war'! As for Faisal's attempt to *"give the Sharh of the hadeeth"* (!!!) then this is nothing but a farce! Better to stick to explanations by *hadeeth* scholars as opposed to self-made 'shuyūkh' and 'teachers' like ("El") Faisal. An hour into the lecture Faisal makes *takfeer* on Abū Usāmah and then fourteen minutes later accuses the brother Dawūd Adeeb of being a *"house nigga"* and of making *"a statement of kufr"* just because the brother Dawūd Adeeb said that a scholar can make *ijtihād* yet err!!? Faisal says:

> "He is telling us, Abū U err... *{sic}* Dawūd Adeeb, that you can't criticise the fatwa of Bin Bāz, which is the crime of the century, to let the crusaders into the Holy Land,[1] if you are not 100% on your deen, so that statement in itself is kufr."

---

[1] They were not allowed into Makkah and Madeenah, which some scholars define as being the *Jazeerat ul-'Arab* (Arabian Peninsula); while some scholars define the Arabian Peninsula to be Makkah, Madeenah and al-Yamāmah; some scholars define the Arabian Peninsula as being Makkah, Madeenah, al-Yamāmah and Yemen. See Shaykh 'Abdul'Azeez ar-Rayyis, *al-Burhān al-Muneer fī Dahd Shubuhāt Ahl it-Takfeer wa't-Tafjeer,*
[The Clear Proofs for Refuting the Doubts of the People of Takfeer and Bombing!], pp.60-68: http://www.salafimanhaj.com/pdf/SalafiManhaj_TakfeerAndBombing.pdf

Firstly, we again see Faisal's utter ignorance of the reality of *shirk* that is currently rampant within the *ummah* and if this is not the real **"crime of the century"** then Faisal has no comprehension of the reality of the crime of *shirk*. There are graves, tombs, mausoleums, shrines and the like all dedicated to the worship of 'Shaykh so and so' or for 'Peer Sāb so-and-so' or for 'Imām so-and-so', for 'Maulvi so and so' and for 'Hajji so-and-so'! If *shirk* is not the greatest crime for Faisal then he seriously needs to re-sit his studies again.

Secondly, Faisal, in his excitement and extremism, stumbles over his words and then he does not *at all* assess Dawūd Adeeb's point about what is found in the books of 'Ulūm ul-Qur'ān and how many scholars have allowed non-Muslims to assist Muslims in warfare. Faisal did not even acknowledge this at all and did not deal with this reality. So beware of Faisal's chicanery and simplistic rulings!

Scholars of the past also allowed the use of non-Muslim, *kuffār* and *mushrik* forces to be drafted upon for Muslims, if there is a benefit in that for the Muslims. Such as:

- Imām ash-Shāfi'ī ﷲ
- Imām Ahmad ibn Hanbal ﷲ
- Imām Abu'l-Qāsim al-Khirqī ﷲ
- Imām Abu'l-Hasan as-Sindī ﷲ
- Imām Bin Bāz ﷲ
- Imām Ibn 'Uthaymeen ﷲ

Therefore, this shows that the issue of drafting *kuffār* forces is something which was ruled upon by scholars in the past, and the scholars who also ruled this in the present era were thus preceded in their rulings. Ibn Qudāmah al-Maqdisī اللہ stated in *al-Mughnī* (vol.13, p.98):

Help is not to be sought from a mushrik, this is what Ibn al-Mundhir, al-Jūzajānī and a group of the people of knowledge stated. There is present from Ahmad what indicates the permissibility of gaining assistance from them (i.e. mushrikeen) and the statements of al-Khirqī also indicate that, if there is a need and this is the school of thought of Shāfi'ī.

Imām an-Nawawī stated in his explanation, vol.11-12, p.403, under *hadeeth* no.4677:

His saying ﷺ: 'Go back, for I do not seek help from a mushrik'; and it is mentioned in another hadeeth that the Prophet ﷺ sought help from Safwān bin Umayyah before his Islām, as a result some scholars give the first hadeeth precedence over the second one. Imām Shāfi'ī and others said: If the disbeliever has good opinion of the Muslims and the need has come to utilize him, if not then it is disliked (to seek the disbeliever's assistance). So these two hadeeths are taken in the light of two circumstances.

Shaykh as-Sindī stated in his explanation of the *hadeeth "I do not gain assistance from a mushrik"*, from the *Sunan Ibn Mājah* (vol.3, p.376, under *hadeeth* no.2832):

It shows that gaining assistance from a mushrik is harām without a need. But if there is a need then it can be done as an exception and this is not opposed.[1]

Shaykh Faisal bin Qazār al-Jāsim in his book *Tahreer ul-Maqāl fī Hukm Munāsarat il-Kuffār fī'l-Qitāl* [Reporting the Statement on the Ruling on Supporting Disbelievers in Combat], p.19 states:

والشاهد من هذه النقول على عدم الكفر في هذه الحال هو اختلاف العلماء في

الإستعانة بالكفار على أهل البغي المسلمين ، فتجويز بعضهم كأبي حنيفة وغيره

ذلك إذا كان الكفار ذميين ويد المسلمين هي الغالبة وهو وإن كان قولاً ضعيفاً ،

وتجويز الجمهور ذلك عند الضرورة يدل على أنه ليست إعانة المسلم للكفار على

المسلمين أو الإستعانة بهم كفراً بمجردها ، إذ لو كانت كفراً مطلقاً لم يختلفوا في

جوازها ، ولم يرخصوا بها عند الضرورة ، وهذ يدل على أن تعاون المسلم والكافر

على بعض المسلمين ليست كفراً مطلقاً ، بل تختلف باختلاف الأحوال

---

[1] Bandar bin Nā'if bin Sanahāt al-'Utaybī, *Wa Jādilhum Bilatī Hiya Ahsan, Munāqishatun 'Ilmiyyatun Hādiyyatun li-19 Mas'alatin Muta'alaqatin bi-Hukkām il-Muslimeen* (Riyadh: Maktabah 'AbdulMusawwir bin Muhammad bin 'Abdullāh, 1427 AH/2006 CE, Fourth Edition), pp.38-42.

What is witnessed from these quotes, regarding the absence of kufr in this case, is that the 'Ulama differed over seeking the assistance of the kuffār against rebellious Muslims. Some of them such as Abū Haneefah and others permitted that: if the kuffār are Dhimmis and the Muslims have the upper hand, even if it is weak word. The majority of scholars permit it when there is a dire necessity and this indicates that this is not a Muslim helping the kuffār against Muslims or that this seeking assistance from them is kufr merely on account of it (the assistance from them). Because if it was absolute kufr the scholars would not have differed over its permissibility and they would not have granted a concession for it when there is a dire necessity. This indicates that a Muslim co-operating with a disbeliever against some Muslims is not absolute kufr, rather it differs based on different conditions...

Faisal continues with his lies to try to discredit the Salafis:

"This person (i.e. Abū Usāmah), along with the rest of the Saudi Salafis, they're always looking down on jihād..."

Then Faisal proceeds with his corrupted, sick and evil *khawārij* methodology:

"Anyone who listens to this tape of this man and doubt {sic} that he's a kāfir you become a kāfir! If you listen to this person Abū Usāmah trying to put Islām down and Muslims down and jihād down, if you have an atom's weight of doubt in your heart that he's a kāfir, you yourself become a kāfir!" (!!!)

Ibn Taymiyyah ﷺ states:

من شأن أهل البدع أنهم يبتدعون أقوالاً يجعلونها واجبة في الدين، بل يجعلونها من

الإيمان الذي لا بد منه، ويكفِّرون من خالفهم فيها ويستحلون دمه؛ كفعل الخوارج

والجهمية والرافضة والمعتزلة وغيرهم.

From the affairs of Ahl ul-Bida' is that they invent statements and make them obligatory in the deen and make such statements articles of faith which have to be adhered to. They make takfeer of whoever says contrary to them in regards to such statements and they made permissible (to shed) the blood of the one (who disagrees with them) as is done by the Khawārij, Jahmiyyah, Rāfidah, Mu'tazilah and others.[1]

Here we see a prime example of Faisal's brainwashing and emotional ploys wherein he tries to terrorise the audience ideologically by forcing them to accept his view, so that the audience will be forced to make *takfeer*. Then Faisal states, in an outburst that typifies his *Khārijiyyah*:

---

[1] Shaykh ul-Islām Ahmad bin 'AbdulHaleem Ibn Taymiyyah, *Minhāj us-Sunnah fī Naqd Kalām ish-Shi'a wa'l-Qadariyyah* (Riyadh, KSA: Imām Muhammad bin Saud Islamic University, 1406 AH, ed. Dr Muhammad Rashād Sālim), vol.5, p.95.

Faisal: "What do you think we should do with this person (i.e. Abū Usāmah adh-Dhahabī)?"

Audience: Kill him!

Faisal: "I can't hear you?"

Audience: "Kill him!"

Faisal: I still can't hear you?

Audience: "Kill him!"

Faisal: OK that makes sense." (!!!)

Look at this uncouth brutality and *Khārijiyyah*, what more is there to indicate Faisal's Khawārij usūl and manhaj? Indeed, from the characteristics of the Khawārij is that they kill the people of Islām and leave the people of polytheists, in one narration it states *"they will kill the people of Islām"* as occurs in the *hadeeth* of Abū Sa'eed al-Khudrī ﷺ.[1]

Now here comes another blunder which Faisal makes in the lecture and if the Salafis are supposed to be *"jāhil in regards to 'aqeedah"* as he regurgitates in this lecture, we were still able to find this blunder of Faisal's! So what does that say about Faisal's own ignorance and distortions of the *deen*?! So pay attention here, Faisal states:

"Now which ayah in the Qur'ān tells you that the moment you give your bay'ah to NATO or the UN you're a kāfir? Who can tell us?"

---

[1] Saheeh Muslim *hadeeth* no.2451.

Okay, so this is the question he asks the audience, who as usual in Faisal's lectures do not respond as most are only uncritical followers, and Faisal also bangs on the table in order to drive home the seriousness of the matter! So now let's look at Faisal's answer to his own question:

"Sūrah Muhammad verse....te...err...(inaudible)...ty-five, Allāh says in Sūrah Muhammad verse twenty five 'those who have rejected faith in what Allāh has revealed...'"

So Faisal again, as has been seen beforehand, stumbles over himself in his excitement and extremism. He also recites verse 25 so quickly that it is unintelligible as to what is being recited and Faisal also makes a mistake in his recitation of verse 25 and misses out a big section of it. So we will reproduce it again here fully for the benefit of the reader:

﴿ إِنَّ ٱلَّذِينَ ٱرْتَدُّواْ عَلَىٰٓ أَدْبَٰرِهِم مِّنۢ بَعْدِ مَا تَبَيَّنَ لَهُمُ ٱلْهُدَى ٱلشَّيْطَٰنُ سَوَّلَ لَهُمْ وَأَمْلَىٰ لَهُمْ ۝ ذَٰلِكَ بِأَنَّهُمْ قَالُواْ لِلَّذِينَ كَرِهُواْ مَا نَزَّلَ ٱللَّهُ سَنُطِيعُكُمْ فِى بَعْضِ ٱلْأَمْرِ وَٱللَّهُ يَعْلَمُ إِسْرَارَهُمْ ﴾

"Indeed, those who reverted back (to disbelief) after guidance had become clear to them – Satan enticed them and prolonged hope for them. That is because they said to those who disliked what Allāh sent down,[1] "We will obey you in part of the matter." And Allāh knows what they conceal." *{Muhammad (47) 25-26}*

The clearest *dalīl* of the tactics of Faisal in defending innovation and its people is evident in this lecture. What is also clear from this sick lecture, which is infected with *khārijiyyah* and *takfeer*, is that Faisal is oddly silent over the fact that 'Umar 'AbdurRahmān praised the *Shi'a* state of Irān and its so-called 'revolution' headed by al-Khomeini as being "a blessed revolution". So Faisal purposely left this out when he played the lecture of Abū Usāmah, trying to hoodwink his audience of blind followers. Faisal thus played only about twenty minutes of Abū Usāmah's lecture yet left out the remaining hour or so![2]

Sample Lecture Number Eighteen: 'Cancers In The Body Of The Ummah'

Before we highlight the absurdity contained in this particular lecture, we wonder if, like us, you have noticed the cynicism and negativity contained in the majority of of Faisal's lecture titles. It is as if Faisal wants his audience to share in his miserable outlook on the Muslim world. Faisal states at the beginning of this lecture, in a statement that seems to be more for name and

---

[1] i.e. the Jews of Madeenah.

[2] Abū Usāmah's refutation of 'Umar 'AbdurRahmān originaly comprised two tapes.

fame and is totally irrelevant to what is supposed to be the context of a lesson teaching Muslims about their *deen*:

> "Today's topic is very provocative and I have many enemies but I will gain even more enemies because I will be calling the criminals by their name."

Faisal states after an hour and fifteen minutes:

> "So the Jews they immediately changed their tune, so the Salafis because they are the yahūd of the ummah, they have all the qualities that the Jews have." (!!!)

This *takfeer* is the real cancer of the *ummah*! Yet Faisal himself is unable to diagnose this acute cancer within the body of the *ummah*! Faisal again tries to show that Imām Bin Bāz's statement about the *Jamāt ul-Jihād* and their being the "brothers of the devils" applies to the *Mujāhideen* completely and refers to anyone who even believes in jihād!

Then Faisal says, in total contradiction to all that we have seen about Faisal, that it is the Salafis who *"have absolutely no respect for scholars"*! It is rather odd for Faisal, of all people, to have the audacity to state this when on most of his tapes he accuses, abuses, slanders, discredits and pours scorn on the scholars and that's when he's not making *takfeer* of them! Faisal then says:

> "The statement of kufr dūna kufr where did it come from? Qurtubī says it come from {sic} Tāwūs! A man who did not even meet the Prophet ﷺ,

266

a man by the name of Tāwūs came up with this statement kufr dūna kufr. So as for the statement kufr dūna kufr Ibn 'Abbās did not make this statement!"

We have refuted this previously in regards to Faisal's lecture *Jewish Traits in the Ummah*. Yet there is more to add here as Faisal has said something which even none of his Takfīrī Shuyūkh say!

Even some of the main Takfīrī theoreticians do not say that Tāwūs invented the statement of 'kufr less than kufr'!! Faisal also leaves off explaining who Tāwūs is, so after discrediting Tāwūs as being *"a man who did not even meet the Prophet ﷺ"* he conveniently neglects to say that Tāwūs was one of the main students of Ibn 'Abbās ﷺ.

Furthermore, Imām Ahmad verified[1] as did at-Tabarī[2] and Ibn Nasr[3], with an authentic chain of transmission from 'Atā bin Abū Rabāh that he said *"Kufr less than kufr, dhulm less than dhulm and fisq less than fisq."* Imām Ahmad[4], at-Tabarī and Ibn Nasr[5] reported with an authentic chain of transmission via Tāwūs that he said *"kufr which does not expel one from the religion."* The students of Ibn 'Abbās ﷺ viewed that the "disbelievers" mentioned in the verses is regarding minor *kufr* and the speech of the scholar is understood from the

---

[1] *Masā'il Abī Dāwūd*, p.209
[2] *Tafseer*, vol.6, p.116
[3] *Ta'dheem Qadr us-Salah*, vol.2, pp.522, 575
[4] *Masā'il Abī Dāwūd*, p.209
[5] *Ta'dheem Qadr us-Salah*, vol.2, pp.522, 574

statements of his students who are more aware of what is narrated from their Shaykh[1] and Imām. Faisal says shortly after this that:

> "Even the layman walking on the street who didn't go to an Islamic university if you ask him 'what about a man who dismantles the sharī'ah?' The layman will say: 'he's a kāfir!'"

We have refuted this simplistic and erroneous insinuation of Faisal previously when we analysed Faisal's attempts to make the laymen's views to be on a par with that of the Mujtahid scholars. As highlighted in the chart, "dismantling the Sharī'ah" is one of Faisal's much-loved terms. We were first made aware of Faisal's abusive use of this concocted phrase through an email that was forwarded to the salafimanhaj.com admin team from a brother in Jamaica. This email highlighted that Faisal claims:

> "It is known of Islam by necessity and it is the agreement of all the Muslims that if you dismantle the Sharī'ah it makes you become a kāfir."

---

[1] For that reason, you'll see that the Imāms of *hadeeth* raise narrations from a Shaykh due to him opposing what his students are upon, as is done with Imām Yahyā ibn Sa'eed who weakened a statement narrated from Ibn Mas'ūd as his followers opposed this. Abū 'Ubayd al-Qāsim bin Sallām said: *"I saw Yahyā ibn Sa'eed deny and criticise the chain of transmission because the companions of Abdullāh opposed it."* See *Kitāb ul-Īmān*, p.22. Also see other examples of this from Imām Ahmad in *as-Sunnah* of Khallāl (vol.3, p.559), so if they raised the narration of a scholar out of him opposing what his students were upon in their understanding, how then can the scholar be understood on the basis of the views of his students?

Abdullāh Faisal then quotes the source for the above quote as being from Ibn Taymiyyah, *Majmū' al-Fatāwā*, vol.8, p.524. Ok, now let us quote the actual Arabic text from Shaykh ul-Islām Ibn Taymiyyah from *Majmū' al-Fatāwā*:

وَمَعْلُومٌ بِالِاضْطِرَارِ مِن دِين المسلمين وَ بِاتِفاق جميع المسلمين ان مَن سَوَّغَ اتباع غير

دين الإسْلام أوْ اتباع شريعة غير شريعة محمد صلى الله عليهِ وَ سلم: فَهُوَ كافِرٌ وَ

كَكفرٍ مَن آمَنَ بِبَعْضِ الكِتابِ وَ كَفَرَ بِبَعْضِ الكِتابِ

It is well-known by necessity from the deen of the Muslims, and with the agreement of all of the Muslims. Whoever makes permissible (sawwagha) following a deen other than Islām or following a Sharī'ah other than the Sharī'ah of Muhammad ﷺ – is a disbeliever and is like the kufr of one who believes in some of the Book and disbelieves in some of it...

This is from: Ibn Taymiyyah, *Majmū' al-Fatawā* (KSA: Tarteeb of 'AbdurRahmān Qāsim, 1997 CE/1418 AH), vol.8, p.524. So we can see that Abdullāh ("El") Faisal, for his own corrupt agenda, translates the word "sawwagha" as "to dismantle" and thus intentionally misquotes Shaykh ul-Islām Ibn Taymiyyah ﷺ. This is clear *khiyānah* (treachery) and an abuse of *amāna* (trust) which deceives those of the Ummah who have no knowledge of the Arabic language. The word "sawwagha" means: *ajāza'* and *abāha'* which means: 'to make permissible'. Firstly, these terms have totally different connotations to "dismantle"; secondly, nowhere in the Arabic quote of Ibn Taymiyyah can one see the verb *'fakkaka'* which means: 'to dismantle'; thirdly, Faisal did not transmit fully what was mentioned by Ibn Taymiyyah and fourthly, the Salafis totally accept what has been mentioned by Shaykh ul-Islām Ibn Taymiyyah ﷺ!

Sample Lecture Number Nineteen: 'Islam Under Siege'

Eight minutes into the lecture he mentions an unauthentic story about the Prophet ﷺ being offered the sun in one hand and the moon in the other. This story, which is found in some books of the Sīrah such Ibn Hishām and the *Maghāzī* of Ibn Ishāq, who relayed it from Ya'qūb bin 'Utbah bin al-Mugheerah bin al-Akhnas, is weak as it is *mu'dal* (a report wherein two or more successive narrators are missing in the chain of transmission).[1] Twenty minutes into the lecture Faisal states, in utter foolishness:

"So as a Muslim it is not for you to fear a coalition, it is not for you to despair. Many of you, when you see the B52 bombers, the Tomahawk cruise missiles, the F16 planes you despair! What about your tawwaqqul, your trust in Allāh ta'ala?"

Then Faisal makes an open error some fifty minutes into the lecture and tries to brush over it. He is corrected by one of his blind followers about whether the

---

[1] Imām al-Albānī states in *Silsilah Ahādeeth ad-Da'eefah*, vol.2, nos.310 and 311: "The chain of transmission is da'eef mu'dal, Ya'qūb bin 'Utbah is of the trustworthy narrators from the Tābi'een who died in 128 AH. I found other routes of transmission of the hadeeth but with a different wording (than the one mentions the sun and moon being given in each hand)."

verse he quoted is in Mā'idah 51 or 56 and he says *"Never mind you can correct your own Shaykh"* (!!) and then states:

"I stand corrected whenever I'm wrong and I tell my enemies for the past eight years, if you listen to my tapes and you find one mistake in regards to fiqh or 'aqeedah, I will take it back publicly! For eight years I'm *{sic}* repeating myself, if you listen to any of my tapes and you find one mistake in regards to fiqh or 'aqeedah, whether it is al-*walā wa'l-barā*, *Tawheed Hākimiyyah*, *fiqh ul-wāqi*, any, seven conditions of shahādah, just one mistake in regards to 'aqeedah I will take it back publicly! For eight years I've been saying that and my enemies haven't been able to find any mistake[1] they only slander me behind my back like nine year old girls…they slander me behind my back like menstruating women. Not like Bin Bāz who they claimed he took back his mistake a minute before he died on his bed, secretely, the tawbah of the Shaykh is not like the layman, did you understand that? Do you understand that? When you pass a dodgy fatwa you misguide thousands and millions, is that clear? So you have to take back your fatwa publicly, but if you are a layman and you make a mistake you can make your tawbah secretly behind closed doors. If you're a Shaykh and you pass a dodgy fatwa you need to take it back publicly because you misguide tens, hundreds, thousands and millions of people."

---

[1] Is he serious?! This book in itself is just a brief attempt to collate a presentation of his horrific errors!

So here Faisal has not only elevated himself to the level of a scholar, by saying that he is prepared to take back any mistakes because this is only for scholars to do this publicly, but he has also raised himself to the level of Imām Bin Bāz ﷺ. Faisal stated that public *tawbah* is only for the scholars, so when Faisal stated that he is prepared to take back any statements openly and publicly, he is insinuating that he also is a scholar, as according to him only the scholars make public and open *tawbah*! This will be something which we revisit in our conclusion. Then Faisal says:

> "It's all because of Shaykh Bin Bāz we have this disaster in the ummah today."

La hawla wa la quwatta ila billāh! So is it due to Imām Bin Bāz ﷺ, just one single man, that *shirk* is widespread in the *ummah*? How much must you hate an individual in order to convince yourself that he is exclusively responsible for the state of the Ummah today?! Is Imām Bin Bāz to blame that some of the Muslim youth are ignorant and only know about killing, murder and injustice? Is it because of Imām Bin Bāz ﷺ that people who study and graduate, after a few years suddenly pose themselves as Shuyūkh? Is it because of Imām Bin Bāz ﷺ that people blindly follow self-styled 'Shuyūkh' and do anything that they tell them? Is it because of Imām Bin Bāz ﷺ that the likes of Faisal are locked up behind bars? Or is it due to Faisal's own irresponsible, ignorant, hateful, 'dodgy' and extremist statements? Imām Muhammad bin Sālih al-'Uthaymeen ﷺ stated, in words which are appropriate for Faisal:

I ask Allāh to support the scholars against what is leveled against them from the tongues of the foolish minded ones, as there are many things which the scholars face.

First: We hear things that are ascribed to the people of knowledge, who are trusted, yet when we check we find out that it is not at all like how it has been said.[1] Much of what is said 'So-and-so is like this...' when we actually check we find out that the situation is not like that at all. This is a great crime and especially if the Messenger of Allāh ﷺ said *'Indeed, lying upon me is not like lying on someone else'*[2] or words to that effect.

So lying about the scholars is connected to the Divine Legislation of Allāh and is not like lying on other people because it includes a Divinely Legislated ruling that is related to a trusted scholar. For this reason whenever the people trust a scholar more, the lies about him will increase and become more dangerous. Because when you say to any common person 'So-and-so said...' they will not respond to you, but if you say 'So-and-so from those who are trusted said...' they will listen to you. So

---

[1] Indeed, therefore, we are not going to blindly follow the writings of the self-styled 'independent Islamic thinkers' and petty columnists who slander the *Salafī* scholars and actually aim to achieve fame from such despicable actions.

[2] Part of a *hadeeth* reported by al-Bukhārī, *hadeeth* no.1291 in *Kitāb ul-Janā'iz (Funerals)* and Muslim also in *Kitāb ul-Janā'iz*, *hadeeth* nos. 2154, 2155 and 2156; from al-Mugheerah bin Shu'bah *(radi Allāhu 'anhu)*. The rest of the *hadeeth* is famous: *"...whoever lies about me intentionally then let him prepare to take his seat in the Hell Fire."*

you will find some people who have an opinion or an idea which they think is the truth and they thus try to establish people upon it, yet the only way they can find to achieve this is to lie about one of the trusted scholars and say 'this is what so and so said,' this is a very dangerous matter, it is not attacking the scholar personally, but it is related to the regulations of Allāh."

<u>Secondly</u>: Blowing up errors out of proportion, as I have just said, is also dangerous and vile, as a scholar is a human who makes mistakes at times and is correct at other times. However, if a scholar makes a mistake it is incumbent on us to contact him and we can ask him: 'did you really say this?' and if he says 'yes' yet we see that it was a mistake we can say to him: 'Do you have any evidence for this?' so if we get into a discourse the truth will become clear. Every (true) scholar is just and fears Allāh, the Exalted and Majestic, and must return to the truth and must make known his retraction also. As for inflating mistakes and then mentioning worse things about the scholar's situation then there is no doubt that this is showing enmity against your brother Muslim, and is also showing enmity against the Divine Legislation, if I am able to say this. Because if the people trust a person and then his trustworthiness is doubted, where will the people turn to? The people will be left wavering without a leader to guide them with the Divine legislation of Allāh. Or are the people supposed to turn to an ignoramus who misguides the people from the

path of Allāh unintentionally? Or are the people supposed to turn to an evil scholar who blocks them from the path of Allāh intentionally?[1]

Al-'Allāmah Sālih al-Fawzān also stated in regards to mockery of the scholars and accusing them of compromising and being 'in the pocket' that:

It is a must to respect the scholars of the Muslims as they are the inheritors of the Prophets ﷺ and making a mockery of them is considered to be making a mockery of their position and inheritance from the Prophet ﷺ, and mockery of the knowledge which they carry. So whoever mocks the scholars, also mocks the Muslims firstly, as the scholars must be respected for their knowledge and position in the ummah. If the scholars are not to be trusted then who should be trusted? And if trust of the scholars is lost to whom shall the Muslims resort to help them solve their problems and explain the regulations of the Divine Legislation? At such a point the Ummah will lose out and corruption will spread. So if the scholar works hard and is correct then he gains one reward, yet if he strives hard and errs he gains one reward, and his error (which is scholarly and based on his attempt to understand the Qur'ān and Sunnah) is forgiven. What is there for the one who mocks the scholars except punishment? History is the best witness of this, past and present and especially if the scholars (that are being mocked) are those

---

[1] Imām Muhammad bin Sālih al-'Uthaymeen, 'Ali bin Hasan Abū Lowz (ed.), *as-Sahwa al-Islāmiyyah – Dawābit wa Tawjeehāt, Vol.1* (Riyadh: Dār ul-Qāsim, 1417 AH/19 CE, Fourth Edition), pp.230-231.

who are referred to regarding issues affecting the Muslims, such as the Council of Senior Scholars (in Saudi Arabia.)[1]

Al-'Allāmah Sālih al-Fawzān was also asked:
Due to events in the past, some of the Muslims ally themselves to the kuffār due to a fatwa heard by some students of Islamic knowledge. What is the ruling on that?

Al-'Allāmah Sālih responded:
I do not think that there is a Muslim who allies with the kuffār however you explain allegiance with a misunderstanding; as the one who allies with them can be ignorant, a non-Muslim or from the hypocrites. As for the Muslim then he does not have allegiance to the kuffār yet there are some actions which you consider to be 'allegiance' when in reality is not allegiance. These are things like buying from and selling to the kuffār, giving and receiving presents from the kuffār and the like which are all permissible and not allegiance to the kuffār. Rather, these things are from worldly interaction and beneficial exchanges, such as hiring a disbeliever for work for example. These are like the beneficial exchanges of the Messenger of Allāh ﷺ when he hired 'Abdullāh bin Urayqit al-Laythī to guide him on the way to hijra, while 'Abdullāh was a disbeliever, in order to help due to his experience on the tracks, so that is permissible. It is

---

[1] Shaykh, Dr Sālih bin Fawzān al-Fawzān, *op.cit.* pp.37-38.

also permissible for a Muslim to hire out his services for kuffār to use if necessary as this is from the door of beneficial exchanges and not from the door of love. To the extent that if a Muslim has a disbelieving father the Muslim must be dutiful to him and this is not from the door of love. Allāh says:

﴿ لَّا تَجِدُ قَوْمًا يُؤْمِنُونَ بِٱللَّهِ وَٱلْيَوْمِ ٱلْأَخِرِ يُوَآدُّونَ مَنْ حَآدَّ ٱللَّهَ وَرَسُولَهُۥ وَلَوْ كَانُوٓا۟ ءَابَآءَهُمْ أَوْ أَبْنَآءَهُمْ أَوْ إِخْوَٰنَهُمْ أَوْ عَشِيرَتَهُمْ ۚ أُو۟لَٰٓئِكَ كَتَبَ فِى قُلُوبِهِمُ ٱلْإِيمَٰنَ وَأَيَّدَهُم بِرُوحٍ مِّنْهُ ۖ وَيُدْخِلُهُمْ جَنَّٰتٍ تَجْرِى مِن تَحْتِهَا ٱلْأَنْهَٰرُ خَٰلِدِينَ فِيهَا ۚ رَضِىَ ٱللَّهُ عَنْهُمْ وَرَضُوا۟ عَنْهُ ۚ أُو۟لَٰٓئِكَ حِزْبُ ٱللَّهِ ۚ أَلَآ إِنَّ حِزْبَ ٱللَّهِ هُمُ ٱلْمُفْلِحُونَ ﴾

'You will not find a people who believe in Allāh and the Last Day, having affection for those who oppose Allāh and His Messenger, even though they were their fathers or their sons or their brothers or their kindred. For such He has written īmān in their hearts, and strengthened them with spirit[1] from Him. And He will admit them to Gardens under which rivers flow to dwell therein forever. Allāh is pleased with them, and they with Him. They are the Party of Allāh, indeed, it is the Party of Allāh that will be successful.'

{al-Mujādilah (58): 22}

---

[1] i.e. "that which gives life", explained as the guidance of the Qur'ān or victory over their opponents.

However, he (who has a disbelieving father) has to be dutiful and good to him, this is from worldly goodness. There are aspects of interaction with the kuffār such as peace treaties, covenants and trusts with the kuffār which are all allowed and do not come under 'allegiance' (to the kuffār). There are some things which some ignoramuses think are allegiance when in reality, are not 'allegiance'. There are situations when the Muslims are in danger and the kuffār avert such a danger from the Muslims, then this is not mudāhanah (compromising) this is mudārah (being amicable and harmonious).[1] So there is a difference between being

---

[1] *Mudārah* literally means to be amicable, affable and harmonious and in the context of the *Sharī'ah* the scholars have noted that it is giving away some of your *dunya* for the preservation of your *deen*. As Shaykh Sālih is emphasizing here, it is known by the scholars that *mudārah* is different from *mudāhanah* (compromising). Imāms Bukhārī and Muslim ﷺ in their *saheehs* within their sections on manners then include chapters on *mudārah*. Al-Hāfidh Ibn Hajar stated: *"..the intent of it is to ward off via kindness."* In *al-Qāmūs al-Muheet* it is stated about the definition of *darā'*: *"To make something a deterrent, and to deter is to rebut, i.e. they rebutted each other in the argument."* Examples of *mudārah* in the Qur'ān are in **"And do not insult those they invoke other than Allāh, lest they insult Allāh in enmity without knowledge..."** *Sūrah al-'An'ām (6: 108)* And: **"Those will be given their reward twice for what they patiently endured and [because] they avert evil through good..."** *Sūrah al-Qasas (28: 54)*
Evidence from the *Sunnah* for this are the *hadeeth* from Abi'l-Dardā' that *"We smile in the faces of people yet our hearts are cursing them."* (*Fath al-Bārī*, vol.10, p.527, *Kitāb al-Adab, Bāb al-Mudārah ma'a'n-Nās*). Also when 'Urwah ibn al-Zubayr reported that 'Ā'ishah told him: "A man sought permission to visit the Prophet ﷺ, and he said, *'Let him in, but what a bad son of his tribe (or bad brother of his tribe) he is!'* When the man came in, the Prophet *(sallallāhu alayhi wassallam)* spoke to him kindly and gently. I said: "O Messenger of Allāh, you said what you said, then you spoke to him kindly." He said, *"O 'Ā'ishah, the worst of the people in the sight of Allāh is the one who is shunned by others or whom people treat nicely because they fear his sharp tongue."* See *Fath al-Bārī*,

amicable and harmonious (mudārah) and compromising (mudāhanah), as compromising is not permissible however mudārah is. So when the Muslims are in danger they obtain mudārah (harmony) of the kuffār in order to avert such danger and this is not allegiance. The matters need to be understood, yet as for explaining every act of interaction with the kuffār to be 'allegiance to them (kuffār)' then this is ignorance and error, or purposefully deceiving the people. So such a person should not enter into such issues which are only for the Fuqahā and the people of

---

vol.10, p.528, *Kitāb al-Adab, Bāb al-Mudārah ma'a'n-Nās.* Ibn Hajar said about these two ahādeeth:

Ibn Battāl said: "Mudārah is from the good character of the believers, to be responsive to people, even with a word, without being coarse with them in speech, this is one of the strongest causes of harmony. Some people think that mudārah is mudāhānah and this is an error, as mudārah is regrettable and mudāhanah is prohibited. The difference is: mudāhanah is taken from the word ad-Dahhān (the painter) who glosses over something and covers what is actually there. The scholars have explained it as lying with a sinner and openly displaying happiness with what he is doing without forbidding him at all. Mudārah is being kind with the ignorant in order to teach him, being kind with the sinner in order to forbid him from what he is doing, without being harsh with him so that he does not expose what he does, and forbidding him with gentle speech and action, especially if his comradeship is needed and the likes of that." (Fath ul-Bārī (Dār ur-Rayyān Print), vol.10, p.545) Imām al-Qurtubī stated:

"The difference between mudārah and mudāhanah is that mudārah is to surrender the dunya for the benefit of the deen and it is permissible and even recommended. Mudāhanah is leaving the deen for the dunya." (Fath ul-Bārī (Dār ur-Rayyān Print), vol.10, p.469)

Ibn Qayyim al-Jawziyyah ﷺ: *"Thus mudārah is praiseworthy and mudāhanah is censured, so there is a differenece between the two. The one who is mudārī uses kindness with a person in order for the truth to manifest from the person or make him retract from falsehood. The mudāhin (compromiser) uses kindness in order for the person to remain established upon falsehood and leaves him upon his desires. Mudārah is for the people of īmān while mudāhanah is for the hypocrites."* (ar-Rooh, p.231)

knowledge. It is neither for the students nor for school teachers to enter into such issues and analyse, prohibit and criticize the people by saying "this is allegiance to the kuffār and they (scholars) do not know the Divinely Legislated rulings" this is dangerous on the one who says such things as he is speaking about Allāh without knowledge.[1]

Faisal continues in his rant of hatred, extremism and excessiveness:

"You have twenty years of Islamic knowledge, or thirty years, you even memorise the Qur'ān and 100,000 hadeeth and your Islamic knowledge didn't cause you to fear Allāh for you to tell the Muslims the truth, for you to wake up the Ummah of Muhammad? You are not a scholar! You are a Shaytān!"

Faisal says again, praising himself:

"You have seen the result of having wicked scholars and apostate leaders ruling over you. Even if you never believed me in the past that they were kāfirs now that they have given their bay'ah to the crusaders to fight against Islām this should have convinced you..."

Indeed, Faisal himself demonstrates here that he is trying to "convince" his audience into *khurūj* and *takfeer*, an archetype of the contemporary *Khawārij*

---

[1] Shaykh, Dr Sālih bin Fawzān al-Fawzān, *op.cit.* pp.54-56

Qa'diyyah if there ever was one. Shaykh ul-Islām Ibn Taymiyyah had mentioned regarding the *Khawārij Qa'diyyah* that:

> They made the abode of the Muslims an abode of disbelief and war and they entitled their abode which they migrate to as 'an abode of eemān' and they considered the countries of Islām as being violable much more than their considering violable the countries of the disbelievers.[1]

Ash-Sharbīnī[2] mentioned in *Mughni al-Muhtāj*:

> The belief of the Khawārij is that whoever performs a major sin has disbelieved, his actions have been nullified and he will reside in the fire forever. They also believe that if the abode of the Imām manifests major sins within it, it becomes an abode of disbelief and legalisation [of spilling of blood]. For this reason they slandered the leading scholars, did not pray behind them and avoided the Jumu'ah and congregation.[3]

---

[1] See *Majmū' al-Fatawā Ibn Taymiyyah*, compiled and arranged by 'Abdur-Rahmān bin Qāsim al-'Āsimī an-Najdī and his son Muhammad, (ar-Ra'āsah al-'Āmah li-Shu'ūn al-Haramayn ash-Shareefayn, n.d.), vol.3, p.28.

[2] Muhammad ash-Sharbeenī al-Khateeb, he was an Egyptian scholar born in the city of Shirbeen in North-East Egypt near Sinai.
He was a scholar of Shāfi'ī *fiqh* and also a *mufassir*, he died in 977 AH/1569CE

[3] Muhammad ash-Sharbīnī al-Khateeb, *Mughni al-Muhtāj ilā Ma'rifat Ma'ānî Alfādh il-Manhaj*, (Beirut: Dār Ihyā Turāth al-'Arabī, n.d.), vol.4, p.124; also available Online: http://www.ahlalhdeeth.com/vb/showthread.php?t=31646
More recent prints were done in 1994 CE and 2000 CE by Dār Kutub 'Ilmiyyah (Beirut) edited and verified by Ādil 'Abdul-Mawjūd and 'Ali Muhammad Muwawwidh. There were also editions printed by Dār ud-Dhakhair (Beirut) in 1377 AH/1985 CE, Dār al-Ma'rifah, 1419 AH/1997 CE and Dār ul-Fikr, n.d.

Indeed, Islām was under siege within this lecture and it was Faisal who was holding Islām and its scholars under siege!

Sample Lecture Number Twenty: 'The Devil's Deception Of The Saudi Salafis'

This is probably the most horrific of all of 'Abdullāh Faisal's lectures of hate. After only the first minute of the lecture Faisal states:

> "The topic we are covering, we are about to cover, is very sensitive...and I have delayed it for three years because I don't want to cover the topic for the sake of nafs [one's own self]..."

Faisal goes on to say:

> "Now the reason why we say "Saudi Salafis", as the term 'Salafi' is used to describe a person who practises Islām the way it was practised by the Prophet ﷺ and his companions, the Sahabahs as well as the other two generations that come after. There are two types of Salafis, the 'classical Salafi'[1] and the fake Salafi, which we classify, which we call the 'Saudi Salafis.' The Muslims this like {sic} the classical Salafis are like Salmān al-Awdah and Safar Hawālī who are sincerely practicing Islām the way it

---

[1] Where on earth did Faisal get this division from? Which scholar has preceded Faisal with this division of 'a classical Salafi' and a 'fake Salafi' and then from this, only including the likes of Safar and Salmān within that classification?!

was practised by the Sahabahs and the Prophet ﷺ,[1] these are the classical Salafis.[2] So if you say that the topic is the 'Devil's Deception of the Salafis' you have mislead {sic} the people....So we have gathered here today to expose one of the greatest fitna to ever emerge in the Ummah of Prophet Muhammad ﷺ."

Faisal then proceeds to use as a basis for this lecture:

"...a book in Arabic which was written by a classical scholar of today![3] I don't want, when I deliver the topic, the people to say that 'Faisal said it.'[4] Now I have in front of me the book of 'AbdurRazzāq ibn Khaleefah ash-Shayijī, he is from Kuwait and he has his Ph.D in Islamic Studies."

---

[1] As for Salmān al-'Awda he has recently praised extremist *Sufis* and also cavorted with Socialists and secularists!

[2] Notice how Faisal only includes these two as being those "who are sincerely practising" as Faisal knows what is in the hearts! Faisal only mentioned these two because they were in prison at the time. So out of all of the scholars in the world, only these two are the "sincere ones"!!? It would be interesting to know if Faisal still considers Salmān al-'Awda as being a "classical Salafi"!

[3] Are there any contemporary Muslim scholars who have testified that ash-Shayijī is 'a classical scholar of today'? It is only Abdullāh Faisal al-Khārijī al-Jamaykī who has stated this! Furthermore, what does Faisal mean by alleging ash-Shayijee to be 'a classical scholar'? It is as if Faisal is just merely trying to insinuate that ash-Shayijī is a scholar who uses the Qur'ān and *Sunnah* as his basis, yet ash-Shayijī is not known to the people of knowledge.

[4] This again demonstrates his deception, as most of the calamities and *Khārijiyyah* within the lecture emanate from Faisal's own mouth and not even from the erroneous views of ash-Shayijī!

As for his use of the works of the *majhūl* (unknown) ash-Shayijī, then this is enough to indicate the weak basis of this lecture! Ash-Shayijī has been refuted by al-'Allāmah Sālih al-Fawzān. Indeed, ash-Shayijī has stated that entering into democratic and parliamentary elections are permissible! Yet Faisal did not mention this at all and rather refers to ash-Shayijī as being "a classical scholar of today!"!! Yet another example of Faisal's selective criticsm, always prepared to remain 'hush hush' when it serves his agenda. Does "a classical scholar of today" call for joining political parties that enter into democratic elections, as ash-Shayijī did? By Faisal's very own views this would necessitate *takfeer* of ash-Shayijī! Does "a classical scholar of today" get himself refuted by the actual classical scholars of the era? Does "a classical scholar of today" include the people of innovation among Ahl us-Sunnah?[1] Then Faisal states an hour and three minutes into the lecture:

"The British were the greatest enemies of Islām and the Muslims and they are the ones who set-up Saudi Arabia, they are the ones who formulated the government of Saudi Arabia, they are behind the kingship of Saudi Arabia, Saudi Arabia is a puppet government governed by the British."

Here then, Faisal agrees and shares the exact same *manhaj* of the Brailwīs, Sūfīs and Tahrīrīs in regurgitating the nonsense that the British supported Saudi

---

[1] The best refutations of ash-Shayijī were compiled by Dr Abū Iyyād Amjad Rafeeq online at the 'Salafi Publications' website in the late 1990s.

Arabia, when the reality is that in the early stages of the state and of the *da'wah* of Imām Muhammad Ibn 'AbdulWahhāb ﷺ, the British were against it with a passion! What indicates that the British were opposed to the "Wahhabi movement" is the fact that they sent Captain George Foster Sadlier[1] to *"congratulate Ibrahim Pasha on his success against the Wahhābis"* – during the war of Ibrahim Pasha in Dir'iyyah. This mission was also to find out to what extent he was prepared to cooperate with the British authorities to reduce what they called *"Wahhābi piracy in the Arabian Gulf."* Indeed, this clearly expressed a desire to establish an agreement between the British government and Ibrahim Pasha with the aim of destroying the *"Wahhābis"* completely. Sadlier made an arduous journey from India to Riyadh to see the ruins in Dir'iyyah, which was razed to the ground by Ibraheem Pasha.[2] Mahmūd Mahdi al-Istanbūlī says, concerning those who make the ridiculous claim that the English hepled to topple the Ottoman Caliphate, which itself is another much circulated fable:

قد كان من واجب هذا الكاتب أن يدعم رأيه بأدلة وإثباتات وقديما قال الشاعر:

وإذا الدعاوى لم تقم بدليلها بالنص فهي على السفاه دليل مع العلم أن التاريخ

---

[1] An officer of the 47th Regiment in the India British army at a time when securing sea routes to India was Britain's main interest. The British were concerned about the rise of the *da'wah* of Imām Muhammad ibn 'AbdulWahhāb and branded any opposer to British colonial rule in India as being a "Wahhabi", this thus contributed to the scaremongering against the *da'wah* of Imām Muhammad ibn 'AbdulWahhāb ﷺ.

[2] Jalal AbualRub, Alā Mencke (ed.), *The Biography of Muhammad ibn Abdul Wahhab* (Orlando, Florida: Madinah Publishers, 1424 AH/2003 CE), pp.224-231.

يذكر أن هؤلاء الإنكليز وقفوا ضد هذه الدعوة منذ قيامها خشية يقظة العالم الإسلامي .

This writer should be expected to produce proof and evidence for his opinion. Long ago the poet said: 'If claims are not supported by proof, they are used only by the fools as evidence.' We should also note that history tells us that the English were opposed to this call from the outset, fearing that it might wake the Muslim world up.[1]

Muhammad ibn Manzūr al-Nu'mānī said:

لقد استغل الإنجليز الوضع المعاكس في الهند للشيخ محمد بن عبد الوهاب ورموا كل من عارضهم ووقف في طريقهم ورأوه خطرا على كيانهم بالوهابية ودعوهم وهابيين... وكذلك دعا الإنجليز علماء ديوبند – في الهند - بالوهابيين من أجل معارضتهم السافرة للإنجليز وتضييقهم الخناق عليهم

The English made the most of the hostility that existed in India towards Shaykh Muhammad ibn 'Abd al-Wahhāb and they accused everyone who opposed them and stood in their way, or whom they regarded as dangerous, of being Wahhābis... Similarly the English called the scholars

---

[1] *Shaykh Muhammad ibn 'AbdulWahhāb fī Mar'āt al-Sharq wa'l-Gharb* [Shaykh Muhammad ibn 'AbdulWahhāb in the View of the East and West], p. 240. Originally translated by Abū Imrān al-Meksīkī.

of Deoband – in India – Wahhābis, because of their blunt opposition to the English and their putting pressure on them.[1]

Furthermore, one should not forget that Faisal says all of this yet he himself, alledgedly, studied at *Imām Muhammad bin Saud University* in Riyadh! So according to his own extremist reasoning and arguments, his own Islamic education, from whence he began to utilize in order to promote himself as a 'shaykh', is in question! As Faisal studied in Saudi Arabia and used that as his main proof to call himself a 'Shaykh'! After an hour and four minutes, the howling Faisal then claims that he can look into the hearts: *"They (the Salafis) are not sincere to their shahādah."* Approximately one hour, nine minutes and 50 seconds into the lecture Faisal states:

> "Now the worse Salafis in this country my brothers, sorry to be specific, but I have to be specific. The worse Salafis in this country are those in south London, more specifically those in Brixton Mosque because they are coming from {sic} very poor backgrounds and they are hungry, so they will kill for Fahd, they break noses in Brixton Mosque on three occasions {sic} for the love of Fahd,[2] one of them was even crying on the minbār! He was giving a khutbah on a Friday and he was crying tears, his shirt was soaked with tears (saying) 'why do you speak bad about

---

[1] *Di'āya Mukaththafah Didd ash-Shaykh Muhammad ibn 'AbdulWahhāb*, pp. 105-106. Originally translated by Abū Imrān al-Meksīkī.

[2] Here again Faisal reiterates the thing about "noses being broken", yet as even the likes of Abū Hamza al-Misrī have stated he only states this as it was Faisal himself who had his nose broken!

Fahd? If you were rich like him you would do the same thing, keep quiet about him.'[1] So he loves him so much that on the minbār he cried hoping that the news will reach in their report. They write reports to Saudi on the da'wah they do every month,[2] so in his report he can write 'I cried for you so increase my salary.'[3] He want {sic} his report to look fancy! Why is it that the African-Caribbean community of Brixton Mosque they are the most vehement in their love of Fahd?[4] The answer is clear, 'Umar said that poverty leads to what? To kufr! Poverty leads to kufr. That's why you only find the very rich Arabs in this movement, you don't find Moroccans, Algerians in this movement! Am I lying? Am I lying? I'm talking in this country do you find Moroccans and Algerians in the Salafi movement? If I'm lying tell me. I want to be corrected. There's a few in this country, but the vast majority are they in this movement? Just one and two. The people who are in this movement are the rich Arabs in the Gulf who have something to lose!"

---

[1] The individual accused here is not clear, as Faisal does not mention his name, so it is very difficult to confirm this claim of Faisal's. However, it has been suggested that it refers to an equally deranged individual, who was later banned from the office of *Masjid Ibn Taymiyyah (Brixton Mosque)* in 1998 CE for his own exaggerations over his personal foilbles!

[2] Do they?

[3] At this, the ignorant audience of blind followers burst into laughter as if they are being entertained by a comedian at a comedy club!

[4] Observe Faisal's propaganda here and use of simplistic reasoning in order to incite the audience to agree with him. *Masjid Ibn Taymiyyah (Brixton Mosque)* is independent and receives absolutely no financial support from Saudi Arabia and never has done, yet due to Faisal's propaganda this has become disseminated around the UK.

Firstly, from what the administraton of Masjid Ibn Taymiyyah (Brixton Mosque) have informed us: in all the years there has never been a report that has left *Masjid Ibn Taymiyyah (Brixton Mosque)*, apart from a report to the Charity Commission. As for the **"money from Saudi"** then the brothers are still waiting for the alleged sum of money that *Masjid Ibn Taymeeyah (Brixton Mosque)* has received. This uncorroborated claim is exactly like a similar claim about Brixton Mosque (*Masjid Ibn Taymiyyah*) that has been circulated on a number of Takfīrī websites and authored by a writer who called himself 'KM'. KM's real name, that he has tried to hide, is Muhammad al-Keenī, as he was originally from Kenya and also known as 'Kenyan Muhammad', but he did not have the gall to put his real name to his article of *bātil*. In 'KM''s account of his experience he states:

> Alhamdulillah, during the process of the hearing, <u>it was established that the Home Secretary had received the letter</u>[1] on the 22nd June 2002 from officials of Brixton Mosque, stating that I was a supposed threat to national security, and he was acting on that information, and that's why I was arrested in Belmarsh.[2]

---

[1] As if the Home Secretary of the Government would receive and read a letter on her/his table from a Salafi Masjid in one of the Ghetto areas of South London! The whole scenario is ridiculous!

[2] The full article can be read here: http://www.cageprisoners.com/articles.php?id=4449

So where is this letter from *"officials of Brixton Mosque"*? Why cannot anyone seem to find such a letter? So Muhammad al-Keenī conducted his interview with the *'Cage Prisoners'* website, who blindly support anyone based on the premise that they have been imprisoned on terrorism charges, yet the interviewer did not bother to even confirm this or even ask *Brixton Mosque* if this was the case.

Secondly, there is a clear contradiction here, as Faisal impugns the African and Caribbean communities of being Salafi due to perceived poverty, yet states that the majority of Salafis are "rich Gulf Arabs"!? Since when have *all* the Gulf countries admitted that they are Salafi? With the exception of Saudi Arabia, most, if not all, of the Islamic ministries of these Gulf countries are not *Salafi* at all!

Thirdly, Faisal again demonstrates his deception and aims to hoodwink his audience who even here did not fall for his lies, when he claimed that there are no Moroccan and Algerian Salafis in the UK. It is well-known that there are many Moroccan and Algerian Salafis within the UK and within the countries, Morocco and Algeria, there are thousands upon thousands of Salafis! Faisal even states that there are only **"just one or two"** (!!?) Moroccan and Algerian Salafis within the UK! Yet Faisal tries to feebly assert that only rich Gulf Arabs are Salafis and this is absolutely bizarre! Indeed, the *Salafi da'wah* is well established within Yemen, Indonesia, Jordan, Nigeria and Ghana, not to mention Algeria and Morocco so the statements of Faisal here are utterly foolish.

Fourthly, one of the brothers who used to listen to Faisal during his early university years in the late nineties has noted to us that when he first went to *Masjid Ibn Taymiyyah (Brixton Mosque)* he found that Faisal's claims were totally unfounded and found loads of Algerians and Moroccans attending the mosque with even the Imām, at that stage, being Moroccan! As a result, the brother realized the exaggerations and dangers of 'Abdullāh ("el") Faisal al-Jamaykī.

Fifthly, Faisal picks out and highlights the African and Carribbean community in particular, due to Faisal's own failure to generally penetrate the Muslim community of this particular ethnic background with his *da'wah*. The reality is that while the Salafī da'wah was being accepted and received from reverts and Muslims from Muslim backgrounds of African origin in London, the wider UK, Jamaica and Africa itself - the *da'wah* of Faisal was going extreme and was based on personal failures and frustrations. Faisal's failure in the Brixton area, which is an area in which many so-called 'revolutionaries' have tried to gain a foothold for their own desires and designs, led him to oppose the Salafīs of Brixton the most and accuse them of *kufr*. Due to this some have even questioned the mental state of Faisal, yet as his mental state is not something which can be corroborated by us, we are sticking with his statements as they stand without the necessity of a psychiatric or psycho-analytical assessment, or the likes.

Sixthly, Faisal applies a racial stereotype which has its origins with the *kuffār* and Faisal has merely accepted it, which is that the Salafīs, and those from African and Carribbean origins *"are coming from very poor backgrounds and are hungry"* - SubhānAllāh! Actually, the latter part of his statement *"...and are hungry"* - is laughable and obviously something that Faisal had just made up on the spot. Not only is this utterly incorrect but it is also an ethnic and racial stereotype that Faisal is regurgitating. From those who attend *Masjid Ibn Taymiyyah (Brixton Mosque)* are doctors, consultants, self-employed businesswomen and men, civil servants, teachers, youth workers, college and university students, IT experts, university graduates and more. Therefore, we totally reject the racist and stereotypical descriptions of the Salafīs of Brixton as being **"poor and hungry"** and **"unemployed"** which constantly dribbles off the vile tongue of Faisal and those Takfīrīs like him. Just four minutes later, he says:

> "I wouldn't be surprised if this is the biggest movement in this country because most of the Muslims are hypocrites."

Hereby, again, making *takfeer* of the Muslims of the UK; then Faisal states, in his utter ignorance and accusations about Muslim women:

> "Women love to marry those who say that there is no jihād anywhere in the world. So you'll find people, hypocrites, they have two wives and

292

three wives and their women are also evil, because a woman is supposed to help her husband go to Paradise, so if I have a wife and I am a hypocrite..."

Allāhu Musta'an! Faisal tries to show that having two or three wives is a characteristic of hypocrisy even though Allāh has legislated for it in His Book:

﴿ فَٱنكِحُواْ مَا طَابَ لَكُم مِّنَ ٱلنِّسَآءِ مَثۡنَىٰ وَثُلَٰثَ وَرُبَٰعَ ﴾

"...then marry those that please you of (other) women, two, three or four..." *{an-Nisā (4): 3}*

Here Faisal accuses the Salafi sisters of being evil, he reiterates this one hour, 16 minutes and 30 seconds into the lecture by stating:

"...But these Salafis their wives don't help them so their wives are also evil. And the reason why they keep quiet is <u>because they are also in it for the money, they are also in it for the money</u> so that they can be able to dress in fancy dresses and so on and so forth. They are dunyafied."

"In it for the money"?! Is Faisal serious? What financial gain is there from adhering to the manhaj of the *Salaf* in the current era?! Are the Salafis of Jordan "in it for the money"? Are the Salafis in Dammāj (Yemen) and in another parts of Yemen "in it for the money"?! Are the Salafis in Morocco "in it for the money"? Are the Salafis in Indonesia "in it for the money"?! A clearly slanderous attack, which is not proven by the reality. How does Faisal know that all these Salafi sisters are "in it for the money"? Did he conduct a survey with them behind their husbands' backs?! Allāh says:

﴿ يَـٰٓأَيُّهَا ٱلَّذِينَ ءَامَنُوٓاْ إِذَا ضَرَبۡتُمۡ فِى سَبِيلِ ٱللَّهِ فَتَبَيَّنُواْ وَلَا تَقُولُواْ لِمَنۡ أَلۡقَىٰٓ إِلَيۡكُمُ ٱلسَّلَـٰمَ لَسۡتَ مُؤۡمِنࣰا تَبۡتَغُونَ عَرَضَ ٱلۡحَيَوٰةِ ٱلدُّنۡيَا فَعِندَ ٱللَّهِ مَغَانِمُ كَثِيرَةࣱۚ كَذَٰلِكَ كُنتُم مِّن قَبۡلُ فَمَنَّ ٱللَّهُ عَلَيۡكُمۡ فَتَبَيَّنُوٓاْۚ إِنَّ ٱللَّهَ كَانَ بِمَا تَعۡمَلُونَ خَبِيرࣰا ۝ ﴾

"O you who have believed, when you go forth [to fight] in the cause of Allāh, investigate; and do not say to one who gives you [a greeting of] peace "You are not a believer," aspiring for the goods of worldly life; for with Allāh are many acquisitions. You [yourselves] were like that before; then Allāh conferred His favor upon you, so investigate. Indeed Allāh is ever, with what you do, Acquainted." {an-Nisā (4): 94}

Ibn Katheer says in his tafseer of the ayah, showing the importance of *tahabbut* (verification):

Al-Bukhārī recorded that Ibn 'Abbās said that the Messenger of Allāh ﷺ said to al-Miqdād,

«إِذَا كَانَ رَجُلٌ مُؤۡمِنٌ يُخۡفِي إِيمَانَهُ مَعَ قَوۡمٍ كُفَّارٍ فَأَظۡهَرَ إِيمَانَهُ فَقَتَلۡتَهُ، فَكَذَلِكَ كُنۡتَ أَنۡتَ تُخۡفِي إِيمَانَكَ بِمَكَّةَ مِنۡ قَبۡل»

294

"You killed a believing man who hid his faith with disbelieving people, after he had announced his faith to you. Remember that you used to hide your faith in Makkah before."

Al-Bukhārī recorded this shorter version without a complete chain of narrators. However a longer version with a connected chain of narrators has also been recorded. Al-Ḥāfidh Abū Bakr al-Bazzār recorded that Ibn 'Abbās said: The Messenger of Allāh ﷺ sent a military expedition under the authority of al-Miqdād bin al-Aswad and when they reached the designated area, they found the people had dispersed. However, a man with a lot of wealth did not leave and said, 'I bear witness that there is no deity worthy of worship except Allāh.' Yet, al-Miqdād killed him, and a man said to him, 'You killed a man after he proclaimed: 'There is no deity worthy of worship except Allāh'. By Allāh I will mention what you did to the Prophet.' When they went back to the Messenger of Allāh ﷺ, they said, 'O Messenger of Allāh! Al-Miqdad killed a man who testified that there is no deity worthy of worship except Allāh.' He said,

«ادْعُوا لِيَ الْمِقْدَادَ، يَا مِقْدَادُ أَقَتَلْتَ رَجُلًا يَقُولُ: لَا إِلهَ إِلَّا اللهُ، فَكَيْفَ لَكَ بِلَا إِلهَ إِلَّا اللهُ غَدًا؟»

"Summon Al-Miqdād before me. O Miqdād! Did you kill a man who proclaimed, 'There is no deity worthy of worship except Allāh' What would you do when you face, 'There is no deity worthy of worship except Allāh' tomorrow?" Allāh then revealed the ayah.

Al-'Allaamah Saalih al-Fawzaan states about the ayah:

Verification (tathabbut) is an obligation without being hasty in judging people except with insight and narration.[1]

In Saheeh ul-Bukhārī (Kitāb ul-Maghāzī) and Saheeh Muslim (Kitāb ul-Īmān) Usāmah bin Zaid ﷺ reported:

The Messenger of Allāh ﷺ sent us to Huraqāt, a tribe of Juhaynah. We attacked that tribe early in the morning and defeated them, (then) a man from the Ansār and I caught hold of a man (of the defeated tribe). When we overcame him he said: *'La ilaha ilAllāh.'* At that moment, the Ansārī spared him, but I attacked him with my spear and killed him. By the time we went back to al-Madeenah, news had already reached Allāh's Messenger ﷺ and he said to me, *"O Usāmah, did you kill him after he professed La ilaha ilAllāh?"* I replied, "O Messenger of Allāh! He professed it only to save his life." The Prophet ﷺ repeated, *"Did you kill him after he had professed La ilaha illAllāh?"*

He went on repeating this to me until I wished I had not embraced Islam before that day (so that I would have not committed this sin). Another narration is: the Messenger ﷺ said, *"Did you kill him after he stated 'La*

[1] Ma'ālī, Shaykh, Dr Sālih bin Fawzān bin 'Abdullāh al-Fawzān, *at-Takfeer wa Dawābituhu* (Algeria: Majālis ul-Hudā, 1425 AH/2004 CE, ed. Abū 'AbdurRahmān 'Ādil bin 'Ali bin Ahmad al-Farīdān), p.11.

ilaha illallah?" I said, "O Messenger of Allāh! He said out of fear of our arms." He ﷺ said, *"Did you cut his heart open(to find out whether he had done so sincerely or not)?"* He continued repeating it until I wished that I had embraced Islām only that day.

Ibn Mulaqqin رحمه الله stated in regards to this hadeeth:

Allāh informed His Prophet ﷺ about the Munaafiqeen who were living among his companions yet did not believe in Islām. The Prophet ﷺ knew about them yet he did not permit that they be killed or dishonoured for they used to manifest Islām verbally. Thus, the ruling on everyone from Allāh's creation has to be based on what is manifest and apparent, not based on what is hidden internally, the likes of this has been relayed from the Imāms.[1]

Shaykh Sālih al-Fawzān states in regards to this hadeeth:

This indicates the obligation of verification (tathabbut) in issues and not being hasty in judging people. The ruling has to be based on knowledge and there has to be verification in regards to a person. Whoever manifests Islām and says the shahādah has to be abstained from as this great story

---

[1] Ibn Mulaqqin, *at-Tawdeeh: Sharh al-Jāmi' as-Saheeh* (Makkah: Umm ul-Qurā University, 1416 AH, ed. Muhammad Ilyās Anwar, MA thesis), vol.1, p.63. See Dr Muhammad bin 'Umar bin Sālim al-Bāzmūl, *at-Takfeer wa Dawābituhu* (Cairo: Dār ut-Tawheed wa's-Sunnah, 1428 AH/2007 CE), p.40.

(of Usāmah bin Zayd ﷺ) indicates, until he nullifies his Islām like the one who associates partners in worship with Allaah, invokes other than Allāh or commits one of the well-known nullifiers of Islām highlighted by the scholars; at that point such a person is judged with apostasy. As long as nothing manifests from him which opposes Islaam then good is to be thought about him and he is judged as having his Islām intact, even if some contrary actions, other than shirk and kufr such as sin or disobedience, manifest from him. He is not judged with kufr until he commits a well-known nullifier of Islām, as highlighted by the scholars, and has no excuse. As he could be ignorant or new to Islām and thus does not know that what he is doing is kufr.[1]

Faisal states just 2 minutes later:

"They claim that the leaders are still Muslims because they see them praying on CNN and so on and so forth...so a person praying is no evidence that the person is a believer, firm in al-Islām, firm with īmān."

This is very dangerous, as it inculcates into the minds of the youth that even though they see a Muslim certainly praying, *"it doesn't mean anything because he is a kāfir anyway and there is doubt"* - this is the logical result from the beliefs of Faisal and it contradicts an important principle of Usūl. As a ruling has to take consideration of what is outward and apparent. Therefore, if we

---

[1] Ibid., pp.12-13.

observe a Muslim praying we have certainty that he is indeed a Muslim, as certainty is not removed by any doubts. Moreover, before *takfeer* can be made we have to take into consideration what is apparent from a person and the apparent action of a person praying is an impediment to *takfeer*. This also contradicts the *aqīdah* of Ahl us-Sunnah wherein *imān* is speech of the heart and tongue and action of the heart, tongue and limbs. The Prophet ﷺ said: *"imān consists of seventy something branches; the highest of them being la ilāha illa Allāh and the lowest of them is to remove something harmful from the path".[1]* This hadīth clearly proves that righteous action is a part of *imān* and an indication of the existence of *imān*. In another narration, the Messenger of Allāh ﷺ clearly defined what is *imān*: *"I enjoin you to believe in Allāh alone. Do you know what imān in Allāh alone is?"* They said: *"Allāh and His Messenger know best."* He ﷺ said: *"To bear witness that there is no god worthy of worship but Allāh and that Muhammad is the Messenger of Allāh; to establish regular prayer; to pay zakāh; to fast Ramadhān and to give one-fifth of the war-booty (al-khums)."[2]* Only Allāh and His Messenger ﷺ have the right to negate *imān* of the heart despite there existing external evidence to the contrary. Allāh states:

﴿ قَالَتِ ٱلْأَعْرَابُ ءَامَنَّا ۖ قُل لَّمْ تُؤْمِنُوا۟ وَلَٰكِن قُولُوٓا۟ أَسْلَمْنَا وَلَمَّا يَدْخُلِ ٱلْإِيمَٰنُ فِى قُلُوبِكُمْ ۖ وَإِن تُطِيعُوا۟ ٱللَّهَ وَرَسُولَهُۥ لَا يَلِتْكُم مِّنْ أَعْمَٰلِكُمْ شَيْـًٔا ۚ إِنَّ ٱللَّهَ غَفُورٌ رَّحِيمٌ ﴾

---

[1] Sahīh al-Bukhāri (9) and Sahīh Muslim (35)
[2] Sahīh al-Bukhāri (53) and Sahīh Muslim (17)

"The bedouins say: 'We believe.' Say: 'You believe not but you only say, "We have surrendered (in Islam),"for Faith has not yet entered your hearts'..." {al-Hujarāt (49): 14}

Faisal then states one hour and twenty-two minutes into the lecture:

"They have a lot of Jewish traits, I will mention about thirteen Jewish traits they have, so they are the yahūd of the ummah, the Saudi Salafis they are the yahūd of the ummah."

Allāh says:

﴿ أَمْ نَجْعَلُ ٱلَّذِينَ ءَامَنُوا وَعَمِلُوا ٱلصَّـٰلِحَـٰتِ كَٱلْمُفْسِدِينَ فِى ٱلْأَرْضِ أَمْ نَجْعَلُ ٱلْمُتَّقِينَ كَٱلْفُجَّارِ ﴾

"Or should We treat those who believe and do righteous deeds like corrupters in the land? Or should We treat those who fear Allāh like the wicked?" {Sād (38): 28}

Ibn Katheer G states in regards to this ayah in Surah Sād, ayah 28:

Meaning: 'We shall not do that.' They are not equal before Allāh, and since this is the case, there must inevitably be another realm in which those who obey Allāh will be rewarded and the wicked will be punished. This teaching indicates to those of a sound mind and upright nature that there must inevitably be a resurrection and recompense. We see evildoers and criminals are prospering and increasing in wealth, children and

300

luxury, until they die in that state. We see oppressed believers dying of grief and distress, so by the wisdom of the All-Wise, All-Knowing, All-Just who does not do even a speck of dust's weight of injustice, there should be a time when the rights of the oppressed are restored with due justice. If this does not happen in this world, there must be another realm where recompense may be made and consolation may be found.

Allāh also says:

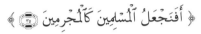

"Then will We treat the Muslims like the criminals?"

{al-Qalam (68): 35}

Imam as-Sa'di ﷺ states regarding the ayah in Surah Qalam, ayah 35:

His (Allaah's) Wisdom does not make the Muslims who stand before their Lord, fulfil His ordinances and follow what please Him – like the criminals who are entrenched in disobeying Him, disbelief of His Signs, stubbornness towards His Messengers and who wage war against His Awliyaa'. Whoever thinks that Allaah equalises the reward between the two of them has thought evil in such a judgement and thus renders the judgement as being void and his view is corrupt.[1]

---

[1] Al-'Allāmah Shaykh 'AbdurRahmān bin Nāsir as-Sa'dī, *Tayseer al-Kareem ir-Rahmān fi Tafseer Kalām il-Mannān* (Beirut: Resalah Publishers, 1421 AH/2000 CE), p.881.

Faisal continues spouting his venom:

> "Salafis oppress their wives and stop them from education...Salafis force women to wear niqāb and stop them from driving cars, <u>all these are examples of how they oppress women</u>. Any hadeeth to give women freedom, liberation and prestige they say the hadeeth is weak."

Contemplate! Blatant lies from 'Abdullāh Faisal, one after the other!

And it is also noticeable how he says all of this but on his lectures entitled *Let the Scholars Beware* and the lecture *Islam Under Siege* he praises the Tālibān regime who closed down women's Islamic schools and actually did force women to adhere to their form of Islamic practice and belief, some of which contained *shirk* and *bida*! An hour and twenty-seven minutes into the lecture:

> "The verdict on the Salafis, I've given you their descriptions, I've given you their 'aqeedah, I will now give you the verdict..."

Before we proceed, here Faisal is about to give a *fatwa*, an Islamic ruling, even though he is not qualified to give this at all, so beware! He continues:

"...Salafis are major hypocrites, there's no difference between a Salafi and a disciple of Musaylimah. Musaylimah exchanged the Sharī'ah and he had people who helped him, supported him, aided him and fought for him. Salafis will fight and kill for King Fahd who has dismantled the Sharī'ah...therefore you're not allowed to pray behind a Salafi, your salah behind them is bātil because they're major hypocrites, they're mega hypocrites. Now you know why I delayed the speech for four years because I make sure you can handle the verdict before I deliver the verdict on you!"

Faisal delivers another incredulous and vile 'verdict':

"Any woman that is married to a Salafi, she has to disassociate herself from him and make barā' from him! How can she co-habit with a man who betray Allāh Ta'ala, His Messenger and the Muslims. She should abhor such a man just to look into his face should make her feel upset and sick. So how can she co-habit with a man, marry man, that a man {sic} and cohabit with him?"

La Hawla wa la Quwwata ila billāhi!

Sample Lecture Number Twenty-One: 'Rules Of Jihad'

Twenty minutes into the lecture Faisal states:

> "What's our relationship with kāfirs? Peaceful co-existence or all-out war? The opinion of Imām Shāfi'ī is that it is all-out war"!!

So he states this without even bringing any *daleel* from where Imām Shāfi'ī ﷺ is alleged to have said this! Which book did Imām ash-Shāfi'ī state this in? Who transmitted it? No evidence is mentioned whatsoever. Refer to the speech of Shaykh Sālih Āl ush-Shaykh *(hafidhahullāh)* under 'Sample Lecture Number Four' above on the categories of disbelievers.

Sample Lecture Number Twenty-Two: 'The Peak Of The Matter'

Faisal continues with his *manhaj* of mass *takfeer*, stating one hour and twenty-five minutes into the lecture:

> "So can you imagine the hundreds and thousands and millions of Muslims who have apostated from Islām without even realising it?!"!!!

Sample Lecture Number Twenty-Three: 'Jihad'

After the first minute he states:

> "If you wage war against a deviant group it's not jihād."

Yet 'Ali ﷺ fought against the Khawārij at Nahrawān and the companions did not make *takfeer* of them. Ibn Taymiyyah stated that in regards to the Khawārij there is a consensus on fighting against them because they are misguided innovators.[1] Ibn 'Aqeel narrated from his Shaykh Abu'l-Fadl al-Hamadhānī (d. 489 AH/1096 CE) that he said:

> The innovators within Islām, along with the liars and those who fabricate hadeeth are worse than the atheists. For the atheists intend to corrupt the deen from outside while those (innovators, liars and fabricators of hadeeth) intend to corrupt the deen from inside. They resemble a people of a city who strive to corrupt it internally while the atheists are like those who have beseiged the city externally. Yet those inside open the fort up to them and thus are far worse to Islām than others.[2]

Muhammad bin Yahyā adh-Dhuhalī stated:

> I heard Yahyā ibn Ma'een say: 'Defending the Sunnah is better than jihad in the path of Allāh.' So I said to Yahyā: 'a man spends out his wealth, tires himself and strives, yet this (defence of the Sunnah) is better than him?' Yahyā replied: 'yes, much better.'[3]

---

[1] Shaykh ul-Islām Ibn Taymiyyah, Muhammad Rashād Sālim (ed.), *Minhāj us-Sunnah an-Nabawiyyah* (Riyādh, KSA: Imām Muhammad bin Sa'ūd Islamic University, 1406 AH, First Edn.), vol.6, p.116

[2] Shaykh ul-Islām Ibn Taymiyyah, Muhammad Muhiyuddeen 'AbdulHameed (ed.), *as-Sārim al-Maslūl 'ala Shātim ir-Rasūl* (Beirut: Dār ul-Kutub al-'Ilmiyyah, n.d.), p.171.

[3] Imām Muhammad bin Ahmad bin 'Uthmān adh-Dhahabī, Shu'ayb al-Arna'ūt (ed.), *Siyar A'lām un-Nubalā'* (Beirut: Mu'assasat ur-Risālah, 1406 AH), vol.10, p.518.

Shaykh ul-Islām Ibn Taymiyyah stated:

Of the famous stories which have reached us is that Shaykh Abū 'Amru
bin as-Salāh commanded that the well-known school of Abu'l-Hasan al-
Āmidī be taken and he said that 'taking it is better than taking 'Akkā
(Acre, a city in Palestine).'[1]

Shaykh, Dr Abū Anas Hamad al-'Uthmān, a contemporary scholar from
Kuwait, comments on this by saying:

Look at this fiqh and manhaj of the Salaf, liberating a school from the
innovators took precedence with them than liberating 'Akkā (Acre in
Palestine) from the Crusaders. Because the innovators deceive the people
thereby corrupting the deen, as for the Crusaders then the people do not
doubt as to their corruption of the religion and worldly affairs.[2]

Ibn ul-Qayyim صلى said about some of the deviants:

Exposing them and their corrupt principles is from the greatest acts of
jihād in the path of Allāh...[3]

---

[1] Shaykh ul-Islām Ibn Taymiyyah, *Naqd ul-Mantiq*, p.156

[2] Hamad bin Ibrāheem al-'Uthmān, *Jihād: Anwā'ahu wa Ahkāmuhu, wa'l-Hadd al-Fāsil Baynahu wa Bayna'l-Fawda* ('Ammān: Dār ul-Athariyyah, 1428 AH/2007 CE), pp.49-50.

[3] Ibn Qayyim ul-Jawziyyah, *as-Sawā'iq ul-Mursalah 'ala'l-Jahmiyyah wa'l-Mu'attilah* (Riyādh, KSA: Dār ul-'Āsimah, 1418 AH/1998 CE), vol.1, pp.301-302.

Ibn ul-Qayyim ﷺ said in *al-Qaseedah Nūniyyah*:

Jihād with the clear proofs and the tongue; Comes before *Jihād* with the sword and the spear.

Al-Wazeer ibn Hubayrah stated similar to this when he stated that fighting against the Khawārij takes precedence over fighting against the Mushriks as fighting against the Khawārij involves preserving Islām's capital while fighting against the polytheists is gaining a profit for Islām.[1] After eighteen minutes Faisal states:

"Our manhaj is the bullet not the ballot! You use the ballot in Algeria and you got a kick in your face. You use the ballot a second time in Turkey and you got a kick in your face. You use it a third time in Nigeria, Abiola, he won the election, yet they put him in prison, poisoned him and you got kick *{sic}* in your face[2] three times!"

In El-Faisal's "tafseer" (!?) of Sūrah al-Kāfiroon he states: *"Our manhaj is the bullet and not the ballot-box."* Faisal also says the same 54 minutes into his "tafseer" (!?) of Sūrah Yūsuf. Did the *Salaf* say that *"our manhaj is the bullet"*, did the *Salaf* say *"our manhaj is the ballot"* did the *Salaf* say anything of the sort like this? The answer is clearly "no", so where is Faisal getting all of this

---

[1] Al-Wazeer Yahyā bin Muhammad ibn Hubayrah, Fu'ad 'AbdulMun'im Ahmad (ed.), *al-Ifsāh 'an Ma'ānī is-Sihhāh*, (Riyādh, KSA: Dār ul-Watan, 1417 AH/1996 CE, 2nd Edn.), vol.1, p.280.

[2] See here how Faisal speaks as if he is talking to the whole *ummah* by using "you used" and "your face", hereby attempting to elicit a collective emotive response.

bātil from? Faisal here has inadvertently helped to bolster the false concept that Islām was spead by the sword. He continues saying twenty minutes into the lecture:

> "Now is there any peace treaty between us and the Hindus? No! So you can go India and if you see a Hindu walking down the road you're allowed to kill him and take his money. Is that clear?"

How did he work out that there was no peace between India and the entire Muslim Ummah? Can a Muslim enter a non-Muslim country under a contract and condition of security, trust and truthfulness and then lie, break the agreement and kill the citizens of that country? This is treachery and not *jihād*, and is ruling by other than what Allāh has revealed. The proofs for this are many, the most important of which is what the Prophet ﷺ stated in the hadeeth of Hudhayfah ibn al-Yamān ؓ in Saheeh Muslim: *"Go! For you have made a promise with them and we seek Allāh's help against them."* This hadeeth is relevant because when Hudhayfah and his father wanted to go to Madeenah the Mushrikeen from the Quraysh seized them and took a promise and covenant from the two of them that they would not go to support Muhammad ﷺ. When Hudhayfah and his father left and arrived in Madeenah they informed the Prophet ﷺ of the matter and the Prophet ﷺ said to them: *"Go! For you have made a promise with them and we seek Allāh's help against them."* Therefore, if a Muslim has an agreement with them the Muslim must fulfil the agreement with them. Abu'l-Hasan 'Ali bin Abī Bakr bin 'AbdulJaleel al-Marghīyānī (511-593

AH/1118-1197 CE)[1] stated in *al-Hidāyah: Sharh ul-Bidāyah al-Mubtadi'*, p.134:

وإذا دخل المسلم دار الحرب تاجرا فلا يحل له أن يتعرض لشيء من أموالهم ولا من

دمائهم لأنه ضمن أن لا يتعرض لهم بالاستئمان ، فالتعرض بعد ذلك يكون غدرا ،

والغدر حرام

If a Muslim enters Dār ul-Harb as a trader, then he is like a Muslim who is Musta'min in Dār ul-Harb, and it is, therefore, not permissible for him to dishonour them in anything in terms of their wealth and blood as he is within Isti'mān which necessitates he does not dishonour them. If he dishonours them after this then this is betrayal and betrayal is harām.[2]

Our Shaykh, Mashhūr Hasan (*hafidhahullāh*) thus states:

Based upon this, it becomes clear to us the accuracy of what has been acknowledged by the 'Ulama of our era in regards to the prohibition of wreaking havoc, hijacking airplanes and killing non-Muslims in their lands which is committed by some young Muslims who enter those lands with Amān (safe-passage and security),[3] in the form of entry visas. For

---

[1] The great Hanafī jurist, was born at Marghiyān in the vicinity of Farghana in Present Day Uzbekistan. He studied with Najmudden Abū Hafs 'Umar an-Nasafī, his son Abu'l-Layth Ahmad bin 'Umar an-Nasafī and other eminent teachers, and excelled in Hadeeth, Tafseer, Fiqh and other studies.

[2] *Kitāb us-Siyar, Bāb ul-Musta'min*

[3] And if they are Mu'āhadeen then the opposition to the *Sharī'ah* would be from two angles, like a person who steals pork and eats it!

this is an example of betrayal and treachery, the prohibition is intensified when it is ascribed to the Sharī'ah and considered as being from "Jihād", as they claim![1]

For more on this refer to what has been noted in our comments of sample lecture no.3 within this study. Then ("El") Faisal says:

> "So the best way to spread Islām is not with da'wah, the best way to spread Islām is jihād."

This statement itself is an utter contradiction, as *da'wah* (jihād with the tongue) is a level of *jihād!* Yet Faisal, as per usual, neglects to mention this to his audiences of uncritical cult followers. Who is Faisal to determine the best way to spread Islām, especially when you take into consideration his lack of knowledge and his thirst for spilling innocent blood? The best way to spread Islam depends on the condition of the Muslims and the attitude of the people they confront. Even when the Messenger of Allāh ﷺ embarked on a military expedition, he still sent someone ahead to invite the people to Islām. Both Bukhārī and Muslim narrate that Sahl Ibn Sa'd ﷺ said : "On the day of Khaibar, Allāh's Messenger said, *'Tomorrow I will give this flag to a man through whose hands Allāh will give us victory. He loves Allāh and His Messenger, and he is*

---

[1] From the edit of Shaykh Muhammad bin Zakariyyā Abū Ghāzī and our Shaykh Mashhūr Hasan Āl Salmān to Imām al-Mujtahid Abū 'Abdullāh Muhammad bin 'Īsā bin Muhammad bin Asbagh al-Azdī al-Qurtubī (aka Ibn Munāsif), *Kitāb ul-Injād fī Abwāb il-Jihād* (Beirut: Mu'assasah ar-Rayān, 1425 AH/2005 CE), vol.1, pp.63-81.

loved by Allāh and His Messenger.' The people remained that night, wondering as to who would be given it. In the morning the people went to Allāh's Messenger and everyone of them was hopeful to receive it (i.e. the flag). The Prophet said, *'Where is 'Ali (Ibn Abi Tālib)?'* It was said, 'He is suffering from eye trouble O Allāh's Messenger.' He said, *'Send for him.'* 'Ali ☼ was brought and Allāh's Messenger spat in his eye and invoked good upon him. So 'Ali ☼ was cured as if he never had any trouble. Then the Prophet gave him the flag. 'Ali ☼ said 'O Allāh's Messenger! I will fight with them till they become like us.' Allāh's Messenger said, *'Proceed and do not hurry. When you enter their territory, call them to embrace Islam and inform them of Allāh's Rights which they should observe, for by Allāh, even if a single man is led on the right path (of Islam) by Allāh through you, then that will be better for you than the nice red camels.'"*[1] In the Fatāwā issued by al-Lajnah ad-Dā'imah (12/14) it states:

الإسلام انتشر بالحجة والبيان بالنسبة لمن استمع البلاغ واستجاب له ، وانتشر

بالقوة والسيف لمن عاند وكابر حتى غُلِب على أمره ، فذهب عناده فأسلم لذلك

الواقع

Islām spread by means of proof, and clear evidences to those who gave a tentative ear and responded to its message, and it spread by means of force and the sword amongst those who were obstinate and arrogant until they were overwhelmed and their obstinacy no longer existed and they submitted to the reality (i.e. Islām is the truth).

---

[1] Bukhāri (3009) and Muslim (2406)

Shaykh ul-Islām Ibn Taymiyyah ﷺ stated:

It is well-known that Jihād comprises fighting with the hand and (jihād) with the proofs, evidences and da'wah, Allāh says:

﴿ وَلَوْ شِئْنَا لَبَعَثْنَا فِى كُلِّ قَرْيَةٍ نَّذِيرًا . فَلَا تُطِعِ ٱلْكَـٰفِرِينَ وَجَـٰهِدْهُم بِهِۦ جِهَادًا كَبِيرًا ﴾

'And if We had willed, We could have sent into every city a warner. So do not obey the disbelievers, and strive against them with it (i.e. the Qur'ān) a great striving.' *{al-Furqān (25): 51-52}*

So Allāh instructed to struggle against the kuffār with the Qur'ān and with a great striving (Jihādan Kabeeran). This is a Makkan Sūrah revealed in Makkah before the Prophet ﷺ made Hijrah and before he was instructed to fight as this was not permitted for him. So this Jihād was with knowledge, the heart, bayān and da'wah and not with fighting. As for fighting then that needs planning and assessment, for it needs courage from the heart and to fight with the hand...Abū Bakr and 'Umar (radi Allāhu 'anhumma) have precedence in all types of da'wah which are not bodily fighting.[1]

---

[1] Shaykh ul-Islām Ahmad bin 'AbdulHaleem Ibn Taymiyyah, Muhammad Rashād Sālim (ed.), *Minhāj us-Sunnah an-Nabawiyyah* (Riyadh: Imām Muhammad bin Saud Islamic University, 1406, 1st Edn.), vol.8, pp.86-87.

Thirty-six minutes into the lecture Faisal says:

"So you want to go to jannah, put up your hands those who want to go to jannah. It's easy, just kill a kāfir, just kill a kāfir!"!!

This unrestricted statement is clear in inciting the murder of innocent non-Muslims and civilians. Bukhāri narrated that 'Abdullāh ibn 'Amr ibn al-'Ās ￼ said: *"The Prophet ￼ said: 'Whoever kills a mu'āhid will not smell the fragrance of Paradise, even though its fragrance can be detected from a distance of forty days.'"* In Saheeh Muslim from Buraydah ￼ who narrated that whenever the Prophet Muhammad ￼ commanded an army general, he ￼ would exhort the army general to have fear and consciousness of Allāh. This is because an army leader is in need of having *taqwā* of Allāh and being reminded of it. In the same way the leader orders goodness for those under him and does not transgress against them. Therefore, the leader of an army has to be one of pious worship, correct *deen* and good manners with his followers. The Prophet ￼ said to an army: *"Do battle and do not steal from the spoils of war, do not betray, do not depart (from the battle), do not mutilate and do not kill young children."* In the two Sahīhs it is mentioned that the Prophet ￼ found a dead woman of the polytheists that had been killed during the battle. He saw the companions surrounding something and then he found out that it was a woman who had been killed during the battle. The Prophet ￼ was angered by this as she had been killed and said: *"This is not one against whom war is to be fought against"* clearly showing that 'this woman did not come to fight against you, so why did you kill her?' He then instructed the other Companion: *"Tell Khālid to not kill children, women or the elderly and frail."*. In the two Sahīhs[1] Ibn 'Umar ☞ narrated: *"A woman was found killed in one of the battles so Allāh's Messenger prohibited the killing of women and children."* The hadeeth is hasan and was authenticated by at-Tirmidhī and Ibn Hibbān from the narration of al-Hasan from Samurah which the 'Ulama differed over in regards to its authenticity, however it is acceptable. It is mentioned in *at-Talkhees*: ***"It was reported by Ahmad and at-Tirmidhī from the hadeeth of al-Hasan from Samurah."*** At-Tirmidhī stated: ***"The hadeeth is Hasan Saheeh Ghareeb."*** Shaykh 'Abdullāh al-Bassām *(rahimahullāh)* stated in *Tawdeeh ul-Ahkām*:

1. It has preceded that the Prophet ﷺ prohibited the killing of women, old men, children, people in places of worship and the likes who have no concern with fighting.

2. These two hadeeths affirm this meaning in regards to the prohibition of killing women and old people who do not aid in war via action or opinion (i.e. strategies).

3. The wars of Islam are neither about oppression nor corruption rather they are wars of mercy and to call to goodness. Al-Māwardī said in *al-Ahkām us-Sultāniyyah*: 'It is not permitted to kill women and children whether during warfare or outside of it, because the Prophet ﷺ forbade killing them just as he prohibited killing the

---

[1] Also in Abū Dāwūd, at-Tirmidhī and Ibn Mājah.

weak. The commander must order his troops with what Allāh has obligated in terms of adhering to His rulings.'[1]

Therefore, the Prophet ﷺ prohibited the killing of women and children and it is known that a clear forbiddance of something *(nahy)* indicates *tahreem* (prohibition). Imām ash-Shāfi'ī stated, as relayed in *al-Faqeeh wa'l-Mutafaqih*, vol.1, p.69:

> The basis of nahy from Allāh's Messenger ﷺ is that all which he forbids is prohibited until a proof comes which indicates that the meaning is not a prohibition.

See how Faisal misguides the Muslims with his ignorant and irresponsible open-ended speech. Faisal then states, in utter contradiction to his usual mass *takfeer* of Muslims and accusing the majority of Muslims of having apostasized from Islām:

"So a man may have a weakness for Vodka or Tenants or he may have a weakness for betting on the National Lottery, one pound every week. But when the Ameer says "jihād" he will be the first to write his name down and put up his hand and go and fight. Is that clear? So if sahabahs drank alcohol and still they had the īmān to fight why should you cut-off your Muslim brothers right now in our midst today? You can't do that to them, that's the khawārij mentality and if you throw him out of

---

[1] 'Abdullāh bin 'AbdurRahmān al-Bassām, *Tawdeeh ul-Ahkām min Bulūgh il-Marām* (Makkah al-Mukarramah: Maktabah al-Asadī, 1423 AH/2003 CE, 5th Edn.), vol.6, pp.371.

the Muslim community which community should he enter into? The Christian community!? That's the khawārij mentality so you should always give hope to the believers as long as they make tawbah."

So where was all of this when Faisal threw the Salafis out of the fold of Islām by referring to them as being *"no different from the followers of Musaylimah al-Kadhdhab"*? Where was all of this when Faisal referred to the Salafis as *"the Jews of the ummah"?* Where was all of this when Faisal referred to the scholars as being *"Rabbis and Monks"*, and his referring to the scholars as *kuffār* that *"should be killed"*? See the quote below. Where was all of this when Faisal referred to the Muslims of today as *"being like the kāfirs of Quraysh"?* Where was all of this when Faisal said *"hundreds, thousands and millions of Muslims have apostated without even realising it"*?[3] As found in the lecture on *'Knowledge'* (!?), sample lecture no.13 in our study, Faisal says:

"So the Muslims in this country (i.e. the UK), the majority of them, they have no īmān and no taqwā, the average Muslim you meet on the street he has no īmān and no taqwā..."

Faisal also stated in his "tafseer" (!?) of Sūrah Yūsuf, 29 minutes into the lecture:

"Most Muslims who leave their countries and come here (to the UK)

---

[1] As occurs in the lecture *'The Devil's Deception of the Saudi Salafis'*, see sample lecture no. 20
[2] As occurs in the lecture *'Rejecting the Tāghūt'*, see sample lecture no.10
[3] As occurs in the lecture *'The Peak of the Matter'*, see sample lecture no.22

have apostated. The nightclub prove too much for them; the betting shop, the National Lottery is too much for them; the alcohol is too much for them; the blue eye {sic} and blond hair is too much for them and so and so forth. The temptations is {sic} too much for them, so they can't practice the deen, they can't. They don't have any īmān to remain on the deen."

After forty-nine minutes Faisal states, making *takfeer* of his own audience:

"Every Muslim would like to kill the kuffār, unless you're a munāfiq and you have no al-walā wa'l-barā' in your heart or you love kāfirs. I wouldn't be surprised if some of you love Hindus and Sikhs and Buddhists and Christians, only munāfiqūn love kuffār."

So hereby, he has accused his own audience of *juhhāl* of being major hypocrites who love the *kuffār*! What sort of nonsense is this? Then he states:

"You can even use chemical weapons to exterminate kāfirs. Now if you have cockroaches in your house would you spray them? Huh? Yes! With chemicals! Who has more dignity the cockroach or the kāfir? The cockroach, the Qur'ān tells you that! Which ayah in the Qur'ān tells you that? Huh?!"

So here, Faisal again makes no distinction among the *kuffār*, as the People of the Book have a certain status in al-Islām to the extent that a Muslim man can marry a woman from the people of the scripture, but can a Muslim man marry a cockroach? Does Allāh allow Muslim men to marry that which has no dignity?! Did Allāh describe in His book the people of the book as being cockroaches or as having no dignity? Are there Christians living now who may go to Paradise? There are no doubt some Christians who live in far, remote, impoverished regions of the world who only know about Christianity and yet only worship Allāh, so for such people Allāh may look into their hearts on the Day of Judgement, and Allāh knows best about this. Imām Muhammad bin Sālih al-'Uthaymeen G stated regarding the verse in the Qur'ān:

﴿ وَأُوحِيَ إِلَيَّ هَٰذَا ٱلْقُرْءَانُ لِأُنذِرَكُم بِهِۦ وَمَنۢ بَلَغَ أَئِنَّكُمْ لَتَشْهَدُونَ أَنَّ مَعَ ٱللَّهِ ءَالِهَةً أُخْرَىٰ قُل لَّآ أَشْهَدُ قُلْ إِنَّمَا هُوَ إِلَٰهٌ وَٰحِدٌ وَإِنَّنِي بَرِىٓءٌ مِّمَّا تُشْرِكُونَ ﴾

"....This Qur'ān has been revealed to me that I may therewith warn you and whomsoever it may reach...." {al-An'ām (6): 19}

This indicates that the evidences are not established upon those to whom the Qur'ān has not been conveyed. Likewise are those whom the Qur'ān has been conveyed to in a distorted manner, the evidences are not established upon them either, but their excuse is not the same as the excuse of those to whom the Qur'ān has not been conveyed at all, because it is upon those whom the Qur'ān has reached in a distorted manner to further investigate. However they may trust the person who

318

conveyed the Qur'ān to them to a point where they do not need to investigate (for themselves).

So the question: 'Has Islām been conveyed to the masses of non-Muslims in a manner which is not distorted?'

Then the answer is: 'No not at all!' And when the affair of those who act without wisdom emerged, it distorted the picture of Islām even further in the eyes of the Westerners and other than them. Those who plant bombs in the midst of people claiming that this is Jihād. The truth is that they harm Islām and further turn people away from it.[1]

Allāh makes a distinction in the beginning in the verse, so even though the people of the book are *kuffār*, Allāh makes a distinction:

$$\lbrace \text{لَمۡ يَكُنِ ٱلَّذِينَ كَفَرُواْ مِنۡ أَهۡلِ ٱلۡكِتَٰبِ وَٱلۡمُشۡرِكِينَ مُنفَكِّينَ حَتَّىٰ تَأۡتِيَهُمُ ٱلۡبَيِّنَةُ} \rbrace$$

"Those who disbelieve from among the people of Scripture (Jews and Christians) and the polytheists, were not going to leave (their disbelief) until there came to them the clear evidence."

{al-Bayyinah (98): 1}

---

[1] *Fatāwā al-'A'imah*, p.55 see:
http://www.madeenah.com/index.php?option=com_content&task=view&id=208&Itemid=2

So if one's mother is a *kāfir*, does the cockroach get more respect and dignity? The key word here is 'dignity' and there is no doubt that *kuffār* still have to be respected, given their dignity, honour and rights and not be treated worse than animals which is what 'Abdullāh ("el") Faisal suggests. In the Hereafter, their end, if they die while still adhering to kufr, will be worse than it is for animals, but as for in this life then they have to be honoured. After one hour and thirteen minutes Faisal says:

> "So one of the aim {sic} and objective {sic} of jihād is to protect your scholars so that the scholars will be able to speak the truth un-watered-down, uncensored Tawheed, authentic Tawheed. But the scholars today they don't tell you Tawheed, they don't tell you al-walā wa'l-barā', they don't tell you about *Tawheed al-Hākimiyyah*... and the scholars of the apostate leaders you have to kill them because if they preach wrong Islām you have to abduct them and kill them...the apostate leaders, the scholars and the armies of the apostate leaders, their army you have to kill them and the layman who supports the army, the layman who supports the army has to be killed aswell...these are the people you kill with jihād." !!

This is enough in proving his falsehood, extremism and outlandish statements! This means, because Faisal makes *takfeer* of the scholars in Saudi for example, the scholars there are all worthy of the above which he has stated! Look at the danger of the statements of Faisal and how it can be understood by the layman.

The Mufti Of Jamaica!? – The Media Activities Of 'Abdullah ("El") Faisal Upon His Return To Jamaica

In Faisal's first media interview upon his return to Jamaica (in 2007), after he was deported from the UK, Faisal appeared to have turned over a new leaf and not make any reference to jihād whatsoever. So from whence Faisal used to boldly claim that he was a "Shaykh of Jihād" he now denied his jihādī persona for Jamaican audiences. There is no doubt that Faisal has done this due to his fear and realisation that he can in no way whatsoever preach the extremism, for which he became so infamous in the UK and the US. What is interesting is that finally Faisal briefly realised the importance of giving *da'wah* within Jamaica although he had never shown any concern for Jamaica prior to his expulsion from the UK and forced departure to Jamaica. Indeed, he did not visit the land for fifteen years, choosing instead to call the Muslim youth in the UK to erroneous ideas of jihād, *takfeer*, criminality and foolery. We'll list some of the observations taken from Faisal's media frolics on the Jamaican TV programme *Religious Hardtalk,* which he gave after he was deported from the UK to Jamaica:[1]

---

[1] The interview can be seen on 'Google Videos' here: http://video.google.com/videoplay?docid=-1028214663151726309#docid=-2232153050792922021

☐ After 7 minutes and 20 seconds Faisal says:

"I have been to 30 countries preaching Islam and I have been warmly welcomed by all of the countries, even by the Chinese Muslims in Hong Kong. But I have to say that the warmest welcome I got was at the Norman Manley Airport by the Jamaican authorities."

Hereby praising a non-Muslim government which Faisal used to say were all 'fair game' for deception. What happened to Faisal's vitriol against the "Kuffār system" that he used always to go on about?

☐ After 8 minutes and 35 seconds he says:

"The Jamaican authorities have been brilliant...the beauty about the Jamaican authorities is that...they did not pre-judge...."

Lauding more praise upon their system, which Faisal now deems as being worthy of praise?!

Accessed 12 October 2010. Also see: http://www.kalamullah.com/faisal.html
Also at www.islambase.info under 'lectures' and then under 'Sheikh Abdullah El Faisal' entitled *Abdullah El Faisal - Interview on Jamaican TV*. The 'islambase' website by 2009 had removed many of their lectures by Faisal, which we had initially found on their site in 2007. But in mid 2010 the 'islambase' website again put the lectures by Faisal back up on their site.

☐ After 9 minutes and 13 seconds, he says:

"There's a reason why the Jamaican authorities took such a stance, if we have heroes such as Sam Sharpe and Manley who are freedom fighters, then it's quite natural...my struggle is exactly similar and I'm not the first Jamaican to be deported for preaching because Marcus Garvey was deported as well from America..."

Hereby comparing himself to freedom fighters, and non-Muslim ones at that. But did not Faisal say that cockroaches were better than non-Muslims?! 49 minutes into the lecture entitled *'Jihād'* by Faisal, he claims that the cockroach has more dignity than a non-Muslim and that the Qur'ān teaches this!? Faisal said in the lecture *al-Walā' wa'l-Barā'* (a)[1]:

"And if you are living in this country and a person approaches you and ask you 'what do you think about the system' and you say to yourself, or you say to the person, 'Alhamdulillāh, it's not a bad system, it's a good system, even though my name is Muhammad I'm allowed to sign on and on top of that I live in the Royal Borough of Kensington and Chelsea, I can't complain.' Now you are in this system and you can't see anything wrong with the system you say 'it's okay'! Just to give that answer 'it's okay' you become a kāfir!" (!!!)

---

[1] The lecture can be heard in full here: www.archive.org/stream/alwala1/alwala.rmvb

Faisal also says in the same lecture:

> "Kāfirs will always be kāfirs, <u>every kāfir</u> will always find a time to make you feel ashamed of your religion, <u>every kāfir</u>!...Kāfirs will always be Kāfirs!"

Faisal states in the lecture *Enjoining the Good and Forbidding the Evil*:

> "The language that the kāfir respects does not come from your mouth, it comes from your Kalashnikov! <u>That's the only language kāfirs respect</u>, this is why the Prophet said jihād is compulsory until Yawm ul-Qiyāmah."

Faisal says 49 minutes into the lecture entitled *Jihād* (which was available on the *'InshAllāh Shaheed'* website):

> "Every Muslim would like to kill the kuffār, unless you're a munāfiq and you have no al-walā wa'l-barā' in your heart or you love kāfirs. I wouldn't be surprised if some of you love Hindus and Sikhs and Buddhists and Christians, only munāfiqoon love kuffār." (!!!)

Faisal then says in the same lecture:

"You can even use chemical weapons to exterminate kāfirs. Now if you have cockroaches in your house would you spray them? Huh? Yes! With chemicals! Who has more dignity the cockroach or the kāfir? The cockroach, the Qur'ān tells you that! Which ayah in the Qur'ān tells you that? Huh?!"

All of this is straight from the horse's mouth!

☐ After 14 minutes and 25 seconds of the *Religious Hardtalk* interview on Jamaican TV, Faisal is asked by the interviewer Ian Boyne: **"Do you support the suicide bombers?"** To which Faisal passes the buck to Yūsuf Qaradāwī saying: **"He is the leading scholar at the moment in the Muslim world, there's no one above him..."** (!!?)

☐ After 17 minutes and 50 seconds Faisal says, with regards to Qaradāwī's view on suicide bombing: **"I do not have the knowledge to refute Yūsuf Qaradāwī's fatwa and even if I debate with him I'm not sure I can win. So I'd rather not debate with him."**

☐ After 18 minutes and 27 seconds Faisal says: **"All the Muslim scholars say you're not allowed to kill innocents, so there is no justification for killing innocents. Even Yūsuf Qaradāwī who passed the fatwa to allow suicide bombing, he specified that it has to be among those who are killing you,** he limited it to those who are killing you." To which Faisal is asked: "So a lot of the suicide bombings which are taking place in Iraq and Israel would violate that and would therefore be contrary to Allāh's will?" Faisal responds: "If they kill innocents it would violate the verdict of the Sheikh (i.e. Qaradāwī)…to kill innocents is a transgression beyond bounds." Faisal then says: "9/11 is an immoral act, I'm saying that, whether it is 9/11 or 7/7." It's as if Faisal has amnesia?! As twenty minutes into the lecture entitled *'Jihād'* (still widely available Online), Faisal said:

> "Now is there any peace treaty between us and the Hindus? <u>No! So you can go India and if you see a Hindu walking down the road you're allowed to kill him and take his money. Is that clear?"</u>

Also let us refer to Faisal's own support of the so-called 'declaration of war' that was issued by Bin Ladin himself which Faisal translated.[1] Faisal in a lecture entitled *'Justice'* states that 9/11 involved the killing of civilians so he is unable to justify it. Yet in the lecture entitled *'No Peace with the Jews'* Faisal justifies bombing and attacking Jewish and Hindu businesses, which would obviously contain non-combatants and innocents and civilians.

☐ After 69 minutes of the *Religious Hardtalk* interview Faisal says that Muslims cannot take the law into their own hands and only the Caliph can implement

---

[1] http://www.archive.org/details/DeclarationWar_SheikhFaisal

the punishments. But in the vile lecture entitled *The Devil's Deception of the 21ˢᵗ Century House Niggers* (!!?) Faisal says to the audience,

"What do you think we should do with this person (i.e. Abū Usāmah adh-Dhahabi)?"

Audience: Kill him!

Faisal: "I can't hear you?"

Audience: "Kill him!"

Faisal: I still can't hear you?

Audience: "Kill him!"

Faisal: OK that makes sense." (!!!)

☐ After 82 minutes and 41 seconds Faisal is asked if he was strong psychologically within prison, to which Faisal boldly responds: **"Yes, <u>well if you're a cleric you have to set an example for other Muslims to follow, you're not supposed to crack up under pressure…"</u>**?! Hereby asserting that he is a qualified "cleric" (!?) as he calls himself, merely regurgitating the language of those he claims to hate so much.

☐ After 86 minutes and 10 seconds, when confronted with the **"abominable"** statements that he made on some of his lectures with regards to advocating the murder of Jews and Hindus, Faisal remarks: **"Well what I was saying to the Muslims on these tapes is that you should rise up and defend yourselves,**

327

this is all I was saying. Because the law of nature says that you need to resist in order to exist..." (!!)

In a lecture by Faisal entitled *Challenges Facing the Youth*, he says:

"If he is a supporter of kufr, a Saudi Salafī, you have to kill him and chop of his head..."!!

Is this "saying to the Muslims that you should rise up and defend yourselves"??! In the same lecture Faisal says in the so-called 'question and answer session':

"You're allowed to take all these benefits that these kāfirs offer you, because everything that the kāfir owns is yours. Every single thing that the kāfir owns is yours so you're allowed to take all the benefits that they offer you and you're even allowed to have four wives and put them on benefit, so hope that they give you a mansion in Hampstead Heath!"

Is this "saying to the Muslims that you should rise up and defend yourselves"??! Faisal says an hour into the lecture *Let the Scholars Beware*:

"The Jews love Judaism more than the Muslims love al-Islām, this is why they have a Jewish state and we don't have an Islamic state. The Jewish Rabbis are more sincere to their false religion more than our Islamic scholars who are not sincere to our religion...Islām is a religion without scholars..."

Is this "saying to the Muslims that you should rise up and defend yourselves"??!
Forty minutes into the lecture entitled *Rejecting the Tāghūt*, Faisal says:

> **"So today the Muslims are like the kāfirs of Quraysh..."**

Is this "saying to the Muslims that you should rise up and defend yourselves"??!
Faisal says in the lecture *Treachery from Within*:

> **"The Saudi Salafis, they are your enemies, in fact they are your greatest enemies because they guise themselves, they hide themselves, in clothing of righteousness and piety with a beard and a white thowb, some of them speak Arabic, yet they use their knowledge of Arabic to cement the throne of the apostate leaders...these are the nine enemies who you have to fight in this world today."**

Is this "saying to the Muslims that you should rise up and defend yourselves"??!
Fifty minutes into the lecture entitled *Knowledge*, Faisal says:

> **"So the Muslims in this country (i.e. the UK), the majority of them, they have no eemān and no taqwā, the average Muslim you meet on the street he has no īmān and no taqwā..."**

Is this "saying to the Muslims that you should rise up and defend yourselves"??!
Faisal says in the vile lecture *The Devil's Deception of the 21ˢᵗ Century House Niggers*:

> **"Anyone who listens to this tape, of this man and doubt that he's a kāfir**

you become a kāfir! If you listen to this person Abū Usāmah trying to put Islām down and Muslims down and jihād down, if you have an atom's weight of doubt in your heart that he's a kāfir, you yourself become a kāfir." !!!

Is this "saying to the Muslims that you should rise up and defend yourselves"??! In the lecture entitled *Jihād* (which was available of the Takfīrī website *'InshAllāh Shaheed'*):

"So you want to go to jannah? Put up your hands those who want to go to jannah. It's easy just kill a kāfir, just kill a kāfir!"!!

Is this "saying to the Muslims that you should rise up and defend yourselves"??! Faisal says in the same lecture, 49 minutes into it:

"Every Muslim would like to kill the kuffār, unless you're a munāfiq and you have no al-walā wa'l-barā' in your heart or you love kāfirs. I wouldn't be surprised if some of you love Hindus and Sikhs and Buddhists and Christians, only munāfiqūn love kuffār."

Is this "saying to the Muslims that you should rise up and defend yourselves"??! So the deception of 'Abdullāh Faisal has not ceased one iota!

Conclusion

Allāh says,

﴿ كُنتُمْ خَيْرَ أُمَّةٍ أُخْرِجَتْ لِلنَّاسِ تَأْمُرُونَ بِٱلْمَعْرُوفِ وَتَنْهَوْنَ عَنِ ٱلْمُنكَرِ وَتُؤْمِنُونَ بِٱللَّهِ ۗ وَلَوْ ءَامَنَ أَهْلُ ٱلْكِتَٰبِ لَكَانَ خَيْرًا لَّهُم ۚ مِّنْهُمُ ٱلْمُؤْمِنُونَ وَأَكْثَرُهُمُ ٱلْفَٰسِقُونَ ﴾

"You are the best nation produced [as an example] for mankind.

You enjoin what is right and forbid what is wrong..."

{Āli Imrān (3): 110}

Forbidding the error of the one who makes a mistake and the one who destroys the *deen* with his misguidance is a great reason for curses to be lifted from the Ummah of Muhammad ﷺ. Allāh says,

﴿ لُعِنَ ٱلَّذِينَ كَفَرُوا۟ مِنۢ بَنِىٓ إِسْرَٰٓءِيلَ عَلَىٰ لِسَانِ دَاوُۥدَ وَعِيسَى ٱبْنِ مَرْيَمَ ۚ ذَٰلِكَ بِمَا عَصَوا۟ وَّكَانُوا۟ يَعْتَدُونَ ۝ كَانُوا۟ لَا يَتَنَاهَوْنَ عَن مُّنكَرٍ فَعَلُوهُ ۚ لَبِئْسَ مَا كَانُوا۟ يَفْعَلُونَ ﴾

"Cursed were those who disbelieved among the Children of Israel by the tongue of David and of Jesus, the son of Mary. That was because they disobeyed and [habitually] transgressed. They used to not prevent one another from wrongdoing that they did. How wretched was that which they were doing." *{al-Māʾidah (5): 78-79}*

331

Such forbiddance results in evil curses being lifted from the Ummah of Muhammad ﷺ. So it is wājib on the whole Ummah to support those who oppose evil; forbid evil; or those who forbid the evil of doubts, innovations and misguidance. We bring to a close the pages of this book with a precious antidote that strengthens the sunnī immune system from all diseases related to misguidance. This antidote comes in the form of wisdom written in ink by a great scholar. The advice interwoven in his words, if understood and applied correctly, can immunise against all strains of deadly misguidance. The Imām of the people of Sunnah, of his era, Abū Muhammad Khalf al-Barbahārī (died 329 AH) said in his monumental work *Sharh as-Sunnah*:

فَانْظُرْ رَحِمَكَ اللهُ كُلَّ مَنْ سَمِعْتَ كَلامَهُ مِنْ أَهْلِ زَمَانِكَ خَاصَّةً فَلا تَعْجَلْنَ وَلا تَدْخُلْنَ فِيْ شَيْءٍ مِنْهُ حَتَّى تَسْأَلَ وَتَنْظُرَ هَلْ تَكَلَّمَ فِيهِ أَحَدٌ مِنْ أَصْحَابِ النَّبِي صَلَّى اللهُ عَلَيْهِ وَ سَلَّمَ أَوْ أَحَدٌ مِنَ الْعُلَمَاءِ فَإِنْ أَصَبْتَ فِيهِ أَثَرًا عَنْهُمْ فَتَمَسَّكْ بِهِ وَلا تَجَاوَزْهُ لِشَيْءٍ ولا تَخْتَرْ عَلَيْهِ شَيْئًا فَتَسْقُطَ فِيْ النَّارِ.

May Allāh have mercy upon you! Examine the speech of every one of the people, particularly in your era. Do not act hastily nor enter into anything until you enquire and observe: did any of the Companions of Allāh's Messenger speak about it, or any of the scholars? So if you find a narration from them, then hold firmly to it, do not go beyond it for anything, nor give preference to anything over it, and as a consequence plunge into the fire.

If only the Ummah of Muhammad ﷺ were to embody this scholarly advice and act upon its injunctions, people like 'Abdullāh El-Faisal would be swiftly contained, quarantined and prevented from spreading their noxious teachings. Understanding the importance of returning back to the companions and scholars of this Ummah, equips one with a deciphering tool that enables the separation of truth from falsehood. A prime and practical example of this can be found in the understanding of the following Noble Verse:

﴿ وَمَن لَّمْ يَحْكُم بِمَآ أَنزَلَ ٱللَّهُ فَأُوْلَٰٓئِكَ هُمُ ٱلْكَٰفِرُونَ ﴾

"And whoever does not judge by what Allāh has revealed, then it is those who are the disbelievers." *{al-Māʾidah (5):44}*

In this day and age, many desire to apply this verse[1] according to its apparent meaning and, but at the same time they wish to restrict its application to the genus of Muslim leaders and declare all of them as disbelievers. However, the true Sunni follower who understands the magnitude of the words: **do not act hastily nor enter into anything until you enquire and observe,** takes a step back and enquires: **did any of the Companions of Allāh's Messenger speak about it, or any of the scholars?** This is the true methodology which governs his understanding of this verse; not mere emotive objectives or obsessions with the ruling class. So the true Sunni follower delves into the books of the Salaf, and he finds statements from them pertaining to the correct understanding of the above-mentioned verse. For instance, he finds that ʾAbdullāh Ibn ʾAbbās commented on this verse by saying, **"It is not the kufr that you are going**

---

[1] For an in-depth analysis surrounding the correct understanding of this verse, refer to salafimanhaj.com, namely an article entitled:
"A Study of the Tafseer of Ibn ʾAbbās (radi Allāhu ʾanhu): 'Kufr Doona Kufr'": http://www.salafimanhaj.com/pdf/SalafiManhaj_KufrDoonaKufr.pdf

towards (in your minds)." And in another narration he states, "It is not the kufr that you are going towards (in your minds); it is not the kufr that expels one from the religion." This is just one example of correct application of Imām al-Barbahārī's invaluable advice, but we need to apply this advice in all spheres of Allāh's religion. Whenever people like 'Abdullāh Faisal speak, we need to give his speech the al-Barbahāri evaluation, and weigh his words against the words of the Salaf.

It is upon 'Abdullāh El-Faisal to be humble before Allāh and make a sincere *tawbah* (repentance) for his past views and seek forgiveness from those whom he oppressed. He must openly recant from his horrific lectures, beliefs and stances and return back to the manhaj of Ahl us-Sunnah as there is no doubt that his arrogance and stubbornness has led him to an array of problems. Faisal himself stated in the lecture *'Islam Under Siege'*, sample lecture no.19 in our study:

> "I stand corrected whenever I'm wrong and I tell my enemies for the past eight years, if you listen to my tapes and you find one mistake in regards to fiqh or 'aqeedah, I will take it back publicly! For eight years I'm {sic} repeating myself, if you listen to any of my tapes and you find one mistake in regards to fiqh or 'aqeedah, whether it is al-*walā wa'l-barā, Tawheed Hākimiyyah, fiqh ul-wāqi,* any, seven conditions of shahādah, just one mistake in regards to 'aqeedah I will take it back publicly! For eight years I've been saying that and my enemies <u>haven't</u>

been able to find any mistake[1] they only slander me behind my back like nine year old girls...they slander me behind my back like menstruating women. Not like Bin Bāz who they claimed he took back his mistake a minute before he died on his bed, secretely, the tawbah of the Shaykh is not like the layman, did you understand that? Do you understand that? When you pass a dodgy fatwa you misguide thousands and millions, is that clear? So you have to take back your fatwa publicly, but if you are a layman and you make a mistake you can make your tawbah secretly behind closed doors. If you're a Shaykh and you pass a dodgy fatwa you need to take it back publicly because you misguide tens, hundreds, thousands and millions of people."

So here Faisal has not only elevated himself to the level of a scholar, by saying that he is prepared to take back any mistakes because this is only for scholars to do this publicly, but he has also raised himself to the level of Imām Bin Bāz ﷺ. Faisal stated that public *tawbah* is only for the scholars, so when Faisal stated that he is prepared to take back any statements openly and publicly, he is insinuating that he also is a scholar, as according to him only the scholars make public and open *tawbah*!

We hope Faisal reads this book, remains true to his words and corrects the multitude of not just errors, but also slanderous remarks and clear-cut lies. Incidentally, we do not know of any instance whatsoever, since 1995, where

---

[1] Is he serious?! This book in itself is just a brief attempt to collate a presentation of his horrific errors!

Faisal has actually admitted an error or retracted any of his statements. Yet Allāh says:

﴿ إِلَّا ٱلَّذِينَ تَابُواْ وَأَصْلَحُواْ وَبَيَّنُواْ فَأُوْلَـٰئِكَ أَتُوبُ عَلَيْهِمْ ﴾

"Except those who repent, rectify and manifest (the truth)..."

{al-Baqarah (2): 160}

Ibn Katheer says in explaining this *ayah*:

> This Ayah refers to those who regret what they have been doing and correct their behavior and, thus, explain to the people what they have been hiding.

Imām as-Sa'dī stated about the *ayah* that it means retracting from sins and being regretful about them, and that one has to rectify their actions which caused corruption in the first place. Allāh has taught us in His book that whoever errs must perform what Allāh mentioned. They have to have repented from the sin, rectify themselves from what they corrupted initially and manifest the truth by saying that they erred beforehand and have now retracted. It is not sufficient to just leave the vile action rather it has to be followed up with good. This retraction cannot be concealed rather it has to be clarified in the open.[1] Imām Ibn ul-Qayyim mentioned this in his book *Iddat us-Sābireen.*

Imām Abu'l-'Abbās Shaykh ul-Islām Ibn Taymiyyah mentioned in *Majmū' al-Fatāwā,* and as did Imām 'Abdul'Azeez bin Bāz ﷺ, that: ***"Whoever errs openly is***

---

[1] See al-'Allāmah Shaykh 'AbdurRahmān bin Nāsir as-Sa'dī, *Tayseer al-Kareem ir-Rahmān fī Tafseer Kalām il-Mannān* (Beirut: Resalah Publishers, 1421 AH/2000 CE), p.77.

to be corrected openly." It is not to be said: "*Leave him and do not criticise him because he has good in him*" and the likes of such unacceptable counter arguments. Rather, whoever errs openly is to be censured openly, as it was mentioned beforehand in the introduction that the Prophet ﷺ censured a spokesman from a group of people openly and he did not take him by the hand to advise him initially and then after that refute him. Rather, the Prophet ﷺ censured him openly without giving advice. Whoever wants to obligate people to advise a person before he can be refuted has to bring evidence for this.

Finally, Allāh says,

﴿ قُلْ هَلْ نُنَبِّئُكُم بِٱلْأَخْسَرِينَ أَعْمَـٰلاً ۝ ٱلَّذِينَ ضَلَّ سَعْيُهُمْ فِى ٱلْحَيَوٰةِ ٱلدُّنْيَا وَهُمْ يَحْسَبُونَ أَنَّهُمْ يُحْسِنُونَ صُنْعًا ﴾

"Say, [O Muhammad], 'Shall we [believers] inform you of the greatest losers as to [their] deeds? [They are] those whose effort is lost in worldly life, while they think that they are doing well in work.'"

{al-Kahf (18): 103-104}

Their intention is good, yet when they were in opposition to the way of the Messenger ﷺ their action was evil. And Allāh knows best.

Jamiah Media Publications

Previous Publications:

1. *Before Nicea.* By AbdurRahman Bowes and AbdulHaq al-Ashanti (2005)

2. *Who's in for Iraq?* By Shaykh Abdul'Azeez bin Rayyis ar-Rayyis (2007)

3. *The Impact of Man-Made Laws in the Ruling of an Abode as Being One of Kufr or Islam.* By Shaykh Khalid al-Anbari.(2006)

4. *A Warning Against Extremism.* By Shaykh Salih Aali Shaykh (2008)

5. *A Critical Study of the Multiple Identities and Disguises of 'al-Muhajiroun'.* By Abu Ameenah AbdurRahman as-Salafi and AbdulHaq al-Ashanti (2009).

6. *The Noble Women Scholars of Hadith.* By Shaykh Mashhur Hasan Al Salman. (2010)

7. *The Creed of Imam an-Nawawi,* By Shaykh Mashhur Hasan Al Salman (2010)

8. *The Beautiful Advice to the Noble Salafis of the West,* By Shaykh 'Abdul-Aziz ar-Rayyis (2010)

9. *Shirk According to the 4 Madhhabs.* By Shaykh, Dr Muhammad al-Khumayyis. (2011)

10. *What the Notables Have Narrated About not Going to the Rulers,* Imam Jalalud-Deen as-Suyuti (2011)

11. *'Abdullah el-Faisal al-Jamayki' – A Critical Study of his Statements, Errors and Extremism in Takfir,* By Abu Ameenah AbdurRahman as-Salafi and AbdulHaq al-Ashanti (2011).

forthcoming Publications:

1. *Guidance on the Ruling on Giving the Khutbah in a Non-Arabic Language.* By Abu Najeed Isam bin Ahmad Saleem bin Mami al-Makki

2. *The Fiqh Madhhab of Ahl ul-Hadith.* By Shaykh Mashhur Hasan Al Salman